NOEL PONTING
GRAHAM CARTER

MOONIES, MOVERS & SHAKERS

THE MOONRAKERS

RAKE DADDY RAKE

Dedicated to the memory of our friend and colleague

MARK SUTTON

(1962-2022)

Published on behalf of Swindon Heritage by
The Hobnob Press,
8 Lock Warehouse, Severn Road, Gloucester GL1 2GA

British Library cataloguing in publication data:
a catalogue record for this book is available from
the British Library.

Design and typesetting by Graham Carter.

The text is set in Times New Roman in 10pt/11pt.

© Noel Ponting and Graham Carter, 2024

ISBN 978-1-914407-72-7

This book is a not-for-profit project; any proceeds from its sale will
be reinvested into other local history projects.

Acknowledgements

The authors would like to give their sincere thanks to the following people
for their help and support in the production of this book:

Bernard Anderson/Great Eastern Railway Society
Mark Andrews (*Royal Arsenal – Champions of the South*)
Mike Attwell
Frances Bevan
Bristol Archives
Noel Beauchamp
Julie Carter
Daniel Chipperfield
John Chandler
Mary Evans (Picture Library/Illustrated London News Group)
David Harvey
Peter Harvey
Shannon Jones
Dick Kirby
Matthew Lloyd
Local Studies, Swindon Central Library (Darryl Moody, Jenny Ackrill & Sara Steel)
Rosa Matheson
Dick Mattick
Dr Julie Miller
Marianne Morgan
Alan Moss (author and historian with a special interest in the Metropolitan Police Service)
Paul Plowman
Libby Rice (London Symphony Orchestra Archive)
Sue Robinson (www.chitternenowandthen.uk)
royal-arsenal-history.com (Ian Bull & Steven Peterson)
Jane Schön (Wiltshire Museum)
Paul Skelton (dover-kent.com)
John Stooke
Jean Thomas (Moore and Burgess Minstrels Archive)
Martin Thomas
Molly White
Paul Williams/The Swindon Society
Wiltshire & Swindon History Centre
Sebastian Wormell (Harrods Company Archive)
&
Mark Hepplewhite and staff in 'Billy Thomas's parlour' (the Glue Pot, Swindon)

Before we start...

As you will come to understand when you read on, this book has a life of its own, starting out as potentially one thing and ending up as another – and following all kinds of unexpected paths, en route to its unpredictable destination.

And if the reader isn't quite sure where it's heading, that's because the authors weren't, either! So prepare to be sidetracked, starting from now.

The thrust of this book is ostensibly a history of *The Association of Wiltshiremen in London*, but there are other themes too, including *cool things you may not have known about Wiltshire*, and its fertile sub-genre, *people you didn't realise were born in Wiltshire*.

So let's start with the news – and it *will* be news for many – that among the ranks of those with the right to call themselves 'Moonies' (on account of they were Wiltshire-born) is one of the greatest architects in British history (and an anatomist, astronomer, mathematician and physicist to boot).

Yes, Sir Christopher Wren was born in East Knoyle, a sleepy village off the A350, between Warminster and Shaftesbury, which (according to Sir Nikolaus Bernhard Leon Pevsner, who, between 1951 and 1974, compiled a 46-volume guide called *The Buildings of England*) 'ought to be the purpose of a visit from every Wiltshire tourist' because of one of its buildings.

This building is not Wren's birthplace, unfortunately – that is long gone, although there is a plaque (pictured) – but rather the village church, St Mary's, which has been described as 'Norman in its bones' and contains a notable feature

from the eve of the English Civil War: decorative plasterwork on the walls of the chancel (pictured, opposite).

Pevsner calls it a 'surprise and delight', and he is not wrong. Created in about 1639, when Wren was seven years old, it is the work of none other than his father, who was rector of the church from 1623, and was also called Christopher Wren.

Seeing his father create the plasterwork surely made an impression on the young son, and who knows what creative and architectural passions it stirred in him?

Christopher Wren the Elder (as he is now sometimes known, to differentiate him from his famous son), was not a Moonie himself, but there is a footnote to his story that is worth visiting briefly.

In 1635 he became Dean of Windsor, and from then on, he and the family only spent part of the year in East Knoyle, while his Windsor day job brought him face-to-face with the Civil War after it erupted in 1641.

When the Parliamentary forces occupied Windsor Castle, he refused to give the keys of the chapel to Captain Fogg, and although Fogg broke open the treasury and plundered it, Wren Senior managed to preserve the records of the Order of the Garter, along with King Edward III's sword, which is still at Windsor.

So those are the roots of our first notable Moonie, but if you think it's the last we will hear of him, you still haven't grasped the unpredictable nature of this book.

Yet another theme of this book is *how things have a habit of connecting up*, so look out for Wren's brief reappearance, once we get into the story proper...

Introduction

One of the many joys of researching into local history is you never know where the journey is going to take you. And that has perhaps never been more true for us than with this book.

We have previously collaborated on two books – both of them about a Swindon-born author, George Ewart Hobbs, whose fascinating writings, mostly in the *Swindon Advertiser*, had largely been forgotten until we discovered them in the paper's archives.

Similarly, it was while researching an article about the Glue Pot (see page 90) for *Swindon Heritage* that we stumbled on another forgotten aspect of the town's history: the annual dinners of *The Association of Wiltshire-men in London*.

Proudly calling up an old legend by nicknaming themselves *The Moonies in London* ('Moonies' being short for Moonrakers, which is still traditionally applied to people born in the county of Wiltshire), they quickly set us, as local historians, a conundrum.

Why (we asked ourselves) was a now-obscure, posh dinner, 80 miles from Swindon, of such interest to local readers that the *Advertiser/North Wilts Herald/Wiltshire Times* not only reported on it, every year, over a long period, but sometimes recorded virtually every word that was said? Like most historical conundrums, there was no simple answer, but the more we delved into it, the more intriguing the subject became.

Frankly, *The Moonies in London* story is, on the surface, the narrowest of niche subjects, apparently concerning a limited number of people from society's elites who happened to hop on a train for an annual shindig in the capital. Even in its time, it seemed far removed from the real lives and concerns of the vast majority of people back home in Swindon and the rest of Wiltshire.

But wait. Scratch the surface and it actually tells us much about Wiltshire people and their achievements, and what bound (and perhaps still binds) them

together. The more we dug, the more we found stories that paint a picture of how and who we were – and therefore how and who we *are*.

The reports of these gatherings tell us much about life in Wiltshire in the past that isn't obvious in other sources: the deep roots of organisations such as *The Moonies in London* (they were one of several); the role of the military in society; the shifting of influence between the upper and middle classes; social etiquette; attitudes to women; attitudes to charity and the 'deserving' poor; the role of apprenticeships in Swindon's railway history; and much more besides.

The reader should expect to encounter some words, beliefs and practices that are, to the modern eye, inappropriate and even offensive; we do not condone them by leaving them unedited, but include them for historical accuracy and to allow the reader to make up his or her own mind about attitudes and prejudices of the times.

Perhaps most surprisingly, the reports reveal the allegiance that people who were born in Wiltshire felt when they got together, and a common pride in the county, even if there was otherwise no obvious bond between them.

So one of the aims of this book is to explain the forces that have shaped Wiltshiremen and their county in the past, and perhaps at least part of the answer can be found in the tradition of the moonrakers itself.

Moonies are a personification of the stereotypical agricultural Wiltshireman, who might seem a bit dim and lack the social niceties of educated and genteel city folk, but whom you underestimate at your peril. Perhaps there is also a link between those yokels and the yoked railwaymen of Swindon, toiling inside their factory, who turned out to be just as clever as their country cousins. And if there really is a kind of alliance between the rural and urban Moonie, then everything about *The Association of Wiltshiremen in London* makes sense after all.

Our journey will take us to Scotland Yard, Harrods, the London Symphony Orchestra, the Royal Arsenal at Woolwich and the earliest origins of Arsenal Football Club, and plenty more destinations besides, and it will throw light on the diverse achievements of eminent people who otherwise had only one thing in common: they were all born (or settled) in Wiltshire.

So were we, and in tracking the journey of the *Moonies in London*, we hope to explain something of the pride that was so evident in *The Association of Wiltshiremen in London*.

And – who knows? – even reignite it. ∎

Noel Ponting & Graham Carter,
May 2024

Origins of Wiltshire societies

A

SERMON

PREACHED AT

St. Mary Le Bow.

Novemb. 27. 1682.

Being the Day of the

Wiltſhire-Feaſt.

By *EDWARD PELLING*, Rector of *St. Martins Ludgate*, and Chaplain to his Grace the Duke of *Somerſet*.

We have no King, becauſe we feared not the Lord, Hoſ. 10. 3.
For the Tranſgreſſion of a Land, many are the Princes thereof, Prov. 28. 2.

Σννωμοσίαι ἢ συςάσεις ὶ ταιρεῖαί τε ἥλιςα μοναρχία συμφέρει.

Conſpiracies, Combinations, and Aſſociations, do not at all conſiſt with Monarchy. Dio. *Cited by Biſhop* Uſher, *Of the Power of the Prince,* pag. 67.

LONDON:

Printed for *John Crump,* at the *Three Bibles* in St. *Paul's Church-yard;* And *William Abington,* at the *Three Silk-worms* in *Ludgate-ſtreet.* 1683.

Wiltshire folk have been gathering together in London and Bristol in a formal setting for some time now: well over 350 years.

The first such event became known as *The Wiltshire Feast* – a get-together of 17th century movers, shakers and wealthy establishment figures – with its primary objective being the placing of children of the deserving poor (ie, those with existing Wiltshire connections) into apprenticeships with City merchants and craftsmen.

Such was the regard that the men of Wiltshire had for this assemblage that it was sometimes lauded as 'the Wiltshire Parliament'.

Despite this being an idea that was subsequently taken up by many other English counties, one of the very first such gatherings was organised for and by Wiltshiremen, and took place on November 9, 1654.

It became the established format that the assembled company would first attend divine service at one of the City of London churches, and then dine together at the hall of one of the City companies (now termed 'livery companies') hired for the occasion.

In his book, *British Clubs & Societies 1580-1800*, Peter Clark explains:

In London, the decisive year appears to have been 1654, when at least three county feasts were held: by the

(Images courtesy of the Wiltshire & Swindon History Centre)

Cheshire men on 6 June; for Wiltshire on November 9; and by the gentlemen natives of Warwickshire on November 30.

The autumn meetings coincided with the assembly of the first Protectorate Parliament (September 1654), and some of the feast participants were, doubtless, in the capital for that session.

Charity was an essential element of county feast activity in the 17th century, as with most other associations. Besides apprenticing boys from the shires, societies frequently maintained poor students at university; the Wiltshire Feast sought to establish petty schools in its area.

The sermon on that first occasion was preached at St Lawrence Jewry, which was redesigned (after the Great Fire of London) by Sir Christopher Wren and completed in 1677, and is still the official church of the Mayor of London.

The sermon was delivered by Samuel Annesley LLD, and entitled *The First Dish at the Wiltshire Feast*, with the dinner that followed taking place at Merchant Taylors' Hall. With the precedent having been set, it then became established as an annual festivity.

In the preface to a printed copy of his own sermon, Annesley wrote:

You have the honour to give the nation a precedent, pray scorn to be outstript by any... And for your county that I may warrantably merit my text. The men of Wilt- ▶

A
DISCOURSE
OF
FRIENDSHIP,
PREACHED at the
Wiltfhire-Feaft,
IN
St. *Mary* Le-Bow-Church December the 1ft. 1684.

By Samuel Mafters B. D. Preacher to the Hofpital and Precinct of Bridwell in London.

6 Ecclef. 14, 15, 16.
A faithful Friend is a ftrong defence, and he that hath found such an one, hath found a Treafure.
Nothing doth Countervail a faithful Friend, and his excellency is in valuable.
A faithful Friend is the Medicine of Life, and they that fear the Lord fhall find him.

LONDON,
Printed by T. B. for *Marm. Foster* and *Awnfham Churchill*, and are to be fold at the *Black Swan* at *Amen-Corner*. MDCLXXXV.

shire which were men that had understanding of the times, to know what England ought to do, about 500 of them met at a feast, and all there [sic] brethren are willing to further their pious projects.

However, Annesley wasn't averse to holding the men of Wiltshire to account for their perceived 'errant' behaviour when he called for a godly reformation of manners in Wiltshire, especially in the suppression of the 'multitude of alehouses in your country'.

Contrary to some reports that the Wiltshire Feast never returned to the capital after the bubonic plague in 1665, we do know that Edward Pelling, Rector of St Martin's, Ludgate, and Chaplain to His Grace, the Duke of Somerset, delivered a sermon 'to encourage Men to be Heartily and Firmly Loyal' at St Mary le Bow on November 27, 1682, and preacher Samuel Masters delivered a sermon entitled *A Discourse of Friendship* at St Mary le Bow, on December 1, 1684.

The following appeared in the *London Post* in December, 1701 – evidence not only that a degree of 'theatre' accompanied the procession to the dining hall, but that the gathering survived in London into the beginning of the 18th century:

This being the anniversary of the Wiltshire Feast, after hearing sermon in St Mary le Bow, the natives of that shire marched thence in good order, to Merchant-Taylors-Hall; A shepherd with his crook, bag, bottle and dog walking before them, with 20 poor children that were to be put out by the Society, and kettle-drums, trumpets, and other musick.

An essentially urban phenomenon, these convivial meetings generally involved a subscription to a given charitable cause. But in a piece entitled *Wilts Leads the Way*, which appeared in the *Pall Mall Gazette* on March 5, 1898, we learn not only of Wiltshire's pre-eminence in such affairs, but also of the value of fellowship amongst ex-pat county folk:

...at one period practically every English county was represented by an annual assemblage of gentry and others, natives of the former, who resided in or about the metropolis. And in the days when the means of communication between the town and the country were few, it is easy to conceive with what interest these gatherings would be regarded. Not only was there the pleasant reunion of those long resident in the great city to talk over the pleasant recollections of old times and friends far away, but every year would bring fresh comers, whose tidings of the most recent doings in the native shire would impart a fresh interest to the meeting.

It must be distinctly understood, however, that though essentially clannish, these gatherings were by no means confined to what are termed the "classes". The great county noblemen drove down to the City in state, the county gentleman posted up from his far distant shire to walk side by side with his banker; the City merchant again rubbed shoulders with companions of his youth, the country tradesman and the prosperous farmer; similarly the clerks and shopmen, the solicitors and other small, professional breadwinners, all met once a year on common ground in the tie of a common county.

One final quote from Peter Clark's *British Clubs & Societies 1580-1800* helps to illustrate the general landscape of benevolence and fellowship in which the Wiltshire Feast, amongst many other county societies, operated:

Sermon after sermon stressed the importance of friendship and solidarity among participants. John Russel, the preacher at the Wiltshire meeting in 1695, identified the four aims of these public feasts: eating and drinking; socializing 'to advance our temporal interest'; 'the reviving [of] good neighbourhood'; and, lastly, charity for the poor.

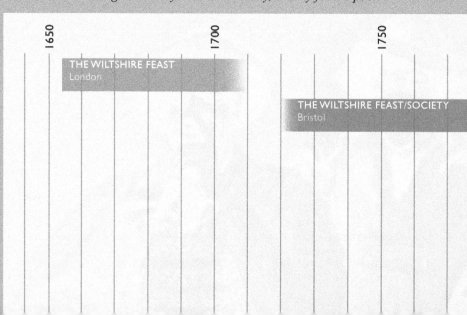

1650   1700   1750

THE WILTSHIRE FEAST
London

THE WILTSHIRE FEAST/SOCIETY
Bristol

Although it appears that the original Wiltshire Society, known as *The Wiltshire Feast*, had gone into hiatus sometime after 1701, evidence shows that it had sprung up again by 1726 – this time in Bristol.

It is unclear if this second iteration of the Wiltshire Society was a renaissance of the original organisation or an entirely new body. Either way, the object of apprenticing the children of the 'deserving poor' to a given trade remained front and centre to its raison d'être.

On August 21, 1729, at All Saints Church in Corn Street, Bristol, the sermon was delivered by the Rev Joseph Horler, Master of the Free School and curate of Wilton, followed by dinner at the Merchants' Hall.

The following are extracts from the printed copy of the sermon.

To my very good friends, Mr James Still, President, Mr Thomas Gibbs, Treasurer, and to the Assistants and all other worthy members and supporters of the Wiltshire Society...

God seems not to want his agent among you already, who have warmly espoused this cause of his, and are bent on carrying it on; who endeavour with a commendable zeal and a bright example to spirit up the members of this Society to answer the end of their annual meeting, to make handsome collections for some poor children, natives of your county, to procure for them some honest and respectable trade, and secure to them a comfortable living in the World...

For the design of our meeting (if I deem aright) was not merely to hear the voice of singing men or singing women, or to eat and drink and rise up to play; but to support a spirit of charity and friendship and brotherly society; that our plenty might put us in mind of other's wants, and that we might remember those that are in affliction acting ourselves also in the body.

It would redound much to your honour and credit to improve that custom, which has lately been revived, of selecting a minor of the household of faith to be the particular object of your bounty, who might date his happiness as it were from this little æra of your Feast, by being plac'd abroad in such circumstances, as never probably could have attended him without your friendly care and assistance.

And a few years later, in 1732, reports confirm that members of the Wiltshire Society walked in procession to Christ Church to hear divine service, and that 'the shepherd with his habit, crook, bottle and dog attended them': clearly a rite or tradition which harked back to the London meetings.

Proceedings concluded with a dinner at Merchants' Hall, and it was stated that 400 people were in attendance.

A notice appeared in the *Bath Chronicle* on August 20, 1761, and its format was typical of those used to gather Wiltshiremen in subsequent years:

WILTSHIRE FEAST

Bristol, August 12, 1761

The Gentlemen Natives of the County of Wilts are desired to meet their Countrymen on Tuesday, the 25th Inst on the Tolzey, at Eleven o'Clock in the Forenoon, to accompany the ▶

President to All Saints Church, to hear Divine Service, and from thence to the Merchant-Taylors-Hall, to Dinner.

James Edwards, President

From 1775, the notice also included the following, thus making it abundantly clear whom would be the intended beneficiaries of the charity:

For the Benefit of poor, Lying-in [pregnant] Women, apprenticing friendless Orphans, and Relief of other distressed Objects of the County.

Discovered in an edition of *Felix Farley's Bristol Journal*, dated August 20, 1768, we learn that:

Thursday last the Gentlemen Natives of the County of Wilts met their President, Mr Cottle, on the Tolzey, and accompanied him to St. James' Church, where an excellent Sermon was preached by the Rev. Mr. Popham, (Son of Edward Popham Esq., one of the Members for the County of Wilts) from whence they proceeded to the Merchant-Taylor's-Hall to Dinner, where a collection of £77 16s was made for apprenticing poor boys; it being the largest ever known on the occasion, by said Society.

The above, though an interesting observation, was not entirely accurate. The record for the sum collected, up to that point, was actually £79 13s, for the year 1765 – and the overall record was achieved in 1773 with a total of £136 11s 6d.

In this account from the *Salisbury and Winchester Journal*, dated May 5, 1766, we learn more of those whom the organisation felt enabled to assist:

We hear from Bristol, that the last President of the Wiltshire Society, Mr

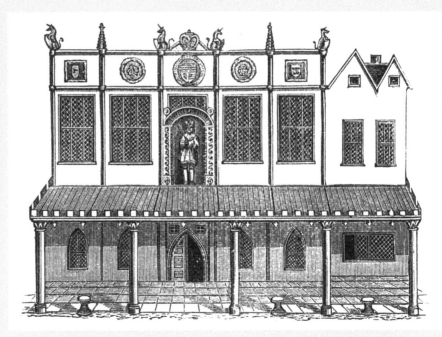

Attendees of the society's meetings in Bristol would be asked to meet 'on the Tolzey' (pictured, above), a covered yet open-sided meeting place that was adjacent to All Saints Church. Thereafter they were to accompany the President of the *Wiltshire Society* to one of the local churches to hear a sermon, later proceeding to Merchant Taylors' Hall in Broad Street, to partake of dinner.

Standfast Smith, made a proposal, which was agreed to by the Committee, allowing 20l [£20] towards the marriage of two young women of sober character, to whose parents it might be some relief to have a daughter thus disposed of.

Lacock in Wilts was the parish approved of to choose from; notice was given in the church, and seven candidates offered for the bounty; the two Church-wardens, two Overseers, and Minister of the parish, chose two on Easter Monday, and made a return of their names. And Monday last, April 21, being the day appointed for the nuptials, thirty or forty gentlemen on horseback, and

five post-chaises, attended the President to Lacock.

Half a mile from the place they were met by a band of music, and went in procession, amidst the acclamations of two or three thousand people, to church, where, after prayers, the ceremony was performed, and the rings given, on which was a motto, "The reward of Virtue".

A sermon was then preached by the Rev Mr Robbins, greatly to the satisfaction of a very attentive audience. After a dinner given to the company by the President, at his own expense, the two fortunes of 10l [£10] each, in half crowns, in two green silk purses, were given. The whole was conducted with the utmost decency, and at six in the evening the company broke up for their return homewards.

The venue for the gatherings in Bristol changed over time.

For the period 1726 to c1739, the Wiltshiremen dined at Merchants' Hall in King Street – home of The Society of Merchant Venturers.

From around 1740 to c1748, they were to be found at the Great Rooms in St Augustine's Back, almost certainly part of the Great House acquired by Edward Colston in 1707.

This is where he later established Colston Boys' School in 1710 (referred to in his will as 'my hospitall') – to prepare boys from poor families for meaningful apprenticeships – coincidentally with the Society of Merchant Venturers appointed as trustees.

Finally, from 1749 to 1783, the dinners moved to Merchant Taylors' Hall, located just off Broad Street, in the centre of the 'old city', re-establishing an association with the Merchant Taylors' Company dating back to the time when the *Wiltshire Society* was active in London.

There are some footnotes to the story. During research conducted by John E Pritchard (of the Society of Wiltshiremen (Moonrakers) in Bristol) in 1926, he discovered that the lyrics of the 14th century ballad *King John and the Abbot of Canterbury* were printed on the reverse of the menu card at the 1779 dinner. He therefore surmised that its singing was part of the tradition at each of the annual gatherings, although as yet, the reason remains unclear (see the Appendices for a version of the song).

The President of the society back in 1779 was John Awdry, and, interestingly,

his great-great-grandson was Col Robert William Awdry JP, who was High Sheriff for the County of Wiltshire in 1928, and President of the third iteration of the Wiltshire Society, in 1929.

In 1784 the activities of the second iteration of the *Wiltshire Society* appear to have ceased abruptly under the presidency of Henry Cruger (1739-1827), himself a former Master of the Society of Merchant Venturers, who had two spells as MP for Bristol and who later also served as a Member of the New York State Senate.

The Wiltshire Society (or, more accurately, *a* Wiltshire society) resumed activities in London in 1817 – recreated from scratch by Wiltshiremen resident in

the capital for the purpose of apprenticing children of poor persons, natives of Wiltshire who had settled there.

The first notice of the inaugural event was to be found in the *London Courier* of January 22, 1817, announcing a meeting for March 26, 1817, at which a prospectus of an intended institution was to be submitted. This was later put back to May 14, and represents the first dinner held by the new organisation:

WILTSHIRE SOCIETY
A MEETING of such Gentlemen as are natives of, or interested in, the prosperity of this County, will be holden at the Albion House, Aldersgate-street, on WEDNESDAY, ▶

A recent image of All Saints Church in Corn Street, the venue for the Wiltshire Feast in Bristol by 1728. It is adjacent to the site of The Tolzey (see opposite), occupied by Café Revival at the time of writing. The church closed in 2015.

the 14th day of May inst, when the Prospectus of an intended Institution will be submitted to them for their consideration.

Dinner on table at 5 o'clock.

Sir BENJAMIN HOBHOUSE, Bart MP in the Chair.

Tickets one guinea each, may be had of the Stewards or the Secretary. A list of Stewards and Temporary Committee, and a copy of the Prospectus may be seen at Albion House.

EDWARD FROWD, Sec Pro Tem Serle-street, Lincoln's Inn-fields.

NB – The object of the proposed Institution is to apprentice the children of the deserving poor belonging to the County of Wilts, residing in London, who might otherwise be destitute of the means of acquiring a comfortable subsistence through life, and afterwards to afford them some assistance to enable them to set up in business.

Addressing the assemblage of 75 'noble-men and gentlemen of Wiltshire', at the first meeting at the Albion Tavern (pictured, above), the President, Sir Benjamin Hobhouse (pictured, opposite), laid out the new charity's plans, but, more importantly for us, paints a vivid picture of attitudes to charity, 200 years ago – at least when it came to the 'deserving poor'.

He said: "Gentlemen, I am greatly obliged to my Noble friend near me [the Society's first patron, the Duke of Somerset] for having proposed my health, and equally so to all constituting this respectable company, for the very handsome manner with which this proposition has been received.

"We are now meeting for the purpose of laying the foundation of a charity, for the prosperity of which I feel no anxiety because I am confident of its success.

"The plan in which it originates I will shorley [sic] state: this nation is no less pre-eminent for its numerous establishments than it is for superiority of civil constitution. And I would beg leave to know whether there is any capital in Europe which possesses so many spacious buildings dedicated to humane purposes, on the principle of benevolence and virtue?

"I submit to you, whether every quarter of this noble city does not abound in asylums, hospital and public charities? Let but a well-authenticated statement appear and be shewn [sic] to exist, there is immediately a rivalry, there is a disposition in all the opulent population of the country to outdo each other in contributing to give it effect. If any proof were wanting, we had it during the course of last winter, when such general and noble exertions to provide, for the labouring poor, employment and subsistence, were made in a way calculated to insure [sic] success.

"It would be slander to suppose, that this Institution, which proposes to administer charity in the very best form, namely, in teaching the children of the poor, and affording ability to provide for themselves, should be found destitute of public encouragement and support.

"The children of the poor of the county of Wilts, residing in London, are to be taught habits of industry before vice has gained an ascendency in their minds, and the means of acquiring a comfortable subsistence through life.

These are the natural effects of charities of this nature.

"While those who are educated are enjoying the fruits of their own industry, public order is promoted. Were such institutions as these uniformly prevalent throughout the country, the progress of pauperism would be arrested and people would not be led to commit acts of violence.

"Gentlemen, if these institutions were prevalent, the people would not be machines in the hands of demagogues, and would oppose all wicked schemes for overthrowing ancient institutions.

"There is another ground, and a very strong one, for inducing me to feel perfect confidence that we shall not fail: I mean that other institutions have been found to flourish.

"I allude to a society instituted of the same kind for Somersetshire – like that Society, we propose to bind the children of deserving poor of the county of Wilts, the children of persons resident in London not equal to the expense themselves, and we propose to do that by a plan calculated to enable them hereafter to provide for themselves; namely, that when their apprenticeships are finished, if they are found to be deserving, to assist them with a small allowance, to be considered as a debt rather than a donation.

"The assistance is proposed to be advanced rather as a debt, because they must necessarily form habits of sobriety and industry, and economy. It is on that account that I think the objects of our meeting are peculiarly deserving our notice and encouragement.

"Although I

have been led to say thus much on behalf of this Institution, let me not be misunderstood, let it not be conceived that I think you will be deficient in zeal. I am perfectly certain that this Institution will be nurtured by every individual until it has attained gradually strength and maturity.

"There is nothing I wish so much as that all this company may live to see the day when those interests they are desirous of promoting will reap the fruits of this noble charity."

The formal prospectus adopted at the first meeting echoed these objectives:

The object of the Wiltshire Society is to raise a fund by donations and annual subscriptions, for the purpose of apprenticing the children of poor Wiltshire parents, resident in London; and also for lending to such as shall be so apprenticed, if their conduct shall have been meritorious, a certain some [sic] of money at the expiration of their apprenticeship, to establish them in business.

Such gentlemen as are natives of, or interested in the prosperity of the county, are invited to contribute to the support of the Society.

The charity would provide help to qualifying ▶

children by inviting applications from those wishing to undertake an apprenticeship. The committee would then vote for those candidates that they wished to assist, and the successful ones would have their apprenticeship premiums (the charge made to the child by the employer providing the training) paid in two instalments, often referred to as *moieties*.

The numbers of children who could be afforded such assistance was determined by the financial flows into the Society: something which could fluctuate from year to year.

Funding for this eminently benevolent, socially progressive undertaking was to come from membership subscriptions and donations, often secured in the convivial environment of the annual festival.

This would comprise an annual meeting of members, followed by a dinner attended by members and guests.

As time passed, the Wiltshire Society would go on to receive legacies from former members and benefactors, and thereafter secure a further income stream by way of interest generated from Government Securities (monies which, under the original trust deed, could only be used to fund London-based cases).

In 1871 it was decided to extend the reach of the charity to include poor children living in Wiltshire itself. The numbers found to be in need of assistance were not inconsiderable, and to augment the Society's funds, the committee decided to invite 'the ladies of Wiltshire' to help in arranging a Wiltshire Society Grand Ball.

The first such event duly took place on May 8, 1871, at the Willis Rooms in St James Street, and continued to be held most years thereafter, up to and including 1889.

Of course, the Society continued to hold its annual dinners as well. Having already celebrated its 50th anniversary at the Albion Hotel on June 8, 1866, it held its 75th anniversary at the same venue on June 16, 1891.

While the 84th annual meeting did take place on June 21, 1900, at the Board of Green Cloth, Buckingham Place, the actual dinner was cancelled 'because so many Wiltshire gentlemen were serving their country in South Africa, and as very few gentlemen had signified their intention of being present'.

An interesting observation was recorded by the society in 1905, when it was noted that apprenticeships in London 'had largely gone out of fashion', with many young people preferring to work in shops or warehouses, rather than take up apprenticeships.

In line with many other similar organisations (including the *Association of Wiltshiremen in London*), *The Wiltshire Society* paused its social activities during The Great War, only reconvening for its (delayed) centenary meeting at the Trocadero Restaurant in Shaftesbury Avenue, London, in May 1920.

Thereafter, in an attempt to revive the popularity of the dinners, the Society elected to hold them in late November rather than June, for fear of it clashing with other events on the social and sporting calendar.

Doubtless prompted by falling numbers, President Eric Long made the following appeal via the press in 1928:

'In order that this Society may be placed on a sound basis, it is essential that it should have as many members as possible. I do appeal, therefore, to all your readers, that even if they cannot see their way to becoming members and sending as generous donations as possible, they will at least send some donation towards this Society. The membership is a guinea a year. A donation of £10 10s, at a single payment, or within a year, constitutes a Life Governorship, an annual payment of £1 1s entitles a person to be a member so long as it continues.'

The 1929 dinner was 'not quite so numerously attended as on former occasions', and at the dinner the following year, only 60 people were present, comparing very badly indeed with the one held, the previous March, by *The Association of Wiltshiremen in London,* which attracted 'over 400' Moonies.

No dinner was held in 1931, nor in 1932, when the Marquess of Ailesbury canceled the dinner scheduled for November 24, 'owing to the small response to the invitation to attend.'

He announced in the press:

'As President of the Society, I very much hope that all members will recognise the financial loss to the Society which will be caused by the absence of the usual dinner subscriptions, and that those who have not done so will be good enough to send to the Treasurer of the Society... a donation equal to the amount they had intended to give at the dinner.'

However, after a gap of three years, it was revived on July 11, 1934, by the then-President, E Harding Newman. It was noted that the society 'relies to a large extent on the contributions of those who attend the annual dinner and all others in whom the report of these proceedings awakens an interest' and that 'the lapse of this annual function has seriously affected the funds of the society'.

The attendance at this particular dinner was not large 'but judged a success', although, in the following year, 1935, the dinner was cancelled due to lack of support.

Despite all this, one further dinner was held, on July 8, 1936, at the Criterion Restaurant, and this was said to be 'very poorly attended' with only 23 people present.

By comparison (and as if to underline the contrasting fortunes of the two organisations), *The Association of Wiltshiremen in London*'s dinner that year was attended by around 300 people.

It may well have been that, put simply, *The Association of Wiltshiremen in London* put on a better show at much less money, which was probably highly significant during a financial downturn. And, as we shall see, they had a 'secret weapon' in raconteur and 'clubbable' after-dinner speaker, JH Thomas MP.

Not surprisingly, doubt was cast on whether to persevere with *The Wiltshire Society*'s annual event. Indeed, the committee would later conclude that this method of raising funds was 'somewhat out of date' and declined to arrange any more, preferring, instead, to solicit financial support directly from members and the wider public.

In tandem with this orientation to financial appeals alone, the meetings of the committee (which had traditionally been held in London since the charity's inception in 1817), switched to Devizes in 1932, and then on to Trowbridge on a more permanent basis.

The Wiltshire Society would continue to evolve as a more Wiltshire-centric organisation, later expanding its objects to encourage 'rural industries such as care and maintenance of agricultural machinery, farriers, thatching, and hurdle making,' having already stated that it would also assist 'children of poor Wiltshire-born persons residing in the County of Wiltshire or in London' by 'enabling them to go to sea or attend any practical science school'.

In 1950 its objects were further widened so that its funds could be used for 'the advancement of Wiltshire-born boys and girls, or one of whose parents are Wiltshire-born, up to the age of 21 years'.

We should not underestimate the role played by the nobility and prominent local politicians, as well as senior, Wiltshire-based military figures, in the success of the Society – by accepting honorary roles (such as President or Steward), and thereby attracting like-minded donors and benefactors.

The Wiltshire Society may have been seen as a rather exclusive organisation for the first century or so of its existence, limited to relatively well-to-do, public-spirited individuals.

It was a charitable organisation which saw a social event as a means to reach out to wealthy donors, whereas *The Association of Wiltshiremen in London* began life as a fellowship organisation, reaching out to old friends, and only subsequently adopting altruistic aims and objects.

And doubtless, class and social standing had a part to play, as well.

The Wiltshire Society was firmly rooted in the Establishment, but *The Association of Wiltshiremen in London* was different. Although it subsequently attracted a growing, aspirational lower middle-class and, in time, many members of the same titled families as had been long-standing supporters of *The Wiltshire Society*, it crucially had its origins as an 'upstart' working-class endeavour.

The most notable of these was George Brudenell-Bruce 6th Marquess of Ailesbury, who was President of *The Wiltshire Society* in 1932: a position which overlapped with his being President of *The Association of Wiltshiremen in London* during the period 1925 to 1948.

In addition, there are numerous examples where Presiding Chairmen at the dinners of *The Association of Wiltshiremen in London* were also, at one time or another, President of *The Wiltshire Society*. These included Sidney Herbert, 14th Earl of Pembroke; Thomas Henry Thynne, 5th Marquess of Bath; Jacob Pleydell-Bouverie, 6th Earl of Radnor; Edward Murray Colston (later 2nd Baron Roundway); and Col TCP Calley.

There are also examples of Stewards (Trustees) of *The Wiltshire Society* taking the chair as Presiding Chairmen of *The Association of Wiltshiremen in London*: Henry Brudenell-Bruce, 5th Marquess of Ailesbury; Lord Edmond FitzMaurice, 1st Baron FitzMaurice; and Evelyn Francis Seymour, 17th Duke of Somerset.

The Wiltshire Society retained a charity number (309531) and continued its charitable objectives until 2008, before finally being removed from the Charity Commission Register on March 31, 2010, when its assets were transferred to *The Community Foundation for Wiltshire & Swindon*.

And so, after more than three and a half centuries, the curtain finally came down on this specific type of organisation in Wiltshire. They formed a key part of the social framework and part of a complex network of benevolent and charitable organisations that were crucial in pre-Welfare State Britain, but continued to be influential and necessary even afterwards.

The histories of these organisations show they are somewhat different to *The Moonies in London* and *The Association of Wiltshiremen in London*. However, they often made proud reference to their ancient origins at their annual dinners. ∎

Reflections on *Wiltshireness*

From our vantage point in the 21st century, you could be excused for wondering why a key aspect of the meetings of *The Association of Wiltshiremen in London* was a deep sense of belonging to their home county.

Thanks to our increasingly global outlook, where borders could be seen as increasingly disposable, Wiltshire's boundaries might seem particularly obsolete.

And this is especially true in Swindon, which was Wiltshire's first new town in more than half a millennium, became a unitary authority in 1998, and in fact never has seemed like it was on the same wavelength as its county counterparts.

The Association of Wiltshiremen in London was an organisation that identified and tried to bolster what we might call *Wiltshireness*, celebrating the achievements of those born in the county, and developing a sense of allegiance – all at a time when they probably sensed that such loyalties were challenged by other circumstances.

However, Wiltshire is a survivor on a grand scale; in some respects it may be the greatest survivor we know. Because when you compare it with aspects of our lives that have undergone profound change over the centuries, our home county has remained a remarkably enduring entity on the map – and it's still there.

It is no surprise that the Association chose the legend of the Moonies as a rallying point. It binds us together like no other single aspect of Wiltshire life, and in the County Championship of emblems, it is right up there with Yorkshire's white rose and Cornish pasties.

One of the problems with understanding and contexting Wiltshire's history is it is *so* ancient, and the prehistoric treasures that survive and define our roots – places like Stonehenge, Avebury and Silbury Hill – are relics of a time before counties were even thought of.

But that's not to say that the concept of Wiltshire is not, itself, ancient.

A must-read book for those looking to understand the county's history and what binds its people together, including – rather appropriately – the origins of the Moonies, is *The Reflection in the Pond*, by John Chandler, subtitled *A Moonraking Approach to History*.

Chandler notes that there was a reference to *Wilsaete* in the year 802, its spelling changing to *Wiltunscir*, later in the ninth century.

This is the earliest known documented reference to the name, but the county had existed since the sixth century, when it was part of Wessex, and that Saxon kingdom was split into shires for administrative purposes: what we now know as the counties of Wiltshire, Hampshire, Dorset and Somerset.

There was a much less friendly arrangement with what we now call Gloucestershire, to the north, because that was part of the hostile neighbouring kingdom of Mercia – and this is key.

It means that while we may have come to consider county boundaries as mostly meaningless relics of administrative expediency born in a distant past, we should understand that when Wiltshire's northern boundary was first drawn, it was a frontier drawn in blood.

That is one of the reasons why the boundary has proved so resilient over a period of many centuries, and it is only in relatively modern times that it has been the subject of amendment, and then only superficially.

The boundary came under threat several times in the 19th century, firstly with a partial redrawing of maps in 1844, and then during the era of *The Association of Wiltshiremen in London*, boundaries being put under the microscope again in both the 1880s and the 1890s.

In the end the changes were only minor, happening mainly around the edge of the county, including what John Chandler calls 'tidying-up', such as the elimination of anomalies like the village of Poulton, which had been part of Wiltshire, despite being entirely surrounded by Gloucestershire, and was now transferred from the former to the latter.

At the same time, parts of Wiltshire's eastern fringes found themselves becoming part of Berkshire.

The potential fluidity of the boundary and a reconsideration of what it meant to be a Moonie could be seen as one of the reasons the Association latched on to county loyalty as strongly as it did.

Other threats to county identity had come with the Poor Law Act of 1834 and the establishment of urban and rural districts in 1894, both of which had the effect of watering down the authority of the old county as a whole.

The division of the county into poor law unions was significant because they took no account of county boundaries. The same was true of sanitary unions,

An artist's impression of 'Jefferies Mill' in Old Town (with the now-demolished Holy Rood Church in the background). Could this be the site of the legend of the Moonrakers?

when they were established in 1872, eroding, still further, the counties' roles.

This was particularly relevant in Wiltshire because of what John Chandler calls 'the Swindon effect'. Until the 18th century, Wiltshire was remarkable for its stability, and if there were any changes to its social life and culture, they were slow.

Then New Swindon happened.

When the Great Western Railway established its works and Railway Village, just north of Old Swindon in the 1840s, it became the first new town the county had seen since the turn of the 13th century.

But not only had it been a long time since it had seen a new town at all,

Swindon was like nothing seen in the county ever before.

Some of the impacts of this industrial urbanisation on the county landscape are clear enough, but others are less obvious.

The nature of the employment in the new Railway Works meant, for instance, that a significant degree of skilled labour needed to be imported, and they came from parts of the country most Wiltshire folk would not have even visited, such as Scotland and Tyneside.

At a time when the rest of the county's population was falling, Swindon's was – and still is – booming.

Ever since the earliest days of the railway town, the question of whether

industrial Swindon's heart was really in the otherwise agricultural Wiltshire has prevailed, and Swindonians inevitably ask themselves how much allegiance they ought to feel to a county it is often out of step with, on many different levels.

This must have been even more of an issue when *The Moonies in London* were formed, because although the separate (and, indeed, rival) towns of Old Swindon and New Swindon had yet to be unified – that didn't happen until 1900 – there is no doubt that the town had grown into a monster with a will of its own.

It would still be generations before it was officially cast adrift from the rest ▶

A photograph of WT Hemsley's moonrakers painting, which was presented to *The Association of Wiltshiremen in London* in 1895 (see page 109). When the original painting wasn't transported to London for the Association's annual dinners, it hung on the wall of the Mechanics' Institute, where it remained for at least 35 years, and possibly until 1977, but is now lost. At the 1896 dinner it was suggested that a photograph of the painting should be made and copies sold 'at a small profit which should form the nucleus for a 'Moonies' Dinner Fund'. This is almost certainly one of those copies. Hemsley's image became the definitive image of the moonrakers legend for many years, and was the basis for colourised postcards (see page 113). (Courtesy of Mike Attwell & Swindon Libraries/Local Studies)

of the county (in terms of administrative boundaries), but the founders of the Association must have sensed Swindon was starting to outgrow Wiltshire.

Ironically, even the most radical, controversial and unpopular upheaval of England's county boundaries, which took place in 1974, left Wiltshire untouched, and its County Council survives to this day. As does the legend of the Moonies, while the idea that being born (or coming to live) in the county unites us, culturally, is nothing if not persistent.

Indeed, the more the idea of counties is threatened, the more important legends like moonraking become.

Not that the basis or moral of the Moonrakers' story is peculiar to any single county or region; it was just that it was in Wiltshire that it stuck fast.

Actually, similar tales were common across the country and beyond, based on two principles. Firstly there was the general idea that you should under-estimate uneducated and seemingly simple-minded country folk at your peril; secondly there is the specific story of smugglers who, when caught trying to retrieve contraband from a pond under cover of darkness, pretend to have mistaken the moon's reflection for cheese, using their presumed idiocy as an excuse for being caught red-handed while trying to rake something from the water.

Some such stories predate the Wiltshire one by centuries, like the old French fable of *Del gupil e de la lune* (*The Fox and the Moon*), in which a fox tries to retrieve a cheese, which he thinks is floating in a pond, by drinking the pond dry. Ironically, its author, the mysterious Marie de France, may actually have lived in England, and one theory is that she was Marie, Abbess of Shaftesbury, who was – even more ironically – a Wiltshire landowner.

Although the evidence would seem to suggest that the moonraking story is apocryphal, and there never was an actual incident of the smugglers outwitting the excisemen in this way, in Wiltshire we are not so sure.

There has long been a train of thought that a real person is at the heart of the legend, with persistent claims and counter-claims about the specific location of the incident, even if there is neither evidence nor consensus on which one, exactly, was the scene of the crime.

The ongoing hunt for the actual pond where the raking took place and any other details has had the effect of the validity of the original story being taken for granted, and this is probably a key reason for the persistence of the legend: the idea that it might one day be resolvable.

Historian Les Reeves identified no fewer than 20 contenders for the location, and John Chandler lists the most-fancied runners as ponds or streams at Poulshot, Collingbourne Ducis, Tilshead and Bishop's Cannings, although the bookies' favourite is the pond in Devizes known as The Crammer.

Of course, any pond in the county might be considered a possibility, and we can, for example, also nominate the mill pond (pictured on page 23) beside the old Holy Rood Church, at the top of Swindon's Old Town, in the knowledge that – legends being what they are – it is impossible to disprove.

Indeed, if one is to make a case for the location of the apparent raking of cheese, logic dictates that it would be more likely to occur in an area where cheesemaking was common, such as Swindon.

Wiltshire was often said to be divided between 'the chalk and the cheese': the fertile chalky parts where arable was common, and the clay-ridden pastures, mostly found in the north and north-west, where dairy farming and therefore cheesemaking prevailed. Devizes might be the favourite as the home of the original *Moonie*, but it is on the dividing line between the two parts of the county, so less likely to be awash with cheeses than Swindon.

Another reason why Wiltshire fits the moonraking story (and another reason why it stuck here) is the county is, indeed, on a smuggling route. Contraband being brought through southern ports and distributed north, or to London, not only would have often been routed through Wiltshire, but it would have been a con-venient stopping-off point for the night.

The first documented reference to the 'Wiltshire Moon-Rakers' appeared in the Western County Magazine in 1791, but the wording suggested it was established at least a generation earlier, so perhaps around 1760. This disproves certain other claims that the legend originated in other counties, those stories either being from a later date, or the supposed location being a pond that did not exist in 1791; so the smart money remains on Wiltshire's moonrakers being the oldest.

One thing is certain in all this: *The Association of Wiltshiremen* (as they were to become) saw moonrakers as a conve-nient and effective 'handle' to latch on to.

Resurrecting the story was the obvious way to reestablish an allegiance to Wiltshire, but maybe they had another motive; perhaps it was also about redemption.

For generations, the story of the moonrakers had been a symbol of supposedly simple-minded country folk being not as daft as others thought them to be, but while the story may have been an example of this, it wasn't evidence.

But whenever *The Association of Wiltshiremen in London* met, they were at pains to list real-life examples of the pre-eminence of fellow Moonies.

After generations when one had to take a Wiltshireman's word for it that he and his neighbours were smarter than you might think, now they provided proof, continually highlighting and toasting men from Wiltshire and their achievements.

In other words, they had a new message: we told you so. ■

Humble beginnings

The inaugural dinner of what was to become *The Association of Wiltshiremen in London* took place on March 13, 1886.

No news report of the event has been found, but the dinner is documented as having taken place on this date in Plumstead, and although the location is unknown, it was probably at the Prince Alfred Hotel, a modest hostelry overlooking Plumstead Common.

The event was evidently a development of a more informal reunion initiative, and although two other men (Charles Spratt and Frank Wallington) were involved, it seems to have largely been a collaboration between two brothers-in-law, namely John Templeman and Henry 'Harry' Batten.

These men are the first Moonies, Movers and Shakers we shall encounter in this story. No known photographs of them exist of the men, they have been overlooked in most histories of Swindon, and they might appear humble, but they are an appropriate example of the vision and talent possessed by certain Swindon men during this era – and deserve some study.

Both Templeman and Batten completed apprenticeships at Swindon's Railway Works before finding new employment at the Royal Arsenal in Woolwich.

John Templeman, who was to be *The Moonies in London*'s first chairman, was born in Swindon in 1852, barely a decade after the foundation of the railway town. He began his apprenticeship as an erector in 1866, completing it exactly seven years later.

The family lived at 24 Reading Street, in the Railway Village.

After his marriage in 1875 (to Harry Batten's sister, Lucy), Templeman moved with his wife to Islington, although by 1886 he was living in Plumstead, and working at the Royal Arsenal.

Templeman would be Chair of *The Moonies in London* for ten years.

At the time of his death on March 19, 1928, at the age of 76, he had moved to the adjacent borough of Woolwich.

Harry Batten, who was born in 1845, apprenticed as an engine fitter. He was originally from Chard in Somerset, but moved to Swindon with his family.

The 1861 census showed him to be living at 6 Taunton Street, in Swindon's Railway Village, then 34 Cheltenham Street in 1871, followed by 36 William Street, ten years later.

During this time he became a well-known figure in Swindon as an amateur entertainer: singer, comedian and multi-instrumentalist.

Between 1878 and 1885 he was a leading member of the *New Swindon Amateur Minstrels* (also known as *The New Swindon Amateur Christy Minstrels*) and was treasurer of the *New Swindon Choral Society*.

He was briefly the licensee of the Fox Tavern in Regent Street, in 1885, but it didn't end well; a benefit concert was necessary in the Mechanics' Institute to pay off his debts, principally to the New Swindon Aerated Water Company.

The following year he left Swindon for good, moving his family to Plumstead and securing a job as a fitter at the Royal Arsenal.

He also became an active member of the Woolwich branch of the Amalgamated Society of Engineers.

Not daunted by his experience in Swindon, in July 1886 he took over as the licensee of the Coopers Arms in Woolwich, and became the resident

pianist at the New Sixty Club, at the Railway Tavern (pictured, above), the venue for subsequent meetings of *The Moonies in London* – in 1888 and 1889.

Batten sang sentimental ballads and comic songs, such as *Where are my schoolmates gone?* (see page 227), and

was a noted comedian, but also a versatile musician, playing the harp, ocarina, pico, piano and piccolo.

At the time of his death in 1899, he was landord of the Pelton Arms, Plumstead.

Frank Wallington, who was the Honorary Secretary from 1893 until 1901, and

continued to attend dinners until 1913 (with the exception of 1911 and 1912), was originally from Gloucester, but served his apprenticeship as an engine fitter at Swindon Railway Works.

By 1891 he had moved to Plumstead to live with his brother's family, before ▶

marrying in 1892. In the 1911 census he is listed as 'engineer (steamship)'.

Wallington eventually emigrated to the United States and died in Eton, Georgia, in 1936.

Charles 'Charlie' Spratt gave his rendition of *Wiltshire Jack* at several annual dinners (see page 95) but although he embodied everything that *The Moonies in London* stood for, he wasn't technically a Wiltshireman. Born in Bridgwater, he came to Swindon as a coach builder, initially lodging at 6 Cambria Place, and later moving to 8 Bridge Street.

His final performance was in 1900, and with the changing focus of the annual dinners, his name was soon missing from future guest lists.

But his death in June 1925 didn't go unnoticed by the *Swindon Advertiser*:

A very old and familiar figure in Swindon for the past half-century or more has been removed by the death, at the age of 77 years, of Mr Charles John Spratt...

"Charlie" Spratt, as he was known to a host of friends, was a born comedian and in his younger days he was always sought after to sing some of the popular comic songs of the day. He was at one time a leading member of the old Amateur Dramatic Society connected with the Mechanics' Institution. Deceased was also one of the first members of the Association of Wiltshiremen in London.

He was a prominent member of the RAOB [Royal and Ancient Order of Buffaloes]... the first treasurer of the GWR Retired Members

Association, and did much good work for the Victoria Hospital.

The inaugural dinner that these men organised in 1886 to try to bring together former Swindon railwaymen who found themselves in London turned out to be a modest affair, with between 15 and 20 people attending.

But the mould was cast.

Almost exactly a year later, on March 12, 1887, they reconvened, this time with the *Swindon Advertiser* reporting the meeting.

Under a headline reading 'Swindonians at Woolwich (1st Annual Reunion Dinner)', the paper reported:

A meeting of Swindonians employed in Woolwich Arsenal was held on Saturday last at the Prince Alfred Hotel, Raglan-road, Plumstead,

when about thirty sat down to a very substantial dinner supplied by the host, Mr Kaenema, the chair being taken by Mr J Templeman, vice chair Mr J Bremner, after which a very enjoyable evening was spent in conviviality. Mr Bailey (harp), and Mr Johnson (clarionet[sic]) accompanied the songs, and the following was the programme:

Selections (accompanists); song, "A Warrior Bold, Mr J Reynolds; song, "Mrs Jones's Musical Party," Mr P Richardson; song, "Little Sister's Gone to Sleep," Mr Parsons; song, "Paris Exhibition," (encore); song, "Our Hands Have Met But Not Our Hearts," Mr Brookman.

At this stage of the proceedings, a letter of apology was handed in from two Swindon celebrities now employed at Belvedere-road, London EC, which caused much amusement.

Song, "Always Pull Together," Mr Jones; toast, "The old Swindonians," which was ably replied to by Mr J Bremner; song, "Sailing," Mr G Calton; solo clarionet, "Auld Robin Gray," Mr Johnson; song, "Welcome Ever, Welcome Friends," Mr Cox; song, "My Sweetheart When A Boy," Mr Baker; song, "By The Dawn," Mr Bremner; song, "Mow Down The Meadow," Mr Richards.

Toasts were next given for the managers and foremen of the Swindon Works, which were suitably replied to by Messrs Bremner, Ferguson, Fisher and Parsons. Song, "When We Were Boys Together," Mr R Watson; song, "My Mother's Welcome Home," Mr Wallington; song, "I Haven't Told The Misses [sic] Up To Now," Mr P Richardson; song, "The Two Great Statesmen," Mr Brookman; duet, "All's Well," Mr Bailey and Mr Reynolds.

A toast was next given to Mr Braid, late schoolmaster of GWR Schools, to which Mr A Wright ably replied; song, "Empty Is The Cradle," Mr A Watson; song, "Lullaby," Mr J Howcroft; song, "Auld Lang Syne," Mr C Ferguson. The Chairman then proposed a vote of thanks to the worthy host, which was heartily given.

The party then broke up, all present having thoroughly enjoyed themselves. ∎

'Where are my schoolmates gone?'

In 1887, *The Moonies in London* toasted the 'late schoolmaster of GWR Schools', their words suggesting the incumbent, Alexander James Braid, was dead.

But the reference was to his post, not the man; he had, in fact, retired ten years earlier, so although he probably could not be said to be alive and *well*, he was certainly *alive*.

Toasts and tributes to Braid would become a recurring theme in meetings of *The Moonies in London*, often accompanied with the wish that he would be able to attend next year's meeting, but ill health prevented him from ever doing so.

The ongoing reverence towards Braid from a number of his former pupils tells us that he must have been an extremely popular teacher, but also an influential character outside the school (pictured, opposite, in the 1870s). Braid, in fact, had played a key role in the formation of the Mechanics' Institution when, in January 1844, he became its first Secretary.

In 1865, he participated in the first of the People's Penny Readings at the Mechanics'. These became a Swindon tradition, the proceeds helping to establish the GWR Medical Fund Society for local railway workers that was to become a blueprint for the National Health Service.

Braid had taken up residency in the schoolhouse, which was attached to the school in Bristol Street, by 1851, long before he actually became schoolmaster; it was a post he held from 1859 to 1877.

Teaching was something of a family affair as his wife, Jane, was a school-mistress, and at least two of the Braids' daughters also worked in the school.

Other historical sources show that although Braid was remembered as a strict disciplinarian – as one might expect from a schoolmaster in this era – there is some evidence of a lighter approach; in 1863, for example, buns and oranges were given to pupils as a Christmas treat.

But quality education didn't end with Braid.

At *The Moonies*' dinner of 1899, one speaker said 'Swindon... possessed the best system of education in the county', which was probably true – but it had been a rocky road.

Even as the new railway maintenance facility at Swindon was being built – it opened on January 2, 1843 – provision ▶

was being made for the incoming workforce and their families.

The first building on the south side of the main line was the GWR school, built in 1844, on land bought from Col Thomas Vilett.

The GWR were intent on retaining control of the school, despite the very close proximity of St Mark's, and even though the two existing schools in Swindon had both been established by churches.

The school was a single-storey building with three classrooms – one each for boys and girls, and a separate room for infants. The two-storey schoolmaster's house was attached, forming an L-shape around separate playgrounds for boys and girls.

The fact that girls were admitted is significant; this was not an era when society as a whole thought girls' education was a priority.

At first all the pupils were GWR employees' children, and as well as 'the three Rs', lessons included geography, history and scripture (religious education).

A major feature of school life was overcrowding; the school wasn't large enough to cope with the demand from the ever-expanding Works and town.

One answer was to build a new infants' school 'extension', which was actually a separate building, south of the main school building and playground, facing on to Bristol Street/Church Place and the park. Although a plaque on the outside of this building claims it was built 'about 1870', in fact it was put up in 1856/7.

The new building alleviated but didn't cure the overcrowding, and in the 1860s rooms in the Mechanics' Institute were turned into makeshift classrooms, and also in 'The Barracks' (later the Railway Museum and now The Platform) in the 1870s, as well as the Rifle Corps' drill hall, in the north-west corner of the park, after it opened in 1871.

In the end, a new school had to be built – in College Street, which opened in 1873 (and is now demolished). This took the girls and infants, while the boys remained at the original school.

Even this was inadequate, and in 1877 the schoolmaster had to turn new children away.

However, in that year, responsibility for education was passed from the GWR to the Local Board (a forerunner of the Council), and four new schools were built in the 1880s: at Sanford Street and Gilberts Hill (in Dixon Street), which still stand, plus Birch Street and Queenstown, which are demolished.

The order to pull down the original 1844 GWR school was made in February 1882, but the infants' school extension of 1856/7 was retained.

Braid's successor as schoolmaster at the GWR School was John Williams, and when it closed, he became the first schoolmaster at Sanford Street.

Williams was a very early and enthusiastic supporter of *The Moonies in London*, attending his first dinner in 1892, and was present for all except one until his final appearance in 1901. During that time he persuaded fellow *Moonies* to grant a sponsorship for pupils at his school.

His death at the age of 53, in 1904, was greeted with much regret, not least from the Advertiser, which reported:

We regret to record the death of Mr John Williams, for 23 years headmaster of the Sanford Street Schools, Swindon, which occurred at Badbury on Thursday last.

As the headmaster for so many years of the largest school in the town, Mr Williams was well-known and highly respected by a host of Swindonians. By his death a prominent figure passes from the stage of Swindon life.

Swindon suffers a loss, particularly the educational section of the town, and Swindon Welshmen mourn the loss of a whole-hearted Cymro.

Mr Williams was born at Swansea on January 13th, 1851. He attended the National School in that town, and remained there to serve his apprenticeship to his profession, under Mr Cole.

From there he went to Cheltenham College, and on leaving in December 1870, he came to Swindon as an assistant master, under the late Alexander J Braid, at the GWR School in Church Place.

On Mr Braid's retirement... Mr Williams succeeded to the headmastership of the school.

He took an active interest in the teachers, and became a president of the local branch of the NUT, represented the local teachers at numerous conferences, and also became a member of the executive of the NUT.

The deceased was a highly successful schoolmaster, and his scholars stood high in the various scholarship lists...

Scholastic duties did not absorb all the interests of the deceased. He was for some time a member of the old Urban District Council. He was also a Freemason for over 20 years. He was a Past Master of the Gooch Lodge, 1295, and a PPG St Br of the Wiltshire Province...

Deceased leaves a widow, but no family, to mourn his loss. And to the widow much sympathy goes out in her bereavement.

The funeral was very largely attended. Mrs Williams was too much indisposed to be present.

A striking evidence of the warm esteem in which the deceased gentleman was held, was to be seen in the fact that there were about 300 of the boys from the School present. ■

The 'inside' story

An apprentice doing a typically menial task in Swindon Works

To understand why *The Moonies in London* came about in the first place, we need to consider what we might call the *inside story* of railway employment in Swindon; more accurately, it should probably be described as the story of being 'inside'.

The term 'inside' was universally understood in the town to be a reference to working behind the high brick wall of the GWR Works, and although strangers hearing this might have sniggered at its suggestion of imprisonment, there was a partial reality in it.

After all, workers spoke of 'serving my time' as an apprentice or having 'done their time', before becoming skilled journeymen, as if it were a sentence.

But it is what happened to them at the end of their apprenticeships that is central to our story, because – far from being a passport to a permanent 'job for life' in Swindon, as one might imagine – for a long period it was the policy of the railway company to dismiss men, once they had been qualified.

From the apprentice's point of view, the policy was significant not just because he found himself unemployed, but because Swindon was effectively a one-industry town, and that almost inevitably meant uprooting one's home and finding work and accommodation, elsewhere in the country.

There is a great irony to all this because job prospects in Swindon during the existence of *The Moonies in London/The Association of Wiltshiremen* were often better than in other parts of the country.

While the world experienced the Great Depression, for example, from the late 1920s and right through the 1930s, Swindon, in relative terms, thrived.

Indeed, this between-the-wars period is what we might consider Swindon's golden age, when it was producing the majestic Castle and King Class locomotives.

So although Swindon was not immune to global economic ups and downs, and there were periods when lay-offs were necessary, there ought to have been a degree of stability among the town's railway workforce that was denied men from other places and other industries.

Dismissal at the end of their apprenticeship was a fact of life for men of many different trades, and something they knew would happen, even before they signed up to be an apprentice.

In terms of employment and career advancement, this was not a problem; the GWR had a worldwide reputation for engineering excellence, and a qualified man leaving Swindon Works often found he had a ticket to a new job that would be valid across most industries, not just railways.

Wherever you would find large industry across Britain, indeed, you were liable to find a Swindon man or two – so it is no surprise to find the likes of John Templeman and Harry Batten (see page 26) working in the Royal Arsenal at Woolwich.

Being able to get another job after leaving the GWR is one thing; the personal upheaval that comes with changing jobs and moving away is another.

We should not lose sight of the fact ▸

that these men were still young. Their apprenticeships commonly started when they were 13 or 14, and lasted seven years (five for latter generations), so they were barely in their twenties when they had to leave behind everything and everyone they knew – for a migration that could take them far from home, and possibly even abroad.

Most of these would have been single, but for some it meant leaving Swindon with a young wife and baby (or babies).

The psychological side of this uprooting is not recorded in Swindon's history, making it easy to overlook and underestimate its impact, and we can probably only imagine how it felt to be a young man forced to leave home in this way.

In some ways, the apprenticeship process anticipated this, and it might even be said that for generations of working-class men who received a short and basic schooling and had no prospect of a university education, they found themselves, instead, enrolled in a 'university of life' in Swindon Works.

We know this because there is a record of conditions and cultures 'inside', put down in the writings of various people who experienced it first hand.

It was really only when Alfred Williams (see page 176) published his book, *Life in a Railway Factory*, in 1915, that we were given the first detailed account of what it was like to be employed in Swindon Works, providing a vivid picture of what working life was like for railwaymen in general, and including the apprentice's lot.

When first employed and still green, it was inevitable that they would be the target of pranks, and it was almost a rite of passage for apprentices, for example, to be sent to the stores for a left-handed hammer, a bucket of steam or a long

weight (wait). But far more valuable induction was to follow, and Williams notes how teenage boys serving apprenticeships often learned a lot more than the trade they had been indentured for.

Some of the things they learned were not necessarily for the best, in Williams's opinion, and for those who had been brought up in the country, like him, there was an additional culture shock to contend with.

He noted that they were 'speedily initiated into the vices prevalent in the factory, and taught the current slang phrases and expressions'.

If they were lucky, however, they found their master to be a father figure, and Williams recounts the example of the foreman of 'the boy turners'. This man was:

a very good formative agent, one who will exercise a healthy restraint on the intractables and encourage the timid'... He very often furnished [the boy] with hints of a personal nature which – whatever the lad may think of them at the time – bear fruit in later life. If the youngster is inclined to be wild and incorrigible, he tries his best to reform him and gives him sound advice... [as well as] a corrective cuff in the ear and a vigorous boot in the posterior, but he usually succeeds in bringing out the good points and suppressing, if not eradicating, the bad.

While Williams provides contemporary accounts of life inside, a comprehensive retrospective of the conditions and culture 'inside' is provided by Rosa Matheson's invaluable book, *Doing Time Inside*, which is subtitled *Apprenticeships and Training in GWR's Swindon Works*.

She notes that 'Here is where the foundations were laid for that

"camaraderie", "companionship" and "being part of one big family", and membership of the "inside" fraternity.'

She notes:

Apprentices learned to adopt this identity very quickly and use it to their advantage. Friendship and camaraderie were essential ingredients in the apprenticeship formula, as they provided the glue that helped many a lad through the less pleasant side of being an apprentice – the dreariness, the drudgery, the poor pay, the rotten jobs, and being 'on the wrong end of the older men's temper'.

All of this would have been valuable experience when the time came for the journeyman to leave home and seek employment elsewhere.

Another useful window into this world is a memoir called simply *Swindon Apprentice*, written by AE Durrant, whose apprenticeship started soon after the end of the Second World War.

By then there was no requirement for apprentices to leave after qualifying, but we still get an insight into the mind of a 21-year-old leaving home, because Durrant had to do two years' National Service. Ordinarily, men started their service at the age of 18, but railway apprentices' call-ups were deferred until they completed their training.

An insight into how much more mature they were, thanks to serving their apprenticeships, is found in Durrant's observation that these slightly older men 'were collectively more mature and immune to NCO terrorism than the usual 18-year-old intake'.

The first part of Durrant's apprenticeship was in R Shop, which dates right back to Daniel Gooch's original railway works and is now the

Steam Museum. Over the generations, many apprentices found themselves in this building, because it contained the 'scraggery', where a number of routine and sometimes tedious turning jobs were carried out, such as the production of nuts and bolts.

It gives us a hint about why the policy of dismissing apprentices when they had served their time prevailed.

Durrant notes that it was in the scraggery that he first realised how 'apprentices seemed to be used as cheap labour, rather than learning anything of use, other than patience'.

This is a theme of Rosa Matheson's study, and she notes that one apprentice from the 1950s, Paul Warren, complained: 'It was slave labour. I did five years and it could have been completed in two. For three of them I was just cheap labour.'

She also notes that Roy Blackford, a coach finisher from a decade earlier, saw that the system provided a ready supply of this cheap labour, describing boys as 'food for the Works, generally'.

But the book also makes a key observation on how apprentices viewed the contract that they had entered into with the GWR (and later British Railways).

By the early 20th century, apprenticeships were not actually indentures, which bound either side to a contract for its full term; subject to giving notice, either side was now free to terminate the contract. So if being 'inside' hinted at a prison sentence, it was misleading, and yet of all the former apprentices that Rosa interviewed spoke of it as being binding, still clinging to the obsolete idea of being 'indentured'.

One of the reasons why completing an apprenticeship in Swindon was valued by other employers was the breadth of the skills learned. Although the qualification referred directly to a particular trade, a feature of many apprenticeships in the GWR was that they were not restricted to a particular shop, so apprentices would often get experience of a range of operations and meet a range of people, sometimes spread across numerous areas of the Works.

Again, this broadened their life experience and bolstered their self-confidence, as well as providing a comprehensive technical training.

They were exposed to a massive range of skills, bearing in mind that Swindon Works could produce almost everything required to run and service a railway, and the shops were split between the very different demands of producing rolling stock for 'loco side', predominantly in metal, and a 'carriage side' that required high skilled working in a range of other materials, including wood and upholstery.

In *Doing Time Inside*, Rosa Matheson points out that one apprentice, Alan Wild, worked in no fewer than 14 different shops, and his experience was not untypical.

Such was the breadth and depth of the skills they had learned that the routine of dismissing newly qualified journeymen seems all the more surprising, until we understand why.

It was simply because it was financially expedient for the company to continually take on low-paid apprentices, rather than pay the rates that a skilled man would demand.

Then, as now, any industry's biggest expense was labour, and with up to 14,000 people working for the GWR in Swindon at its peak, it was a very costly commodity indeed. With shareholders looking to maximise their investment, it was inevitable that the company looked for savings in wages, and with Swindon and the surrounding district providing an ever-ready supply of new apprentices to replace them, it was a sound financial policy to jettison journeymen as soon as they qualified and could demand a full salary. ▸

DOING TIME INSIDE

APPRENTICESHIP AND TRAINING IN GWR'S SWINDON WORKS

ROSA MATHESON

There was, though, a price for the company to pay.

When apprenticeships first emerged in Britain, starting as long ago as the 12th century, they were largely a means of industries protecting their trade by carefully controlling and restricting the way that skills were passed on to new generations.

This was the background to early Freemasonry (see page 38) and often led to the foundation of guilds, but later the role was taken up by unions, because although the obvious role of a union is to protect workers against employers and win better conditions and pay, they also exist to protect the trades of their skilled and qualified members against unskilled labour.

So while the GWR relied on apprenticeships for economic reasons, the company was also feeding this idea of protectionism, demarcation and closed shops, where employment was dependent on being a member of a union (although, ironically, apprentices were usually not required to be a member of a union, even in a closed shop).

All this took place against a growing unionisation and militancy in industrial relations in general, and it is perhaps no coincidence that railway unions had a reputation for being among the more militant.

Jimmy Thomas MP, whom we will meet later in the story, is a reminder of this.

(21-1)

1901.
Great Western Railway.

Locomotive, Carriage & Wagon Department.

CHIEF MECHANICAL ENGINEER'S OFFICE,

Swindon, Wilts. August 22nd. 1922.

32894.

Certificate of Apprenticeship.

I hereby certify that

Leslie John PONTING.

born on the 4th. July 1901. has been employed as an Apprentice in this Department as follows:—

Period of Apprenticeship Six years from 4.7.1916 to 3.7.1922.

Trade Boilermaking.

Works at which employed Locomotive Department, Swindon. Ponting bears a good character, and has completed his term in a satisfactory manner.

1922 to 1965

CHIEF MECHANICAL ENGINEER.
G.W.R. Loco, Carriage & Wagon Department

(500. R52 10.21.L. 666)

So it can be seen that the formation of *The Moonies in London*, with its intention of bringing together displaced former railwaymen who now found themselves isolated, was a direct result of apprenticeships and the migration of skilled men from Swindon.

And it is easy to see why the association took the form of a reunion for Swindonians at first.

As we shall see, it soon evolved and mushroomed into a social and welfare organisation, concerned with softening the impact on these young men who found themselves in a strange city, so far from home – and if they needed a model, the tradition of benevolent societies for displaced people in general and for Wiltshire in particular, was a readymade one.

However, *The Association of Wiltshiremen in London* (as it would become) developed its own unique character, telling us much about the sense of belonging felt by people from Swindon and the rest of the county, and becoming a vehicle for expressions of fraternity, loyalty and pride that became a kind of outpouring.

For the student of history, the reports of the Association's annual dinners in the local press provide a surprising and often touching insight into what it meant to be a Swindonian and a Moonie over a period spanning 70 years. ■

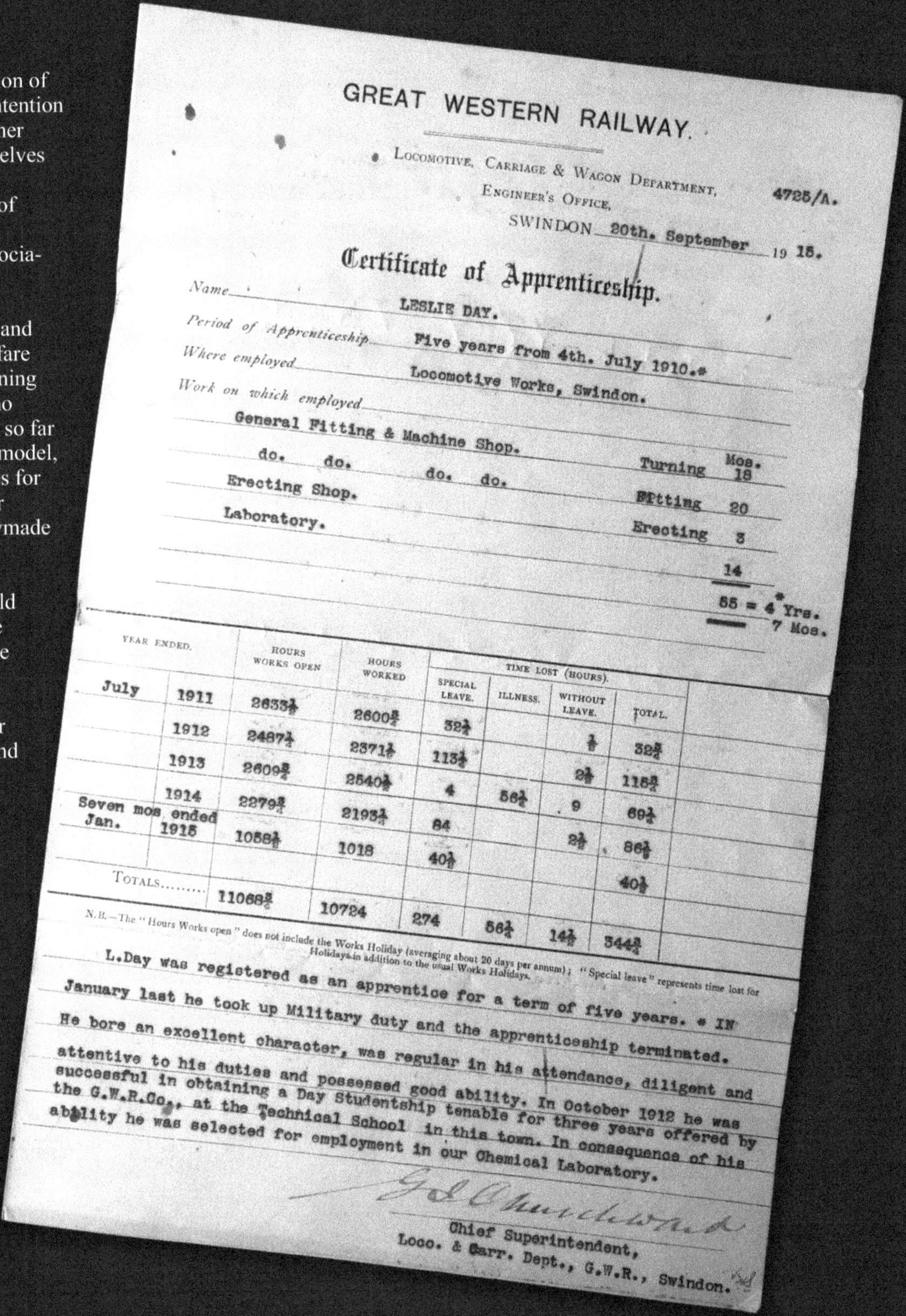

GREAT WESTERN RAILWAY.

LOCOMOTIVE, CARRIAGE & WAGON DEPARTMENT, 4725/A.
ENGINEER'S OFFICE,
SWINDON 20th. September 1915.

Certificate of Apprenticeship.

Name LESLIE DAY.
Period of Apprenticeship Five years from 4th. July 1910.*
Where employed Locomotive Works, Swindon.
Work on which employed

		Mos.
General Fitting & Machine Shop.		
do. do. do. do.	Turning	18
Erecting Shop.	Fitting	20
Laboratory.	Erecting	3
		14
		55 = 4* Yrs. 7 Mos.

Year ended.		Hours Works open	Hours Worked	Time lost (hours). Special Leave.	Illness.	Without Leave.	Total.
July	1911	2633½	2600¾	32¼		½	32¾
	1912	2487¼	2371½	113¼		2½	115¾
	1913	2609¾	2540½	4	56¼	9	69¼
	1914	2279¾	2193¼	84		2½	86½
Seven mos ended Jan.	1915	1058½	1018	40½			40½
Totals.........		11068¾	10724	274	56¼	14½	344¾

N.B.—The "Hours Works open" does not include the Works Holiday (averaging about 20 days per annum); "Special leave" represents time lost for Holidays in addition to the usual Works Holidays.

L.Day was registered as an apprentice for a term of five years. * IN January last he took up Military duty and the apprenticeship terminated. He bore an excellent character, was regular in his attendance, diligent and attentive to his duties and possessed good ability. In October 1912 he was successful in obtaining a Day Studentship tenable for three years offered by the G.W.R.Co., at the Technical School in this town. In consequence of his ability he was selected for employment in our Chemical Laboratory.

G J Churchward
Chief Superintendent,
Loco. & Carr. Dept., G.W.R., Swindon.

Apprenticeship papers for co-author Noel Ponting's paternal grandfather (opposite) and maternal grandfather (right).
Note the signatures by Chief Mechanical Engineers Charles B Collett and GJ Chruchward respectively.

We have already seen that *The Association of Wiltshiremen in London* was neither unique nor original in its purpose and aims, but came from a long tradition of similar organisations based in Wiltshire.

It is also important to understand that, in the generations before the birth of the Welfare State and the evolution of the national (and even international) charities that we are familiar with today, many other fraternal and benevolent organisations existed as part of a complex support network in the county, of which the Association was only part.

This remarkably diverse network includes all kinds of organisations devoted to supporting the 'deserving poor', from workhouses and almshouses to churches, with both the Church of England and non-conformists (who were particularly strongly anchored in Swindon life), providing relief.

Other charity-minded fraternities have long histories too, and some still survive today, such as Rotary and Round Table.

It would be difficult to find a town in the whole of Britain where the appetite for forming organisations for mutual benefit was more prevalent than in Swindon.

This is most obvious in the two key organisations that existed from the 1840s to support railwaymen and their families, namely the Mechanics' Institute and the groundbreaking GWR Medical Fund (whose baths complex (now called the Health Hydro) in Milton Road, is pictured).

The latter had already celebrated its centenary when it provided the blueprint for the formation of the National Health Service in 1948, allowing the rest of the country to finally catch up with Swindon's comprehensive medical support system. ▸

Strength in numbers

While emphasising that both these organisations were essentially created *by* the workers, *for* the workers, it should also be said that the GWR's support for the Mechanics' and the Medical Fund also helped to further this Swindon tradition of benevolence, charity and brotherhood.

Meanwhile, a number of friendly and building societies became firmly established in the town, and the Co-operative movement took root in Swindon in 1850, just six years after the formation of the pioneering Rochdale organisation.

Sadly, no comprehensive history of these organisations has so far been published, despite their crucial role in forming the town's character and even what we might celebrate as an enduring 'Swindon spirit', and it is beyond the scope of this book to chart them all.

It is useful, however, to log the history of one of these organisations, the Freemasons, and the irony is that despite the often-levelled accusations against their secretive nature, their history is well documented.

It is important to look at the Freemasons so that we can put *The Association of Wiltshiremen in London* into context, not just because of the obvious similarities between them, but also because a number of the characters we will meet in the following pages (and some we have already met) were either known to be Freemasons, or probably were, and the man who is sometimes called the 'father of New Swindon', Sir Daniel Gooch (pictured, opposite), was a prominent Freemason too.

There is also some common ground between the growth of apprenticeships (see page 31) and the rise of Freemasonry.

That's because they also evolved from guilds: specifically those of stonemasons and cathedral builders, established in the Middle Ages. At the core of the origins of Freemasonry is the regulation of the stonemasons' trade and the running of apprenticeship schemes that set minimum standards of workmanship, thereby safeguarding the economic interests of its members, as well as providing protection and mutual aid.

In this respect, their purpose seems to mirror the role of trade unions, another part of the welfare network, and one that found fertile ground among Swindon's railwaymen as that movement grew, particularly in the early 20th century.

The Freemasons' roots, however, are ancient. From the 13th century onwards, and maybe even earlier, stonemasons congregated in 'lodges', the workrooms attached to a building in the course of construction.

But as a consequence of the decline of cathedral building, some lodges of operative (ie, working) masons began to accept 'honorary' journeymen and master craftsmen as a way to boost their declining membership.

By the beginning of the 1600s, relatively few such groups remained in existence, and those which had survived were instead meeting in public houses and taverns. Yet isolated and independent Lodges of Freemasons were starting to spring up in London and elsewhere, composed mainly (if not entirely) of non-operative masons, and these adopted the rites and trappings of ancient religious orders and chivalric brotherhoods.

For example, it is believed that Sir Robert Moray, a founder and first President of the Royal Society, was made a Freemason of 'The Lodge of Edinburgh' at Newcastle in 1641. According to his Wiki entry, 'this is the earliest extant record of a man being initiated into speculative Freemasonry on English soil.'

Furthermore, it is recorded that Elias Ashmole, the celebrated Antiquarian, was made a Freemason at Warrington in 1646. His diary entry for October 16 in that year reads: 'I was made a Free Mason at Warrington in Lancashire, with Coll: Henry Mainwaring of Karincham in Cheshire.'

These isolated, speculative Lodges were operating entirely independently of any central control, with each of them observing their own formal, ceremonial rituals, each of a very prescribed and solemn nature.

However, much was to change in June 1717, when four Lodges, meeting in London at the Goose & Gridiron Tavern, agreed to form themselves into the 'Grand Lodge of London & Westminster' (an association of Lodges) and elected their first Grand Master.

While many people will look to this one event as the birth of Freemasonry as we know it today (ie, the creation of what would later become the Grand Lodge of England) it must be remembered that the very first Lodges were actually to be found in Scotland. To quote from an article published in 2016 by Amanda Ruggeri:

By the late 1500s, there were at least 13 established lodges across Scotland, from Edinburgh to Perth. But it wasn't until the turn of the [17th] Century that those medieval guilds gained an institutional structure – the point which many consider to be the birth of modern Freemasonry.

For the first six years of its existence, the Grand Lodge (in England) concentrated its efforts on growing 'the craft' in and around London, although by 1724, Lodges were also being constituted in Bristol, Bath and in Norwich. And

within a year or so it is said there were about 70 Lodges under the central control of the Grand Lodge, comprising around 1,400 Brethren.

The movement was relatively slow to catch on in Wiltshire; by 1727, only two speculative working Lodges were thought to be operating in the county.

One was in Salisbury (later to be known as Salisbury Lodge No 109), while the other met in Devizes (known simply as 'Lodge at the Crown Inn').

During the very same year, the Grand Lodge in London began the process of grouping the various disparate Lodges across England into Provinces.

Freemasonry in Wiltshire saw a period of growth from broadly this point onwards, resulting in the formation of the following Lodges (receiving their formal Warrant of Constitution on the dates shown in brackets): Sarum (Salisbury) (1732), Warminster #1 (1735), Chippenham (1763), Melksham (1765), Marlborough (1768), Warminster #2 (1770), Devizes (1770).

This activity in the county ultimately resulted in the formation of the Provincial Grand Lodge of Wiltshire in 1775, under the authority of the first Provincial Grand Master, Col Sir Thomas Fowke.

However, there is no evidence that any meeting in the county was ever held under his direction. Indeed, it is thought he didn't even visit Wiltshire during his period in office.

With no discernible progress being made, the Grand Lodge instead appointed Thomas ▶

Dunckerley as Superintendant in Charge, in 1777, and he gets the credit for convening possibly the first ever meeting of the Provincial Grand Lodge for Wiltshire, on September 22, 1777, although only Salisbury Lodge is mentioned in the records as having been in attendance.

It is thought that the early Warminster Lodge and one at Marlborough had been erased from the Grand Lodge Register by this time, and any others are assumed to have closed down. Even the lodge at Devizes, while still in existence, appears to have been a no-show.

Dunckerley stood down in 1792, and there followed a further extended period of uncertainty as to the future of 'the craft' in Wiltshire. Indeed, it was stated in 1823 that Freemasonry in Wiltshire was 'sinking into nothing for want of a helping hand to cheer and support it'.

Two years later, John Rock Grosett, the MP for Chippenham, took over as the second Provincial Grand Master, but showed little interest, and a further period of apathy set in.

It took until the appointment of Frederick, 2nd Baron Methuen as the third Provincial Grand Master, in 1853, for the Province of Wiltshire to emerge from stasis.

Installed in Swindon on September 6, he went on to hold office for 38 years, and under his stewardship Freemasonry saw something of a revival, increasing from only four active Lodges to 11, with a total membership of over 500.

Quoting from *A History of Freemasonry in Wiltshire*, published in 1880, Lord Methuen is accorded particular praise by the author, Frederick Hastings Goldney:

> *The popularity and high standing of the craft in this Province of Wiltshire, so different from what it*

was but a few years ago, when it could boast of but two working lodges and a score of subscribing members, is, in a great measure, due to the exertions of the PGM, Lord Methuen, who for upwards of a quarter of a century has had the Province under his charge, and who, by his unwavering interest in the maintenance of good order and harmony in the lodges, by his courtesy towards the brethren, by his constant attendance at the meetings of Provincial Grand Lodge, and by his impartiality in the discharge of the duties devolving upon his high office, has so materially aided in increasing the numbers of the lodges and brethren, and establishing that genuine feeling of loyalty towards himself, and good-will towards one another, which is here so happily displayed.

The author also sought to pay due regard to the three brethren who had served under Lord Methuen as Deputy Provincial Grand Master: Sir Gabriel Goldney, Lord Henry F Thynne MP, and one of the most important men in Swindon's history, Sir Daniel Gooch.

It was said of Gooch that his 'fame as a Mason is almost as widespread as his great reputation in the outer world' and that he 'bore the heat and burden of the work of the Province for 16 years from the time of his lordship's appointment, and rested not from his labours until in 1869 he was summoned to fill the higher office of Provincial Grand Master for Berks and Bucks, whither his great popularity amongst the brethren has followed him.'

There is often much speculation and mystery associated with the aims and objectives of Freemasonry, its membership criteria and its initiation rites.

From about 1725 the ceremonial trappings associated with marking the passage of an individual as he progressed through 'the craft', developed into a series of three degrees. All were of a very solemn character and had their own special teachings, namely reaching the

moral and social duties of Man to God, his Neighbour and Himself; searching into the hidden mysteries of nature and science, inculcating fidelity and trustworthiness with true fellowship in this life; and finally, emphasising life after death, or the immortality of the soul.

In the *Freemason's Pocket Companion*, published in 1735, William Smith relates many of the tenets of the craft, a prerequisite of which is a reverence to an unnamed, neutral Creator, also referred to as The Great Architect of the Universe.

The responsibilities conferred upon new initiates included aims and tenets that we will often see echoed in the meetings held by *The Moonies in London/The Association of Wiltshiremen in London*:

- Doing as you would be done by
- Acting with honesty
- Avoiding all intemperances and excesses
- Behaving as a peaceable and dutiful subject
- Being a Man of Benevolence and Charity, not sitting down contented while his Fellow Creatures, but much more his Brethren, are in want, when it is in his Power (without prejudicing himself or Family) to relieve them
- Becoming a lover of the Arts and Sciences, and taking all opportunities to improve oneself therein

The Royal Sussex Lodge of Emulation No 355 was consecrated on 1st May 1, 1818, making it Swindon's first Lodge; the unveiling of a blue plaque, in 2018, to mark the event, is pictured, opposite. Its formation is particularly auspicious, given that it pre-dates the town's railway era. It is also the second oldest active Lodge in Wiltshire.

Some background history of the Lodge appears in the book *A History of Freemasonry in Wiltshire* by Frederick Hastings Goldney, himself a former Senior Provincial Grand Warden. He notes:

The number of the lodge upon the books of the Grand Lodge was ▶

originally 702, which was altered in 1832 to 453, and in 1863 was brought forward to 355... It appears that the lodge met at the Goddard Arms Inn, Swindon, and that there were between 20 and 30 members, including Brothers T Calley MP, of Burderop Park, Rev D Williams, of Avebury House, and Richard Miles, of Morden House.

Today, this lodge meets at the Masonic Hall, at The Planks in Old Town.

Freemasonry records show a clear crossover between it and membership of *The Wiltshire Society*, and they enjoyed huge support at senior level from within the nobility and the landed gentry, and patronage extended, in due course, to the top table of *The Association of Wiltshiremen in London*.

For example, Frederick Henry Paul Methuen, 2nd Baron Methuen (1818-1891) was both Provincial Grand Master of Wiltshire (1853-1891) and President of *The Wiltshire Society* (1848 & 18870; William Pleydell-Bouverie, 5th Earl of Radnor (1841-1900) was Provincial Grand Master of Wiltshire (1891-1900) and President of *The Wiltshire Society* in 1875 (as Viscount Folkestone); Jacob Pleydell-Bouverie, 6th Earl of Radnor (1868-1930) was Provincial Grand Master of Wiltshire (1900-1928) and President of *The Wiltshire Society* (1894 & 1921), plus Presiding Chairman of *The Association of Wiltshiremen in London* (1906 & 1921), as well as being Lord Lieutenant of Wiltshire (1925-1930); Major General Thomas Charles Pleydell Calley (1856-1932) was Provincial Grand Master of Wiltshire (1928-1932) and President of *The Wiltshire Society* (1911), plus Presiding Chairman of *The Association of Wiltshiremen in London* (1913).

We have already noted a willingness for Swindon people to form mutually beneficial and charitable organisations, and a glance at the list of leading business, military and civic figures from in and around the town from the Victorian period onwards also reveals a particularly strong commitment to charitable causes and community service from them.

We could contend that much of this was fostered by their links to Freemasonry, as well as by their individual faith and moral imperatives.

Just taking a sample of members from one Swindon Craft Lodge and its associated Royal Arch Chapter as an example, all of the following individuals left their mark on the town's history:

Royal Sussex Lodge of Emulation No 355 (selected Worshipful Masters):
1869: Alexander James Braid
1876: William Affleck
1882: Harry Bevir
1890: William Edward Nicolson Browne
1901: Henry William Thomas
1911: Thomas Charles Pleydell Calley
1924: WE Morse
1932: JL Calderwood
1938: TC Newman
1943: JR Hewer
Wiltshire Chapter No 355 (selected First Principals):
1874: Alexander James Braid
1876: Lord Frederick Methuen, 2nd Baron Methuen
1897: TO Hogarth
1911: Thomas Charles Pleydell Calley
1912: JS Protheroe
1915: Charles Riddiford Thomas
1918: Henry William Thomas
1930: HC Preater
1933: EW Beard
1935: JL Calderwood

Further afield in the county we find other examples of Freemasonry and the influence of the nobility.

Residing these days in Corsham, Lodge of Rectitude No 335 traces its history back to February 12, 1812, although its actual warrant extends yet further back, to 1734 and a 'Lodge No 16' (then located in Norwich) which forfeited its warrant in 1809.

Having originally held its meetings in Westbury, it subsequently transferred to Melksham in 1817, then to Box, Bath, Monkton Farleigh and finally, in 1860, to the Methuen Arms in Corsham.

It moved to the Masonic Hall in Bath Road, Pickwick, in around 1994, sharing premises with the resident Corsham Lodge No 6616, and is said to be the oldest continuously active Lodge in Wiltshire.

A further interesting footnote is that the present Masonic Hall once formed part of the Pickwick Estate, which was broken up and sold in 1948, following the death of Sir Frederick Hastings Goldney (1845 – 1940) of Beechwood House.

Sir Frederick, who inherited the baronetcy in 1925, was not only a former Provincial Grand Treasurer and Deputy Provincial Grand Master of Wiltshire, but went on to become Grand Steward of England.

He was made Mayor of Chippenham for both 1874 and 1888, and became High Sheriff of Wiltshire in 1908.

And what of Freemasonry in Wiltshire in 2024? From the official website of the Provincial Grand Lodge of Wiltshire, comes the following summary:

In Wiltshire, 44 Lodges meet in centres around Salisbury Plain from Swindon and Highworth in the north, Downton in the south, Marlborough in the east, and Bradford on Avon in the west. Membership is in the order of 2,300, and increasing year by year. ∎

'Swindonians at Woolwich'

When *The Moonies in London* sat down for their third gathering on March, 10, 1888, the *North Wilts Herald* thought it significant enough to provide a report of the proceedings, even though there were only around 40 people in attendance.

Despite a headline referring to 'Swindonians at Woolwich', it noted that the gathering took place in the adjacent town of Plumstead, at the Railway Tavern, where they sat down to partake of an 'excellent spread'.

Then it went on to reveal the details of the musical offering that was provided, and this gives us an outline of what passed for formal light entertainment in late Victorian Britain, as well as a measure of the apparent coyness and tweeness of the songs, with the report stating:

After dinner, Mr J Templeman having been chosen chairman and Mr J Reynolds vice-chairman, the musical portion of the programme was opened with the "Boulanger March" by the band. A song with harp accompaniment, "The Harp that once through Tara's Hall," was rendered by Mr JR Howcroft, after which Mr H Kirk informed the company that "He had not told the Missus up till now."

We also get a measure of the formality that dominated such occasions, and the lengths that it was necessary to go to to make sure due respects were paid to one's 'superiors', inbetween the entertainment:

The Managers and Foremen of the Swindon Works were then toasted, among those whose names were mentioned being Mr Carlton, Mr Haydon, and Mr Brittain. Messrs Bremner, Reynolds and Howcroft acknowledged the toast.

Mr J Templeman then sang "I'm off to California", Mr J Richards gave "The Minstrel Boy", and Messrs Horsington rendered the duet, "We are in London now". At this point a telegram was received from Swindon friends wishing success to the gathering. Mr A Richards then sang "When Other Lips", and Mr P Richardson wished the company Good Evening, and, in response to an encore, announced that he had to Meet a Lady.

Mr H Dan sang that "He Couldn't", and after a very appropriate piano solo, performed by Henry of Battenberg, Messrs Richards and Wilson gave a capital song and dance; songs by Mr J Reynolds and Mr J Bremner closed the programme.

A vote of thanks having been accorded to the Chairman and Mr H Batten, the promoter of the dinner, a very pleasant evening was brought to a termination with "Auld Lang Syne".

It is necessary to note the name Horsington in the report; it will reappear later in a surprising footballing context. We also believe that the so-called Henry of Battenberg was a comical persona of 'Harry' Batten, one of the founders of *The Moonies in London*.

There were no press reports of the meeting the following year, 1889, but it certainly took place, and a notice appeared in the *Swindon Advertiser* on February 23, 1889, in advance:

We are asked to state that the third anniversary dinner inaugurated by the Swindonians at Woolwich, will take place on Saturday, March 9th, at the Railway Tavern, Plumstead. All friends in Swindon wishing to attend should communicate with the hon sec Mr J Templeman, 6, Swetenham Place, Plumstead, not later than Saturday next, March 2nd.

We know that the attendance had risen to about 60, and the necessity for a 'hon sec' to be appointed by a committee emphasises how established the Association had become in its short life so far.

With the new decade, however, *The Moonies in London* really seemed to take off, and although the attendance of the 1890 dinner had risen only to 72, the proceedings were reported at length in the *Advertiser* on March 15, 1890.

For the first time those present were referred to as *The Moonies in London*, and the report also underlines how it was very much in the spirit of a proper reunion:

SWINDONIANS IN LONDON – The fourth annual dinner of the "Moonies" in London was held at the Bridge House Hotel, London Bridge on Saturday evening last and proved most successful in every respect. Originally started by former employees of the Great Western Railway Company at Swindon who had migrated to the Royal Arsenal at Woolwich and of whom a gentleman ▶

so well known in connection with Swindon local entertainments in times past as Mr Harry Batten, and also his "brother-in-law," Mr J Templeman, were the moving spirits, the idea of Swindonians in London meeting together once a year in friendly reunion has become more and more popular each succeeding year, and culminated, as the Chairman (Mr Templeman) explained in his opening remarks, by the largest meeting being held on Saturday last.

Hitherto the dinner has been held in Woolwich, but as it was desirous that every facility should be given to Swindonians residing in other parts of London, the committee resolved that a more central position would meet the requirements of all alike, and fixed on the London Bridge Hotel as the rendezvous.

Their choice was amply justified by the grand style in which the caterer of this celebrated banqueting house had supplied "every requisite for a good appetite" (apologies to George Eliot) and the bright and cheerful style in which the tables were decorated.

But, perhaps the most interesting part of the evening was that previous to the dinner, when old school "chums" and old shopmates who had not seen one another for years again met, and, after a hearty shake of the hand, compared notes as to their doings since leaving "the dear old town."

Many were the enquiries as to absent friends, and reminiscences of days gone by and the associations thereby given prominence to. It was very agreeable to find that all were doing well, and that several had managed to reach positions of trust and importance – a fact that cannot be otherwise than gratifying to the "authorities" at the Swindon Works where most of those present had "served their time," and been enabled to enjoy, in the first place, the inestimable advantage of a good school education, and afterwards the more appreciated, because better understood and valued, facilities afforded them for practical and theoretical study at the evening classes in connection with the Mechanics' Institute.

A striking proof of the keen appreciation of these educational facilities which existed amongst the company was exemplified in the enthusiasm with which the name of Mr Braid, late headmaster of the Great Western Schools, was received later on in the evening.

In accordance with the usual practice, the selection of chairman was made when all the company had assembled, and the unanimous verdict was that Mr John Templeman, who has filled the office on previous occasions, should occupy the position, which he accordingly did, as also Mr James Bremner the vice-chairmanship.

The dinner over, harmony was the order, interspersed with a few toasts of a brief description. The Chairman, in proposing the first toast, "The Moonies," said that at the dinner inaugurating the movement at Woolwich they had thirty present; at the second, forty; last year, sixty; and now this year, with company exclusively composed of those who had been connected by residence with Swindon, they had seventy-two (applause).

Mr Howcroft, the hon sec to the committee, then read a number of letters of apology from foremen and other friends at the Swindon Works, and elicited much enthusiasm on giving Mr Braid's "greeting" to them all – conveyed by telegram...

Mr Batten responded to the toast of "The Moonies," remarking that he was glad and proud to say he was a "Mooney," and he thanked them all for associating his name with the toast. He had always thought they should meet once a year, and show their appreciation of the dear old town. It was one of his happiest moments to see them all there and so well and prosperous (applause).

The proceedings went on to pay its respects to the railway company's heirarchy, back in Swindon, but the report suggests rather less a blind deference and rather more a genuine warmth:

The Chairman proposed the health of the "Managers and Foremen at Swindon Works," which was well received. He coupled with the toast the name of their vice-chairman as the son of the late Mr Bremner, a foreman who was well-known and respected at Swindon.

Mr Bremner, in reply, referred to the pleasant recollections he had of foremen at Swindon, many of whom had passed away. In making mention of several of these by name, he elicited marks of sympathy and respect, and concluded by passing a eulogium on the last to depart – Mr Lazenby. He considered it was a great thing for a foreman to treat one and all alike.

During his twenty years' absence from Swindon, he had not met with *foremen to equal those he had known at Swindon (applause).*

The year's musical offerings were then detailed, revealing a rather refined selection that included 'a selection on the piano' and solos on clarinet and piccolo.

There was also the usual curious list of songs, including *I Will Stand By My Friend*, *Swinging In The Lane*, *Thy Face I Never See*, and *Volunteer Fire Brigade*, for which local names and places were introduced to 'the patter', followed by *The Old Brigade*:

The Chairman then briefly proposed "Old Swindonians," and had pleasure in calling upon Mr Miles, the oldest Swindonian present, to respond. He had been his (the Chairman's) first drawing master.

Mr Bremner, having nicely sung, Teddy Malone, Mr Miles (a well-known inhabitant of Swindon some twenty-five years ago), responded to the Chairman's toast. It struck him as a most happy idea this meeting together. He could remember so many old faces at Swindon, and that night he saw them reproduced in the younger ones present. He had met with Swindonians in many parts of the world, and it had always been a great pleasure and advantage to him to do so, and keep up old friendships.

We also learn of Mr Miles's advice to those apprentices who faced the prospect of leaving the GWR after completing their apprenticeships (here suggesting that it was not, at that time, compulsory to move on):

It had always been his advice to young men, and he strongly advised it now, directly they were out of their time, to "clear out."

Not that Miles's departure had been straightforward:

Preceding, he referred to the incident in connection with his leaving Swindon, caused by his connection to a drum and fife band there, and the offence they gave over one particular engagement, culminating in apprentices being sent to prison, and journeymen being discharged from their work. He left Swindon because he "had to go." Having to go in this manner, he was not in possession of the necessary tools, and it was a source of pleasure to him to know that his fellow workmen supplied him with many. These tools, and particularly a scribing block, given him by the father of their vice-chairman, he had taken about with him in various parts of the world, and they were always momentos of the kind friends he had left.

It was always a great pleasure for him to go back to Swindon and see his old friends; and when they were all gone, he could still go, and would be glad to speak to the dear old trees, and the dear old church. In conclusion, and referring in feeling terms to so many he remembered but who had gone to another world, he hoped the young men would appreciate, and work upon, the foundations left by them (applause).

What had been 'an exceedingly agreeable and pleasant evening' was finally brought to an end by votes of thanks to the committee, which, it was noted, comprised 'Messrs W Wallington, J Innes, J Green, D Cox, H Batten, TF Jones and J Templeman, with Mr J R Howcroft as Hon Sec.'

But perhaps the most topical and – for us – enlightening part of the evening came with a reference to two Swindon-born players and the significant part they played in the early history of what would become one of the biggest, richest and most famous football clubs in the world... ∎

Left: St Saviour's Church, Swindon (pictured in 2014), 'the wooden church', another inititative by railwaymen in the 1880s, opened in 1890.

The men who changed football

When *The Moonies in London* met at the Bridge House Hotel, London Bridge, on March 8, 1890, one of the after dinner toasts made reference to two former Swindon railwaymen who had played in a key football match in London, earlier in the day.

According to the *Advertiser*:

The health of two of the company, Messrs Horsington and Offer, who had greatly distinguished themselves at football in the final tie for the London Challenge Cup, played that day at The Oval, between Old Westminsters and the Royal Arsenal, was drunk with enthusiasm.

This single sentence, near the end of the report, is just one of many of the perfunctory toasts that characterised the meetings over *The Moonies in London/The Association of Wiltshiremen in London*'s entire existence.

One might also think it was notable only because of the novelty of two former Swindon Town players being picked to play for Arsenal, and the happy coincidence that on the very day that *The Moonies* were in town, Horsington and Offer were playing in a big final.

Indeed, if any of those present at the dinner had taken the opportunity to go to the match in the afternoon (kick-off: 3.30pm) – and we must assume that some did – they could not have known the full significance of what they had just witnessed.

However, they probably gleaned some hint of an precedented football fever that was building in London.

It is only with the gift of hindsight and the benefit of extensive research that the

The Arsenal first team line up for the photographer – probably before the home game aganist Great Marlow in February 1890, a month before the cup final that drew the attention of *The Moonies in London*. Former Swindon Town players Richard Horsington (left) and Henry Offer (right) are seated on the ground.

deeper story is revealed: the part that Richard Horsington and Henry Offer played in the history of Arsenal, and the rapid development of football in the south of England that ultimately turned it into the national game.

Although the match that day cannot be said to be the one that transformed

football in the south, contemporary reaction to it suggests that it was the proof, if it were needed, that the nature of football had changed. As we shall see, the media's and public's obsession with football was now beyond doubt.

In terms of Swindon's history in general, and its football club's history in particular, by delving deeper into the background to the match, we can state that Horsington was the first true Swindon-born football 'star', that Offer was very close behind, and in a sense, they were also the town's first professional footballers.

Other former Swindon railwaymen who found themselves in London and were being supported by *The Moonies in London* may have left home to find work in industry, and indeed both Horsington and Offer moved to Plumstead to be employed in the Royal Arsenal Ordnance Factory at nearby Woolwich, but the real reason for the move was not to do with their industrial skills, but rather their football prowess.

And this is not just the story of local men made good. The fact that they played for Royal Arsenal is significant because of that club's central role in the development of football; one history of Arsenal is called *The Club That Changed Football*, and it is no exaggeration.

To understand why, one has to look at the state of the game in London, only a few years earlier, and how what is known, these days, simply as Arsenal Football Club was born in the summer of 1886.

English football was well established by the mid-1880s, with its ability to draw large crowds – but not yet in London.

The game had effectively been invented in 1857 with the establishment of 'association rules' that differentiated it from its rugby origins, and after the foundation of the FA Cup in 1871, it grew sufficiently in popularity for the formation of a professional Football League in 1888.

However, the new league was made up exclusively of clubs from the industrial north and midlands, underlining how it ▶

TUESDAY, MARCH 11.
†At Richmond, St. Bartholomew's v. St. Thomas's (Inter-Hos-
pital Cup).

UNDER ASSOCIATION RULES.

†THE LONDON ASSOCIATION CUP.

OLD WESTMINSTERS v. ROYAL ARSENAL.
FINAL TIE.
VICTORY OF OLD WESTMINSTERS.

The experiences of the match on Saturday at the Oval between the Old Westminsters and the Royal Arsenal, to decide the possession of the London Association Challenge Cup for the next twelve months, cannot fail to be particularly gratifying to those who take interest in the development of the Association game in the metropolitan district. The success, too, of Saturday was gained, be it added, under certainly not the most favourable circumstances. There was in the first place a great counter-attraction in the fixture at Richmond between the Corinthians and Preston North End, a meeting watched with more than ordinary interest from the fact that each club had already been successful on one occasion during the present season. In the second, the heavy rain during the morning, accompanied by a high wind, were certainly calculated to act as a deterrent rather than an encouragement to spectators. Long before the time fixed for commencing, though, it became evident that the gathering would be larger than had been expected by the management of the Surrey Ground. Though the kick-off was not until half-past three, by two o'clock there was already a knot of enthusiasts in possession of the centre of the ground, and so steady was the inflow during the hour and a half that remained, that by the advertised time there were certainly over six thousand present. A few minutes before half-past three a hearty cheer announced the appearance of the Old Westminsters, and this was quickly followed by another heralding the advent of the Arsenal team, who had a strong following. The toss was won by the latter, and as there was a stiff breeze blowing almost directly down the ground, their supporters were naturally jubilant when it was seen that they would have the aid of such a powerful ally for the first half. With commendable punctuality the Westminsters started the ball to the minute, and it soon became evident that the Woolwich men, who, it was fancied, would show to better advantage in the matter of combination, would have all their work cut out. A run by Horsington on the right gave the Arsenal backs, who at the outset were kept hard at it, temporary relief, but the Westminsters, with Bain, Peck, and Street well in the van, quickly resumed the attack, and Peck lost a chance by a wild kick which sent the ball over the Arsenal bar. Offer retaliated by taking the game once more into Westminster territory, and Moon, whose goal-keeping throughout was again of the first character, had to use his hands to clear his goal. Just after this Horsington was unlucky enough to slip his knee, and the Arsenal team had for a few minutes to play without him. Though the Westminster backs were sadly handicapped by the high wind, which brought the ball back whenever it was lifted to any height, they still offered a determined resistance, and the Arsenal forwards found their defence almost impregnable. A high kick by Fox bore the ball back well over his head, and the wind took it directly in front of the Westminster goal, which was, however, splendidly saved by Moon. Just after this Robertson also had a favourable chance, but his final kick was faulty, and a minute or two later Moon again stopped a smart shot by Offer. The Westminster forwards now in their turn became the aggressors, and some pretty play by

Richard Horsington (pictured) played in Swindon Town's first FA Cup match – and would go on to write himself into the record books at Arsenal, for the same reason. In fact, he played in the first four of Swindon's games in the competition.

The first was a 1-0 first round victory, away against Watford Rovers, on October 23, 1886, followed by a 1-7 second round away defeat to the Slough-based team, Swifts, on November 20, 1886.

The following season saw him play again as Town lost 0-1, away, to Old Brightonians, on October 8, 1887.

And the following year they were beaten 2-5 at home by Great Marlow, on October 27, 1888.

Horsington had also been in the team when Town won the Wiltshire Association Challenge Cup in its augural season, 1886-7, with a 1-0 away victory over Trowbridge Town on March 19, 1887.

Although he was a right winger, he failed to get his name on the scoresheet in any of these matches, but he may have made enough of an impression on someone who was watching; within three months of his fourth FA Cup match for Swindon, he was playing for Royal Arsenal.

And within a year he was playing at The Oval in the final of a major London cup competition, an ill-fated match that was watched by *Moonies* who were in town for their annual dinner, later that evening. ∎

was yet to make much impact in London and the south, where it remained a game closely associated with its public school origins.

In London, the sport that took the attention of the public and the press in the winter was rugby – the Greenwich-based Blackheath team were one of the most prominent in the country – and in the summer it was cricket; so it is quite fitting that the Arsenal football club would be born out of a cricket club.

It was originally called Dial Square Football Club, an offshoot of a cricket team of the same name that was made up of workers at the Dial Square gun finishing workshop.

That was part of the Royal Gun Factory, which was one of the three sections that made up the huge war machine that was the Royal Arsenal Ordnance Factory (the others being the Royal Laboratory and the Royal Carriage Department).

The football team was formed after the end of the cricket season in the autumn of 1886, as a means of occupying the Dial Square players during the long winter months to come.

Workers in the Royal Arsenal were asked to make donations to help the fledgling club, and part of this fund was used to purchase their first

football, which was used during practice on Plumstead Common. Those players who did not already own a red shirt were instructed to purchase one from a shop called Lewin's of Plumstead, and red has famously been the club colour ever since.

For now there was comparatively little interest in football in that area, and because of this (and because there was no local league), finding local opponents for the new works team at the Royal Arsenal was a challenge.

But Dial Square travelled to Millwall for its first match, against Eastern Wanderers, on December 11, 1886, and ran out 6-0 winners.

It was probably the only match Dial Square ever played, because within a month they changed their name to Royal Arsenal Football Club, in an attempt to attract players from all parts of the ordnance factory, rather than a single workshop.

It was a masterstroke.

Royal Arsenal's first game was at home, against Erith, on January 8, 1887 – just two years (almost to the day) before Richard Horsington played his debut.

The 'home ground' was actually a public space, Plumstead Common, which was borrowed for the day, but they soon moved to the Sportsman Ground, on Plumstead Marshes, about a mile north of the common, where they could charge an entrance fee to spectators.

By the end of the year their matches were attracting around 300 paying customers.

In September of the same year, they successfully applied to be members of the Football Association, and on October 29, 1887, the club played its first competitive fixture, a London Senior Cup tie against Barnes, which they lost 0-4.

Flooding and drainage problems with the club's home ground, caused by its close proximity to the Thames, and the smell – it was part of a pig farm – led to the club moving to a new home, Manor Ground (or Manor Field), in the spring of 1888, its first match there attracting a crowd of around 500.

These were comparatively humble beginnings, but the club was about to experience a meteoric rise, and over the next couple of years, Royal Arsenal would attract much more media interest – to the extent that, in Deember 1889, the local *Kentish Independent* newspaper reported that 'there is probably no subject so much talked about around us'.

By then, both Richard Horsington and Henry Offer had moved from Swindon to Plumstead, to play key roles in this new phenomenon.

Born in Swindon in 1866, Horsington appeared on the 1881 census at 8 Exeter Street, in the Railway Village, where the 14-year-old's occupation was recorded as 'engine fitter apprentice'; his father was also employed in the GWR Works, as a brass finisher.

Young Horsington didn't just show a talent for football; he was a well-known all-round sportsman. The *North Wilts Herald* of November 14, 1884 shows that he played rugby, and had kicked 'a splendid goal' for Swindon Victoria against Marlborough, in front of 'a large number of spectators' in the GWR Park, New Swindon.

And there is evidence that one of the things that made Richard Horsington such a good winger on the football pitch was his speed.

Throughout the spring and summer of 1885 and 1886, he entered various 120-yard and 440-yard (quarter-mile) handicap races. We find him representing Swindon in Birmingham, Cheltenham and Bristol, and in various events in his home town. During one sports day he took part in, at the GWR Park in 1885, which was organised by the GWR Cricket Club, another heat featured an H Offer – almost certainly Henry Offer, his future Arsenal team-mate. Also running that day was J[ames] Kibblewhite (see page 83).

Around the same time, an R Horsington – almost certainly Richard again – appears in reports of cricket matches, and in the *Swindon Advertiser* in March 1888, an R Horsington is mentioned as a boxer. He was clearly filling much of his spare time playing one sport or another – but not all of his time.

As if working full-time for the GWR and then all his sporting exploits weren't enough, Richard's name also appears in newspaper reports in connection with ▶

By Horsington's and Offer's day, football had evolved from the rugby-like game it had been in the 1860s; the FA Cup was established, and the rules had finally also been standardised.

Not that they were necessarily the same as we know them today.

For instance, three (not two) opposition players needed to be between an attacker and the goal line for a player to be onside, and penalty areas were not introduced until 1891, following the introduction of the penalty kick.

Before then, the role of the goalkeeper went through various changes as the game evolved from rugby to football.

A year after the first outlawing of any handling of the ball in 1870, the rules were changed again, to allow a goalkeeper to handle the ball 'for the protection of his goal', although how that was defined is unclear. It was another two years before the laws stated that the goalie was not allowed to carry the ball, and in 1887 (the year after Swindon Town's first appearance in the FA Cup), it was necessary to bring out another rule – to prevent them handling the ball in the opposition's half of the field.

Quite how or why they were 'protecting' their goal so far up the field, is another mystery. It would be 1911 before keepers' handling of the ball was at last restricted to the penalty area.

Another innovation was nets on the goals did not become compulsory in competitive matches until 1891 – so the match referred to at *The Moonies*' dinner would have been played without nets (although crossbars had been established way back in 1865).

During Horsington's career, matches were controlled by umpires: one from each side. They signalled their decisions by waving white flags or handkerchiefs (no whistles). It was only in more important matches that a referee, who was off the field, gave the casting vote if umpires could not agree with each other.

Tactics also changed during the 1880s, when the long ball game that had been the standard from the beginning and was obviously a relic from rugby, was gradually replaced by more sophisticated passing, and teams deliberately playing their opponents offside.

For Royal Arsenal's home matches, spectators were separated from the pitch by ropes, and for bigger matches, wagons were borrowed from the local army garrison as makeshift grandstands.

And just to underline the difference between football of this era and the modern game (but also its quaintness): in those days the team captain didn't just have responsibility for leading the team on the pitch; it was also his job to collect together the gate money, before the start of the match. ∎

his membership of the 2nd Wilts Rifle Volunteer Corps, where he is listed as being duty bugler several times.

The Horsingtons were a sporty family; around this time there were also numerous reports of a J Horsington – almost certainly his elder brother, John – also playing rugby for Swindon teams.

It was in 1885 that Richard first began to appear in newspaper reports as a footballer, beginning on October 16, in a report of a 5-2 win for Swindon Town over a Gloucester XI, in which he scored the fourth goal with 'a long shot'.

One measure of the primitive, casual and informal nature of football at the time is that Horsington once guested for a Wantage side that turned up without a full team for a match against St Mark's Young Men's Friendly Society, in November 1885; the home team's captain also failed to show because of some misunderstanding over the fixture. It took place in an unnamed field 'kindly lent to the Friendly Society FC for the season by JEG Bradford'.

In early 1887, Horsington represented Wiltshire in matches against Berks & Bucks, 'Somersetshire' and, perhaps significantly, Kent, the county in which Plumstead, the home of Royal Arsenal FC, was situated, on the outskirts of Greater London.

If it was an opportunity for club officials to see Horsington in action, he probably didn't make much of an impression that day; Kent ran out 5-1 winners, and Horsington was not Wiltshire's scorer.

Later in the same month, he was in the Swindon Town team that won the Wiltshire Cup with a 3-1 victory over Trowbridge, and for the first time, both he and Henry Offer, his future Arsenal teammate, were in the starting line-up of a competitive match together.

At the end of March 1887, it was reported that Horsington 'fell a cropper', breaking his collar bone while playing for Swindon Town in a game against Reading Town. It was the first reported incidence of what would become an injury-prone career, but by July Horsington had recovered enough to continue his summer pursuit, and he represented Swindon in an athletics meeting at Windsor.

During the 1887-8 season, he continued to play for Swindon Town and also represent Wiltshire, scoring in a 4-0 win over Oxfordshire in November 1887.

Newspaper reports now regularly singled him out for playing 'a grand game' and suchlike: the first signs that he was the star of the team, and perhaps beginning to outgrow his hometown club.

As yet there was no league for Swindon Town to play in, so most of their matches were friendlies, the only games qualifying as competitive senior matches in those days being in the FA Cup – and Horsington played in each of the first four ties in the club's history.

Football was booming, and although sleepy Wiltshire was a long way from the sport's hotbeds, it wasn't immune to the game's rapid growth in popularity.

The *North Wilts Herald* started to struggle to give accurate attendance figures for Swindon Town matches, reporting, on March 31, 1888, that there were 'about 1,000 spectators' at the club's home ground, The Croft, for a match against arguably the quaintest-named of all football teams: Mr C Lacey-Sweet's XI. The match reporting was just as quaint:

Horsington and Pearce, getting possession of the leather, began to make matters

The OS map of Plumstead, c1893. Surveyors left the large area at the top (containing our text) blank, for security reasons; it was the site of the Royal Arsenal Ordnance Factory. Arsenal's two home grounds of the era are circled; Henry Offer played at both, Horsington only at the Manor Ground. After retiring, Horsington lived at the Fountain pub, at 132 Plumstead Road, which is in the centre of the page, close to the factory site. For a time, Arsenal's changing rooms were in the pub next door, called the Railway Tavern.

dangerous for their opponents. Baines, however, was equal to the occasion, and saved a clinking shot from Horsington in pretty style.

He did eventually get on the scoresheet in the 3-1 win – after he had again 'secured the leather… put in a brilliant spin on the right wing, and finished up with a "hot 'un" which Baines failed to stop.' The *Wilts and Glos Standard* saw the game rather differently, not least because they had the opponents down as Clifton. Their estimate of the attendance was 700, and they said that, in scoring his goal, Horsington dribbled the whole length of the ground to beat Baines'.

In October 1888, he lined up for what would turn out to be his final competitive game for Swindon Town, a 2-5 defeat at home to Great Marlow in the FA Cup, when 'about 2,500 persons lined the ropes at the time of starting'.

It was the third season they had competed in the FA Cup, but the first time they had been drawn at home.

Horsington had a new role when Town entertained St George's Bristol at The Croft in December 1888, as he was named as 'umpire'. He was perhaps recovering from another injury, but was back in action in Town's 9-0 defeat of Chippenham on December 15, 1888. He surely scored in that game, but no record exists of the scorers.

A week later he represented Wiltshire against 'Somersetshire', reports again sadly neglecting to name the Wiltshire scorers in a 3-5 defeat.

But when Swindon Town took to the field against Clifton at The Croft in January 1889, the *Advertiser* noted that the home team were 'minus the services of RT Horsington', apparently unaware of the reason for his absence.

In fact, he had joined Royal Arsenal, and made his debut for the then Plumstead-based team in a 1-1 draw ▶

New Manor Ground
(Probably Ainsdale)

Invicta Athletic Grounds

against Vulcans at Willesden on January 9, 1889. No details of Horsington's 'transfer' were reported, but with hindsight the manner of it seems highly significant.

As the definitive history of the club, *Royal Arsenal – Champions of the South* (by Mark Andrews, Andy Kelly and Tim Stillman) explains, while it was originally a prerequisite for Royal Arsenal players to be employed in the factory in order to qualify for the works team, the club's growing ambitions meant there had been a crucial change. At some point the sequence became reversed, men now being brought in to play for the football team as the priority, with a job in the Royal Arsenal arranged for them, to make their move financially viable:

> *The team consisted mostly of 'bogus' amateurs – quality footballers who had been promised well-paid work in the Arsenal if they played for the football team. This was effectively confirmed by the* South Eastern Herald *on 19 September 1890 [20 months after Horsington's move] when they reported: 'I hear that the whole of the team will be kept regularly on the day shift. This will be a great advantage to them, as a night shift takes all the football out of a man.'*

It was certainly club policy by Easter 1889, when the *Boston Guardian* indignantly reported the case of John Julian, who captained Boston Town to a 4-1 win over Arsenal on Good Friday, and then promptly (although no transfer fee seems to have been involved) 'signed' for the opponents. The paper explained that 'work at 50/- [£2.50] a week was obtained for him in the Arsenal, and Julian left us on Sunday night.'

So it is probable that Horsington went to Arsenal in similar fashion, only his move was three months before Julian's, so it is possible that he was the first player to move to the club under these circumstances, putting him at the vanguard of a policy that transformed Royal Arsenal from a Works' team into something much bigger.

As we have seen elsewhere in this book, the completion of an apprentice-ship with the GWR was often a watershed in a young Swindonian's life, owing to the long-standing policy of the newly qualified man not being offered a job in the Works.

However, it was probably different for Horsington. He must have been kept on after completing his apprenticeship in 'engine turning' in May 1887, more than 18 months before departing for Arsenal.

During that time he was still playing for Swindon Town, which would have been impossible if he had moved away.

So it would have needed to be quite an incentive for him to leave his well-paid job with the GWR, uproot and move to Plumstead. The factory's management and the football club board must have got together and made him an offer he couldn't refuse.

What is beyond doubt is that Horsington was simultaneously the first Swindon-born player and the first Swindon Town player (of many) to effectively be transferred to a bigger club, lured by the prospect of a more lucrative career than could be achieved by staying in Wiltshire.

For this reason, and because he had, after all, made something of a name for himself in Town colours, it seems appropriate to call him Swindon's first football 'star', even if the term had not yet been conceived.

Just to put Horsington's move to Arsenal into historical context: 1888, which ended with him playing his last match for Swindon Town, was the year of the first murder by the serial killer later dubbed Jack the Ripper (who operated over the river from Plumstead, in Whitechapel).

More significant, however, is the foundation, by a dozen clubs, of the Football League. Even if they could not yet compete with these professional clubs, Arsenal's day was coming.

Horsington did not score in his first match for 'the Royalists', but was said to be 'conspicuous' – which must have been difficult considering the match was played in thick fog!

But he certainly made an impression in his next game, against Ilford, which ended in a 1-1 draw. This time the match was played in a strong gale, with Horsington providing a 'splendid pass' (according to the *Kentish Mercury*) for Saul to score. That game was played at the Manor Ground (sometimes called Manor Field), in Plumstead, where he would spend the rest of his life.

The weather still conspired against the new arrival as he tried to make his mark, a 'bitterly cold wind accompanied by a driving snow' being the main feature of a 0-1 defeat by Ilford in February 1889.

He was again in the team when the new season kicked off with a match against London Caledonians in September 1889.

In the same month he scored the first goal in a 2-0 win over Casuals, in front of a crowd of 'nearly 2,000'.

Then, on September 21, 1889, Horsington wrote himself into Arsenal folklore by not only playing in the 10-1 hammering of Tottenham, but scoring the fifth goal. It was before the days of intense rivalry between the two clubs – they were not yet neighbours, Arsenal still playing in eastern London – but it still stands (and probably always will) as the biggest victory over the old enemy.

Another landmark in Arsenal's history soon followed, on October 5, 1889, when Horsington, who had once played in Swindon Town's first-ever FA Cup tie, was picked to play in Arsenal's. It was in a preliminary round against Lyndhurst, and the team that who would go on to raise the trophy a record 14 times (by 2024), ran out 11-0 winners, in front of an enthusiastic home crowd of 2,000.

Horsington provided 'a well-placed centre' for Hope Robertson to score the club's first FA Cup goal, and scored the ninth goal himself, with a long-range shot 'from the touch line'.

Horsington also played in the next round when Arsenal travelled to Norwich Thorpe on October 29, 1889. They drew 2-2, but progressed to the third round by virtue of the fact that their opponents could not afford to take the trip to Woolwich for the replay.

He was missing from the line-up in the following round, when they ran out 5-2 winners over Crusaders after extra-time, despite the protests of the referee, who was encouraging the two captains to stop playing because of bad light!

Neither did he play in the next round, on December 7, 1889, which saw Royal Arsenal lose 1-5 to one of the leading clubs of the day, Swifts, who fielded four internationals.

The story has now brought us back to the match noted at the annual

By this time Horsington seems to have been an automatic choice on the Arsenal team sheet, and any absences were probably due to injury, so it was no surprise to see him back in the side, after missing recent games.

But it didn't take long for his bad luck to resurface, because he was (in the words of one reporter) 'lamed, early in the contest'.

'Horsington was unlucky enough to slip his knee,' said another report, 'and the Arsenal team had for a few minutes to play without him'.

Then, with about 20 minutes gone, and soon after Old Westminsters had taken the lead: 'Arsenal were unlucky enough to lose the help of Horsington, who again had to leave the field, and this time permanently, being unable to take any further part in the game', adding that he was 'sorely missed'.

Another report said:

They were, of course, most unlucky in losing for more than an hour of the game the services of apparently one of their best forwards, Horsington, who, until his leg gave way, had shown himself particularly conspicuous on the right wing. ▶

POLYTECHNIC.—A. Hunt (goal), J. E. K. Studd (captain) and A. Brimmell (backs), W. Offord, W. Potter, M. C. Jones, J. Sullivan, C. Stanning, S. Dorrington, J. T. Pryce-Jones, and J. Newman.

†ROYAL ARSENAL v. TOTTENHAM HOTSPUR.

That the Reds, as the Royal Arsenal Association team of footballers are termed, are likely to play an important part in the various matches in the metropolis during the present season was again manifest on their own ground at the Manorway, Plumstead, on Saturday, as in the presence of about fifteen hundred spectators they beat their old opponents, Tottenham Hotspur, by ten goals to one. Owing to the heavy showers that fell previous to the match commencing, the ground was in rather a slippery state, but with the exception of this slight drawback, everything was favourable for a fast game, there being scarcely any wind to interfere with the players. The visitors, winning the toss for choice of ends, elected to defend the goal nearest the road during the first half of the game. Barbour set the ball in motion for the home club, and they had not started many minutes ere the same player, by a splendid shot, sent the sphere between the uprights, gaining the first point for the Reds. The visitors tried hard to retrieve their loss, the ball being worked from one end of the ground to the other two or three times very quickly, each goal keeper having to repel attacks from the opposing forces until Robertson secured a second point for the home club, after which Meggs scored twice. The visitors, however, nothing daunted, played up in a determined manner, and had the satisfaction of reducing their opponents' lead by a point obtained by Parker, but before crossing over Horsington still further increased the score of the Royal Arsenal, the score standing five goals to one. In the second half the game was more of a one-sided character, the Reds having matters nearly all their own way, adding five more goals to their total, Robertson obtaining two, Meggs two, Barbour one, the game terminating as stated above. Umpires, Messrs. M. Jackson and Hatton; referee, Mr. W. Parr. Sides:—

ROYAL ARSENAL.—F. W. Beardsley (goal), H. Offer and J. M'Bean (backs), D. Howatt, J. M. Bates, and J. W. Julian (half-backs), R. T. Horsington and J. W. Meggs (right wing), H. Barbour (centre), H. R. Robertson and J. Crighton (left wing).
TOTTENHAM HOTSPUR.—J. Anderson (goal), H. Griffith and J. E. Jull (backs), G. Baldock, E. Pracey and J. Ayres (half-backs), F. C. Cotterell and M. P. Cadman (right wing), D. A. Tyrrell (centre), W. B. Buckle and G. A. Parker (left wing).

UNDER RUGBY RULES.

MIDDLESEX WANDERERS FOOTBALL CLUB.
The annual general meeting will be held to-day (Monday) at ... taken at eight

---

dinner of *The Moonies in London*, the final of what is mostly known as the London Senior Cup (but went by various versions of the name), played at the Oval, on March 8, 1890.

Even worse than losing one of their best players: substitutes were not yet allowed in competitive matches, so they were forced to struggle on with ten men against a side containing two internationals, including the England goalkeeper.

So it is no wonder they lost 0-1.

Those present in the crowd were seeing the end of Horsington's football career, because he would never play in the first team again. But as contemporary reports indicate, they were also witnessing something of a footballing phenomenon.

Newspapers had already begun to report more fully on games, fill the voids between matches with off-the-field news, and comment on incidents inside the ground, not just what was happening on the pitch. But at The Oval on that day, the size and the mood of the crowd still took them by surprise.

The very fact that the attendance was estimated as anything between 5,000 and 8,000 tells us that reporters had previously had little experience in estimating the size of crowds on such a scale.

By today's standards, of course, the crowd was tiny, but in 1890 such a turn-out was a revelation to those who hadn't experienced it before. The size of the crowd was also surprising because on the same day there was a match taking place down the river at Richmond, between Corinthians and Preston North End.

The latter were the current FA Cup holders and were known as 'The Invincibles' because they were the greatest team of the era, so reporters noted how this would have been a huge 'counter attraction' for neutrals.

Not that neutrality was much in evidence at The Oval, which proved an eye-opener to certain sections of the press, such as *The Field* ('the country gentleman's newspaper').

Its reporter pointed out that 'the excellent form shown by the Arsenal men made their partisans particularly sanguine', while 'outside the ground the scene was almost as animated as that inside, breaks and many other descriptions of vehicles lining the fence for a considerable distance, a large number hailing from Woolwich.'

Another reporter noted that 'of the popularity of the Arsenal there can be no question', but added:

The company... was not what we have been accustomed to see on the Surrey ground, and the rough element was noticeable; indeed, many of the spectators seemed anxious to umpire the game for themselves, and used language not calculated to do the sport too much good. When feeling runs high, a little extra enthusiasm may of course be excused, but many of those present on Saturday went beyond reasonable limits. ▶

The 1889-90 Royal Arsenal squad, with Richard Horsington second from the left in the middle (standing) row. For reasons unknown, despite being a key player, Henry Offer is absent from the picture. The only final they didn't win that year was the one played on the day of *The Moonies*' dinner.

In other words: if the potential for the game to turn spectators into passionate and partisan supporters, gripped by allegiance to a single team, had not yet been recognised, this match left them in no doubt that football fever had broken out in the capital.

And, just in case anyone had any doubts about football's new-found ability to raise blood pressures on the terraces, it also noted its ability to create real drama on the field:

> *For a new club, the Arsenal have done extraordinarily well this season, and few of those present on the Oval on Saturday will forget the grand effort they made at the finish to equalise.*

Football had well and truly been set on the course that would make it the sport we know today, and if *The Moonies in London* wanted to see a single game that embodied what football was becoming, they could not have picked a better example.

Meanwhile, Horsington's injury produced ripples outside the game, because it was apparently the catalyst for an article that appeared in – of all places – *The Pall Mall Gazette*, under the headline 'IS FOOTBALL DANGEROUS?'

This stated: 'Horsington, forward, in Royal Arsenal v Old Westminsters, injured his head, and had to leave'.

As well as the fact that (as seen above) Horsington clearly suffered injuries to his leg, not his head, the article is also curious in that it linked this unfortunate but unremarkable injury to a bizarre list of other serious and sometimes fatal misfortunes sustained as the result of football:

> *At the close of the Association ties, I jot down (writes a correspondent), for the benefit of those who are interested in the above question, some of the casualties of the 1889-90 football season. I must say at the outset that the following statistics have been compiled from the ordinary daily papers, and are only those that meet the eye of the general reader. I have not gone out of my way to consult the sporting journals or the day books of the British hospitals. Had I done so, no doubt the butcher's bill would have been a much more ghastly one than it is...*

Although a number of the 'accidents' that were listed were fatal, the danger seems to have been rather exaggerated in many respects, and some of those on the list were from rugby matches, not association football. They included one that followed an argument during a match at Kidderminster, which led to one player hurling a brick at another, 'smashing his skull in a terrible manner' and causing his death, a few hours later.

Inaccuracies, melodramatic stories and fantasies aside, the article is revealing in at least two ways. For a start, it seems to underline that footballers in general and, here, Horsington in particular, were now enjoying fame that reached beyond the sports pages.

But it also confirms what a phenomenon football had become in London, because you can be sure that any new craze has reached cult status when the media becomes obsessed by its imagined dangers.

If any *Moonies* at the fateful match felt short-changed by the early departure of Swindon man Horsington on the right wing, however, there was another former local man on the left wing, ready to take over.

Although Horsington is the first Swindon Town player deserving the accolade of 'star', Henry Offer was close behind, and it is even possible the pair left on a double 'transfer' (not that the term was yet in use, and no fee would have been paid to Swindon Town).

Offer did not make his debut for Arsenal until eight months after Horsington, however, providing another possibility: that he followed on his former team-mate's recommendation.

Born on July 16, 1869, at Devizes, Henry Offer would make his mark and write himself into the record books for several reasons, and go on to be arguably the first truly professional footballer (in the modern sense) from Wiltshire.

As we shall see, he was also central to circumstances that led to Royal Arsenal becoming a professional team, providing them with the potential to compete with pioneers from the north.

Listed wrongly in the 1871 census as Tom Henry (instead of Henry Thomas) Offer, he was then living with his parents and two siblings at Rowde, Devizes. His father, Thomas, was a Chelsea pensioner and a sergeant in the Royal Wiltshire Militia.

By 1881 the whole family had moved to 24 Newport Street, Swindon, where Henry lived with his parents, three siblings and three lodgers.

There are a few reports of him batting and bowling for 'Swindon Town Cricket Club', and playing as a defender in a local team, but in 1887 and 1888 he joined Horsington in the line-up for Swindon Town's FA Cup ties.

The first of his more than 50 appearances in an Arsenal shirt was in September 1889, when he played alongside Horsington in that record-breaking match against Tottenham, and Offer's name features several times in Arsenal's and other football records.

Ironically, while it was Horsington who

had supplied the pass for the club's first-ever goal in any FA Cup match (a game that Offer also played in), it was Offer who scored Arsenal's first-ever goal in the first round proper.

That was in a 1-2 defeat against Derby County (one of the original members of the Football League) on 17 January, 1891, on any icy pitch, in front of a crowd of 8,000.

It is a measure of Offer's ability and standing that, a week earlier, he had played for the South of England in a representative game against the North, at Nottingham (losing 0-3).

During his Arsenal career, he played as a back (defender), half back (midfielder) and forward (striker) – the original utility player – and at only 5 feet, 4.5 inches (1.64m) tall, and weighing in at just 9 stone, 2.5lb (58.3kg), he was instantly recognisable on the field.

His popularity with supporters was clear from another new phenomenon, the matchday programme, which emerged during this time, and included, in 1890, a poem about the team, and the lines:

And brilliant little Offer deserves a word of cheer

No man is more respected and none more honoured here;

He never leaves the leather, our critics all confess,

That Offer oft reminds them of the famous Scotch express.

The same poem, incidentally, comments on Horsington's absence, hinting there was a growing realisation that his injuries could be insurmountable:

May next season find our champions the subject of our theme

And may gallant Meggs and Horsington be number'd with the team.

On April 25, 1891, Offer claimed another club Arsenal 'first' – in a friendly against illustrious professional visitors, Sunderland, a new member of the Football League.

An Arsenal player was injured after just 20 minutes and had to leave the field, but the home side were still holding their own at half-time, with the score at 1-1.

In those days, substitutes weren't allowed in competitive games, but it was a friendly, after all, and perhaps to appease the large crowd of around 7,000 who sensed a famous home victory, during the interval it was agreed that Arsenal could restore their team to eleven men.

And so it fell to Henry Offer to become Arsenal's first ever substitute. Not that it did the club much good; the visitors scored twice in the second half, to win 3-1.

Although (for unknown reasons) he was not in the starting line-up against Sunderland, by the spring of 1891, Offer was virtually ▶

Henry Offer, pictured during his spell with Southampton, and a cutting detailing his historic substitute appearance against Sunderland

SUNDERLAND v. ROYAL ARSENAL.

In the presence of some 7,000 spectators, the above teams met at the Invicta grounds, Plumstead, when a rather vigorously contested game resulted in favour of the visitors by three goals to one. Half-way through the initial portion of the match Howat was hurt, and had to retire. Offer was allowed to take his place in the second half. Campbell kicked off for the visitors against the wind at 3.45 p.m. An attack on the left was put aside by Bates, but after some ten minutes' play from a general attack, Miller sent the ball past Bee, and so placed the Sunderland-ites a goal ahead. Connolly, after a clipping run, equalised, with the result that at half-time the game stood one goal all. Immediately on re-starting the visitors commenced to press corners; these fell to both sides, but were unproductive. In quick succession Campbell and Hannah each sent the ball past Bee, and nothing further being scored, the match resulted in a win for Sunderland by three goals to one.

ever-present in the team, and as they had now enjoyed two seasons of remarkable success, they were facing a dilemma.

Ironically, considering how they had enticed (or as Swindon Town fans might have put it: 'poached') players from smaller clubs in the previous two or three years, now Royal Arsenal found the tables turned, with the threat of League clubs luring their stars away to sign professional contracts.

The alarm bells began ringing following a friendly against a professional club, Gainsborough Trinity, on November 22, 1890, played in front of a crowd of up to 8,000, at Arsenal's new Plumstead ground, called Invicta.

The match was covered widely in newspapers across the country, but closer to home, in the *Kentish Independent*, the report simultaneously emphasised the level to which Arsenal were now playing, Offer's major role in their success, and the dilemma they were facing:

For the second time this season the Royal Arsenal has encountered a professional football team and come out of the struggle undefeated. In the battle with South Shore, Blackpool, they managed only to score a tie. In the match last Saturday against the Gainsborough Trinity Club they did better, winning by two goals to one. This we regard as the best thing they have done yet. The Trinitarians were the smartest lot all round that we have ever seen at Plumstead, and their play and combination so good that most of the experts present considered that they ought to have won… The Arsenal lads also played their very best, and Offer especially is to be complimented… We are glad, of course, when our side wins, but, irrespective of the result, the play with such a fine club as that which came so far to see us last Saturday, was a splendid lesson for the team.

However, in the following weeks it emerged that, amid the hospitality after the match, Gainsborough officials had approached some Arsenal players. And after a column by a correspondent in the *South Eastern Herald*, one fan was angry enough to write to the editor on December 5, 1890:

Sir – I was a good deal surprised to read in 'Invicta's' notes last week that the Gainsborough Trinity, after being kindly and hospitably entertained by the Arsenal team, endeavoured before they went away to induce some of our best

Richard Horsington's impressive grave in Plumstead reflects his success as a businessman, as well as a sportsman. He left an estate worth more than £18,000, which was a small fortune in 1928. (Courtesy of David Harvey)

players to leave the club. It certainly strikes me that if 'Invicta' is correct in his remarks – as I understand he generally is – this is not particularly honourable conduct on the part of the visitors.

But it was a controversial subject, and the club was divided on the question of whether the solution was to turn professional.

Part of the issue was with certain people within the club being too invested in the notion of football being a gentlemanly sport, best suited to amateurs – a sentimental view apparently driven by memories of its public school origins; they clearly did not want their

club to become like the big professional northern and midland clubs, with their loud working class fanbases.

Another argument against turning professional was the threat that local officials and amateur clubs would effectively boycott Arsenal if they turned professional.

But there was a better reason for doubt in Arsenal's case, because it emerged that professional players weren't necessarily

protected if they failed to make the first eleven or – and they need look no further than Richard Horsington's recent experience for an example – they were injured. However, if an Arsenal player currently found himself out of the team, for whatever reason, he would still have his job in the Royal Ordnance Factory, and therefore an income.

January 1891 saw the question

officially addressed when the Vice-chairman broadly hinted, at the club's half-yearly meeting, that they were now seriously considering going professional at the end of the season.

And just two weeks later it emerged that, straight after their FA Cup meeting, three Arsenal players had been offered professional contracts with Derby County. The *South Eastern Herald* reported that the visitors had come pre-armed with contracts and even signing-on fees, and it is likely that Henry Offer, who scored Arsenal's goal in the match was one of those approached.

According to one source, Offer was indeed tempted to turn professional, the following month – not by Derby, but Burnley, and supposedly signed for them. But he failed to break into the first team.

In fact, the census of the following April showed he was still living at 48 Crescent Road, Plumstead, where his occupation was listed as 'wheeler', and the Arsenal records show that he finished the season with them.

Another source, suggesting that he played a trial for Burnley, is probably more accurate.

They were a well-established professional club, one of the original members of the Football League, and one of six from Lancashire, as well as the holders of the Lancashire Cup, having defeated local rivals Blackburn Rovers, the previous season. So it would have been a very big move indeed.

Arsenal did, indeed, turn professional during the 1891 close season (joining the Football League for the 1893/4 season), but there is much irony to the outcome, especially from Offer's perspective. ▶

Royal Arsenal - v - Old St. Mark's
Football Match at the Oval
on
Saturday last.

R. Florance
"Fisting" a ball out
of the Old St. Mark's
Goal.

Dodging with the
Ball.

A High Kick.

The Hon. Doctor of the Surrey County Cricket Club.
(Dr Blades) attending to Canby's
Ricked Ankle.

A "Throw-in"

For a start, turning professional meant an immediate influx of new players, who were recruited from the likes of Aston Villa and Sheffield United, and although Julian, the club captain, indicated that the majority of current players would sign professional contracts, Henry Offer either wasn't offered one (which seems unlikely) or he turned it down.

Perhaps his experience at Burnley, Horsington's injuries and the prospect of moving and then not making the grade weighed heavily on him; perhaps he resented the fact that the whole team, given their success over the past two years, would not go forward as a unit.

There is nothing that provides us with a definitive answer, but we do know that despite being at the top of his form, Offer chose to return to Swindon Town, an amateur side, for the following season.

But there was soon to be a change of heart, and he did turn professional after all: not with Arsenal or Burnley or Derby County, but Southampton St Mary's.

Shortly to become known simply as Southampton, they (like Arsenal) had big ambitions to compete with the northern giants of the game, and came in with a professional contract for Offer in the summer of 1893, a year ahead of the club becoming founder members of the Southern League in 1894 (along with Swindon Town).

It was enough to persuade him

Left: a cartoon that appeared in the *Penny Illustrated Paper* on October 25, 1890. Henry Offer played in this match, which Royal Arsenal won 4-0.

Remarkably similar to shops in the Railway Works at Swindon, this is part of the Gun Carriage Works at the Royal Arsenal in 1874. Henry Offer worked here as a wheeler. (Courtesy of www.royal-arsenal-history.com)

to leave Swindon for a second time, and it was Offer (the scorer of Arsenal's first goal in the FA Cup proper) who was the man to score Southampton's first League goal – on October 6, 1894, in a 3-1 home win over Chatham.

A week later he played in another record-breaking match, scoring twice in the 14-0 demolition of Newbury in the first qualifying round of the FA Cup, which remains the biggest win in Southampton's history.

But his stay at the club would be short. Despite scoring ten times in 18 appearances, Southampton finishing the season in third place, and Offer still only being 26 years old, he retired from professional football at the end of the season.

Why is not known, but he resumed his career of joiner, and settled on the Isle of Wight, where he died, aged 77, in 1947.

Meanwhile, although (and perhaps because) Horsington was denied the opportunity to be a full-time professional

footballer, he became a highly respected local figure, first working as a publican.

He lived out the rest of his life with his Swindon-born wife, Kate, and their family, although their son, who was also called Richard, was killed in action in Rawalpindi, India (now Pakistan) in 1922.

Horsington was successful enough as a businessman to acquire a mineral water company from George Weaver, the owner of the Invicta ground, where Arsenal ▶

played home matches after moving from the Manor Ground. Indeed, they would have played their first League season there (1893/4) if Weaver hadn't tried to raise the annual rent to £350 from the £200 he had charged in the previous two seasons. Weaver was also controversial because he was behind a failed takeover bid at the football club.

Horsington was a member of at least two Freemason lodges, and turned out to play football in local charity matches in fancy dress. He even bought a handful of shares in the football club when it changed its name to Woolwich Arsenal and became a limited company in 1893 (their move from east London to Highbury in north London was in the summer of 1913).

So both Horsington and Offer were

important names in the history of Arsenal, but their short careers were also part of a bigger picture.

It is rather fitting that these two working class, former Swindon railwaymen were key players in the short period when football was suddenly transformed from its public school roots (which still dominated the game in the south) to not just the national sport, but the favourite sport of working men.

And you couldn't invent a better-equipped club than Arsenal to spearhead these developments.

The 1890s saw the reduction of industrial workers' hours from 54 to 48 hours per week (and down to as little as 42 hours for some white-collar workers). This provided arguably the single most

important catalyst for the growth of football in its entire history.

It meant a change from a six-day working week to five-and-a-half, with many workers now finishing at lunch time on Saturdays, leaving them free to either play football or – even more significantly – *watch* matches on Saturday afternoons.

It cemented the future of professional football and was particularly significant for Arsenal because they began as a works team, with the ordnance factory providing a fertile, readymade fanbase.

The factory was actually a conglomeration of departments with a combined workforce of more than 11,000 (at that time), giving it a similar social background to clubs in the industrial heartlands of the north and midlands, which already had established professional teams; in many ways it also mirrored the Railway Works and social infrastructures at Swindon.

During the research for this book, the authors discovered that Richard Horsington's loser's medal from the very day he was a guest of *The Moonies in London* still exists.

A *London Evening Standard* report in 2010 said the medal, from the defeat by Old Westminsters was coming up for auction. Believed to be the oldest Arsenal medal in existence, it was expected to fetch up to £6,000.

So we set about tracking it down. However, despite contacting the auctioneers, the Arsenal Museum and several of the football club's historians, we could find

no trace, nor knowledge of its whereabouts.

We then mentioned it to David Harvey while asking him for permission to use his photograph of Horsington's grave (see page 56).

David said he didn't know where it was, either.

However, a couple of days later he phoned – to say it had been found.

David had

mentioned the medal to his brother, Peter, and by an extraordinary chance – which even David was surprised to discover – it was Peter who bought the medal in the auction.

Contemporary newspaper reporters and modern historians disagree about what the cup they played for that day is actually called. Although the medal says otherwise, it is most often referred to as the London Senior Cup, but is also seen in

Other demographics were also on Arsenal's side; Plumstead was booming as – once again like Swindon – there was a large and sustained influx of skilled workers from all corners of the country. Between 1881 and 1891 – exactly the time when Horsington and Offer arrived from Swindon – the number of people living in Plumstead who had been born outside the area increased at double the rate of locals.

There were even similarities between Arsenal's and Swindon Town's rise into league football and professionalism, although Swindon's development was too little and too late to keep Horsington and Offer in Wiltshire.

Along with its rapid speed, the most important aspect of Arsenal's rise was the sustained

period of success they enjoyed on the pitch, just before turning professional.

In the 41 matches they played during the 1889-90 season, with Horsington (when not injured) and Offer virtually permanent fixtures, they won 31 and drew five, so if there had been a league table, they would probably have topped it. In the following year, with Horsington gone but Offer virtually ever-present, their success was almost as impressive.

Anything less might have dampened the fans' enthusiasm and the club's ambitions, but it proved the perfect launchpad for a big club, even if injuries ensured that Horsington would be looking from the sidelines.

One final thing to consider about Horsington and Offer is their relationship with each other.

They played together in two different teams and, as we have seen, Offer may have gone to Arsenal on Horsington's recommendation.

But they probably didn't move in the same circles off the pitch.

While Horsington later became a publican, Offer may well have been teetotal, if the team he played for before joining Swindon Town is any measure. They were called Temperance FC, and existed at a time when the Temperance Movement was hugely popular nationally, not least in Swindon. So it is fair to assume that if he played in their football team, he had also joined the movement – and its followers were required to 'sign the pledge' not to drink.

So when *The Moonies in London* toasted them in 1890, Offer would have responded with a glass containing something less intoxicating than his team-mate and the rest of those present. ∎

combinations of 'Challenge', 'Senior' and 'Association', or even just the London Cup.

The report on *The Moonies'* gathering called it the London Challenge Cup, which suggests the reporter may have just read it off one of the players' medals, and thus we can say that the one pictured opposite almost certainly attended the dinner!

If the re-discovery of Horsington's medal is fortuitous, then the next part is even more astonishing.

At the same time that he bought Horsington's medal, Peter Harvey bought another: one belonging to (of all people) Henry Offer.

It is from a different competition: the

London Charity Cup, the final of which was also against Old Westminsters, and played at the Oval, but a month later, in April 1890.

This time, Arsenal – minus Horsington, but fielding 11 players for the whole match – won 3-1, one of the goals scored by Offer.

Someone later converted the medal into a badge, and we

would like to think it was Henry himself, so he could proudly wear it on his jacket.

As well as being Arsenal fans, David and Peter Harvey are also railway enthusiasts, who visit Swindon's Steam Museum regularly – and when they do, they always find time to visit (of all places) the Glue Pot (see page 90). ∎

Front and back views of medals won by Richard Horsington (opposite) and Henry Offer (left) in cup finals in 1890 (courtesy of Peter and David Harvey)

Inside the Woolwich war machine

There is a certain irony to the fact that it was emigrant Swindon railwaymen working at – of all places – the Royal Arsenal Ordnance Factory at Woolwich who were the inspiration for the organisation that became *The Association of Wiltshiremen in London*.

As we have seen (see page 31), newly qualified apprentices and others left Swindon to find employment in factories and workshops all over the country, their GWR backgrounds being a measure of the quality of their training and work, and a ticket to working in all kinds of light and heavy industries, not just railways.

Where they landed and what they found when they moved there was something of a lottery, but it is safe to say that few places would have provided the social structures and support mechanisms that they had been accustomed to since being born in (or moving to) Swindon.

At Woolwich, though, they would have found as good a mirror of the Swindon set-up as anywhere in the world.

Indeed, while it is way beyond the scope of this book to include a comprehensive history of the Ordnance Factory, which spans the best part of 500 years, it is pertinent to point out the parallels between Swindon and Woolwich.

Far from feeling as though they had been plunged into their new homes without support, in fact anyone from Swindon finding employment in the Royal Arsenal would have considered themselves relatively well looked-after and in a working and living environment that must have felt surprisingly familiar.

Just as those working behind the walls of Swindon's giant railway complex talked of being 'inside', so the Royal Arsenal was effectively a self-contained unit, and because of the necessary security prevalent in and around this gigantic war machine, historians today still talk in terms of it being 'a secret city within a city'.

Even more significant than the geography of this huge operation was its self-sufficiency.

Just as they would have experienced in Swindon, workers in Woolwich would have found most of their accommodation, leisure and welfare needs served by a range of organisations provided (or at least supported) by the management of the Arsenal itself, or workers' bodies.

We can therefore come to the conclusion that the foundation of *The Moonies in London* was inspired not by a relatively poor provision of mechanisms and systems that were designed to support workers at Woolwich, which would have been the case in other industrial centres. Rather, it was the spirit of support and co-operation that former Swindon railwaymen found there that appeared to be the catalyst, and it must have seemed ▶

Right: the Royal Arsenal's impressive 'radial crane'. Built in the 1880s, it was enclosed in the pictured building in 1892. (Courtesy of www.royal-arsenal-history.com)

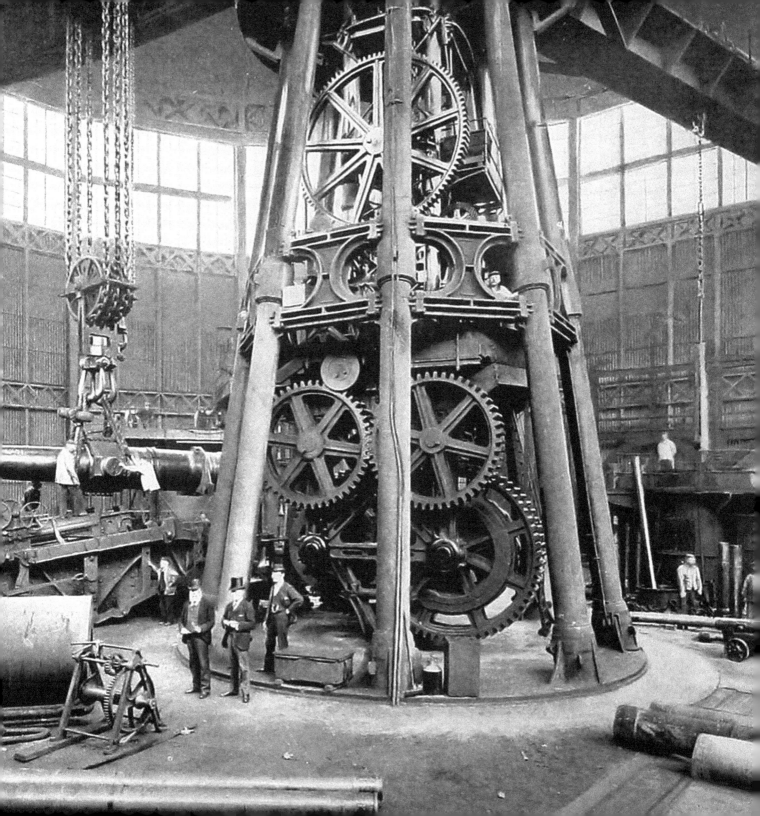

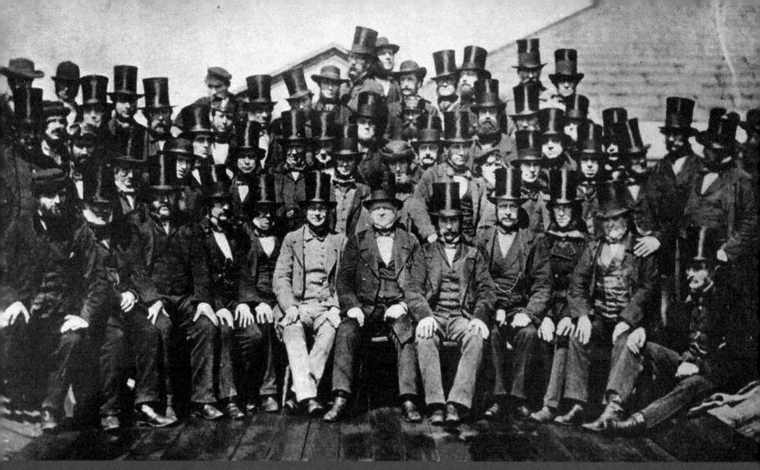

Above: gun carriage designers in 1870. Opposite: the Gun Carriage Works in 1874 (an external view of these Works as they appear today can be found on pages 70-75). (Courtesy of www.royal-arsenal-history.com)

a natural and even an obvious step to create another new support organisation as an additional prop to what already existed.

By the time former Swindon workers began arriving at the Royal Arsenal and *The Moonies in London* were formed in the 1880s, it was already well on the way to becoming the largest munitions factory in the world – and it had already been a very long road.

Whereas Swindon's GWR factory traced its origins only to the 1840s, with a major expansion (the Carriage and Wagon Works) quickly following in 1868, the Royal Arsenal's origins go back way

before even the Industrial Revolution. Born out of the Royal Naval Dockyard's (unstaffed) gunwharf at Woolwich, the Royal Arsenal began when a small plot of land beside the Thames was purchased in 1518 for the equipping of newly constructed warships.

And the site underwent a major expansion in 1670.

Although some explosives (mostly fireworks) were produced there, the Arsenal didn't manufacture armaments until around 1696, and the first cannon didn't come out of Woolwich until the latter part of the 18th century.

There was a longer history, however,

of first holding and then producing gun carriages. Just like the separate Carriage and Wagon Works at Swindon (a supplement to the 'Loco side'), the Royal Carriage Department illustrates the wide range of materials handled, the diverse operations undertaken and the many skills found behind the walls of the Arsenal, and how it provided work across an impressive myriad of different occupations.

Because the Arsenal was spread over more than three square miles and had a workforce, at its peak, that even dwarfed the one at Swindon, reaching close to six figures in wartime, behind its walls it was necessary to divide the operation into a number of smaller units.

In 1805, when it was first given the name of Royal Arsenal, these departments still retained a measure of independence, and by the time *The Moonies in London* were formed, there were effectively three arms: the Royal Gun Factory (originally the Royal Brass Foundry, but renamed in 1855), the Royal Laboratory (a manufacturing facility, built in 1856, later to be a key research facility) and the Royal Carriage Department (with a long history, formalised when it was given its new name in 1803).

These three departments were broken down into more than 30 sub-divisions, including The India Office, War Department Chemist and Royal Electrical and Mechanical Engineers.

Like the GWR Works in Swindon, where not just rolling stock but almost everything necessary to equip and service a whole railway was produced, so the Royal Arsenal was much more than a factory for guns.

Behind its walls at different times in its history, and especially as it expanded and developed, one could find major logistical and storage systems; research and testing units; military administration; uniform production; and the manufacture and handling of a wide range of supplementary military equipment, such as tents and ammunition boxes. As well as larger hardware such as field guns, howitzers, mortars, torpedoes and even early rockets, the site also made a dazzling array of small arms, from bayonets and swords to muskets, rifles and pistols.

This 'secret city' needed to be maintained and serviced, so various units were created to answer to its needs; fire prevention, for instance. Swindon had its own fire station, but Woolwich had several firefighting centres across the site. Not surprisingly, the various explosives and other volatile and dangerous materials that were routinely made, stored and stockpiled across the site made not just *fire* prevention but *explosion* prevention absolutely crucial.

In yet more parallels with Swindon Works, the Arsenal had a gasworks and other power generating facilities, a dedicated telephone exchange and its own ambulance.

Medical and accident considerations were as advanced as they were in Swindon, although at Woolwich they were provided and organised by management, rather than through workers' co-operation, as was the case with the GWR's Medical Fund.

The Woolwich set-up was clearly designed to cater for the inevitable accidents that would befall workers on the site, with a surgery (which is sometimes referred to as a hospital) placed close to the main gates.

It had X-ray facilities, a fracture clinic and an eye clinic, where the standard of surgery was said to be 'second to none'. There was a dispensary and also a mortuary, for when the accidents proved fatal. A couple of other 'sub-surgeries' were also provided, elsewhere on the site.

But medical provision was not restricted to accident and emergency functions. Many employees routinely consulted the doctors at the surgery, and it was also where workers were vaccinated against contemporary perils, such as smallpox and tetanus.

Although the Arsenal did not have the luxury (as was the case in Swindon) of a hospital containing wards, its status as a military site meant that workers were entitled to be in-patients (or have more serious injuries treated) at the military hospital (Herbert Hospital, renamed The Royal Herbert Hospital in 1900), which was two miles away, at Shooters Hill.

It is worth detailing the rules that were in place at the Royal Gun Factory in 1884, which show both how extensive the medical provision was, but also its limitations for newly arrived employees:

All persons engaged in the Arsenal who have been employed three years ▸

continuously and reside within one mile radius of a point equidistant from the main and Plumstead gates of the Royal Arsenal are entitled to medical aid at their residences should they be unable to attend personally. Men [with] under three years [service] are not entitled to medical assistance, except in case of injury or sudden illness while at work. When fit to resume work, they should attend at the Medical Department to have their names withdrawn from the sick list... Any man incapacitated from performing his work through an injury received whilst in execution of duty, or by sickness clearly attributable to the nature of his work, is allowed full pay for three

months continuously, if necessary.

Ironically (for former Swindonians working there), the Arsenal also had its own railway. Beginning with horse-drawn wagons in the 1820s and evolving into three separate systems, it used two different narrow gauges, but also standard gauge rolling stock, those lines linking with the South Eastern Railway from the 1850s. The system was eventually amalgamated to form a single railway in 1891, called Royal Arsenal Railways, and comprised 147 miles of track compressed into two square miles.

It is claimed that this made it the densest railway network in British history, although former

Swindon men might have pointed out that the countless sidings and other rails inside the GWR Works, if counted as separate to the network, was probably larger.

A dearth of historical personnel records means it is almost impossible to pinpoint where any particular former Swindon man might have worked (with the exception of Henry Offer, see page 46), but it seems likely that some of them would have ended up looking after the site's railway.

Not that railways were the only means of transport inside and into the Arsenal,

Main Gates, Woolwich Arsenal

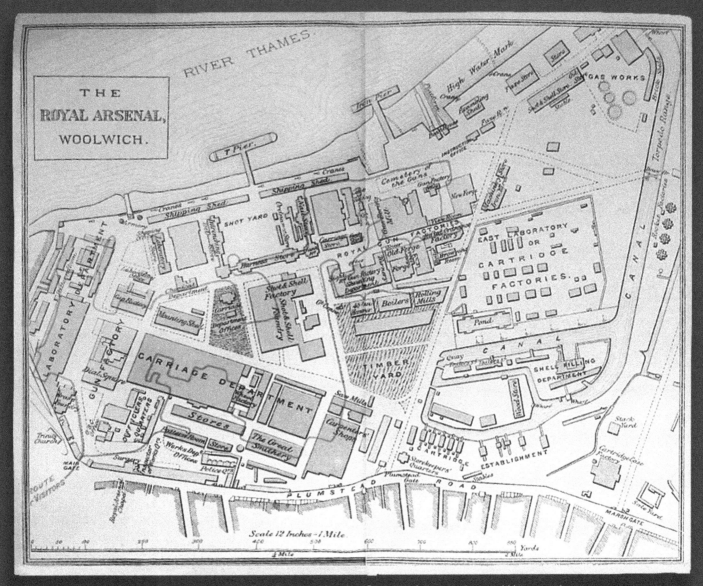

The site in 1887, the year after the first meeting of *The Moonies in London* (Courtesy of www.royal-arsenal-history.com)

where there were two piers serving the Thames, effectively making up the site's northern boundary, and a canal. The canal doubled as a test bed for torpedoes, and one found there when the water was drained in the 1980s is now on display at the Royal Navy Submarine Museum in Gosport.

The Royal Arsenal was a constantly changing landscape in many respects. Although always busy, for instance, activity naturally increased dramatically during times of war, such as the Boer War (which will feature elsewhere in this book). ▶

Change also came about as new technologies appeared, and these were often as a result of research and development carried out at Woolwich. Sometimes experience from military action was the catalyst for the change, which brings us back to the Boer War.

Serious faults in the ammunition used by the British Army during that conflict, along with an arms race and the growing complexity of weapons in the first years of the 20th century, all led to the establishment of the Chemical Research Department at the Arsenal in 1907.

To most newcomers, it must have appeared as an ever-changing, confusing and somewhat daunting place, but at least Swindonians who found themselves working there would have seen the parallels with what existed at the GWR Works back home. And in its social frameworks, too, they would have felt quite at home.

Where Swindon's Railway Village, for instance, provided 300 homes for railwaymen and their families, so up to 300 people found official accommodation provided for them at Woolwich. These were actually housed on site, behind the walls of the Arsenal, and included houses and flats for 44 police constables and two inspectors, and a house for the Magazine Foreman. But they were the tip of a very large iceberg.

The workforce is believed to have numbered around 11,000 in the late 1880s, and they largely found homes for themselves and their families in adjacent urbanisations, most significantly in Plumstead and Woolwich.

However (yet again mirroring Swindon), towns and villages further afield would also have provided homes for some of the workforce, their often rural characters impacted by influxes of industrial working-class people from many different parts of the country. And as the workforce swelled during wartime, it caused a housing crisis, with communities of prefabricated homes springing up to meet the demand.

In terms of leisure, Swindon's work-force could avail themselves of various facilities, such as (from the 1930s) a dedicated sports ground; sport also filled some of the free time of employees in Woolwich, with a range of teams playing under the Royal Arsenal banner, as well as the famous football team.

One member of the team, Richard Horsington, who moved from Swindon to work in the Arsenal and play for its football team (see page 46), would have been immediately aware of the existence of arguably the most impressive part of the social provision for employees: its own co-operative farm, which covered 56 acres and grew crops that provided some of the workers' food.

In January 1889, just five days after Horsington played his first match for the team, this farm made national news. Even though it was claimed to be working at a loss, a Plumstead vicar insisted that the farm should pay a tithe, an ancient tax of ten per cent of output, levied by the Church. This caused an outcry that turned into 'an anti-tithe demonstration' in which 'a large crowd assembled with a band playing *The Dead March*'. The vicar refused to back down, and two vans had to be auctioned to raise the necessary fee.

The incident perhaps underlines yet another parallel with Swindon at the time: a growing militancy.

Something of an echo of the pioneering and influential Mechanics' Institute at ▶

Opposite and following pages: the Royal Arsenal site today

Swindon, the co-operative society was formed in 1869, and by 1889 it had 6,200 members.

Perhaps this, above all other parallels, best demonstrates how the GWR Works at Swindon and the Royal Arsenal at Woolwich reflected each other – and why anyone arriving from Wiltshire to find new work on the south bank of the River Thames might have felt more at home than we might have imagined.

Even today the former Royal Arsenal reflects Swindon's former Railway Works because, following a slow and painful decline and closure in 1967, it has been converted into numerous units with various functions, including some catering and retail (like the Swindon Outlet Village). Other areas have been redeveloped for new housing.

Woolwich, too, has its share of former industrial buildings looking for a new purpose, as is the case in Swindon, but also people who are passionate about researching its history and educating present and future generations about the industrial site's former importance, its lasting legacy and its source of pride.

At the Royal Arsenal this burden falls mainly on the shoulders of Ian Bull and Steven Peterson, whose exemplary work and commitment to heritage requires them to be not only archivists and publishers of an extensive RAH website (www.royal-arsenal-history.com), but they also conduct guided tours.

A measure of the scale of the place and its rich history is that the 'standard' tour takes three or four hours, but if visitors want to find out even more, including a detailed description of the gun-making process, they can join another tour lasting all day.

Anyone interested in industrial history and our national and military heritage should make a point of joining a tour

there, and seeing the remarkable site for themselves.

When the co-authors of this book were both fortunate to attend one of the 'standard' tours as part of our research, it provided us with modern photos of the Arsenal as it is today, but we are indebted to the RAH for providing the historical images used here, too – and for giving us one final link between Swindon and Woolwich.

Our guide confirmed that the high quality of former railwaymen's work and the finer tolerances they worked to in the GWR meant they were not only welcomed at the Arsenal, but (it is believed) sometimes even specifically recruited or 'poached' from Swindon (and if they were also blessed with a talent for playing football, it was a bonus).

For completeness, although a full history is beyond the scope of this book, it should be mentioned that Swindon also contributed proudly to the war effort, and in the First World War, some of it was related to the work of the Royal Arsenal.

Charles Collett, then Assistant Works Manager, but later to become Chief Mechanical Engineer of the GWR, was awarded the OBE for his services to the country's war effort as the Railway Works produced ambulance trains, bombs and shells, and a Ministry of War National Drying Kiln was set up in the Works to dry wood for use in the production of Sopwith aircraft.

Meanwhile, the 1915 Munitions of War Act allowed the Government to create National Factories to help with the production of arms and ammunition.

Until then, they relied on production at the Royal Arsenal, two other government locations (the Royal Small Arms Factory, at Enfield and the Royal Gunpowder Factory at Waltham Abbey) and private ▶

companies such as Vickers Armstrong, but their combined efforts were insufficient to meet demand.

So, a major facility opened in Swindon in 1917, at what is now Kembrey Park, covering 67 acres. Now often referred to as the 'powder works', its official designation was His Majesty's Explosives Factory (HMEF) Stratton, Swindon. Broadly speaking, HMEFs manufactured the explosives that supplied the 174 National Filling Factories where bombs, shells and mines were assembled.

There were four key types of explosives: cordite, a propellant invented at the Royal Arsenal and first used in 1889; Lyddite and Tri-nitro-toluene (TNT), which are high explosives used to fill shells; tetryl, used in fuses; and ammonium nitrate.

Swindon's role was to produce ammonium nitrate, which had historically been used as an agricultural fertiliser, but could be added to the much more expensive TNT to make it go further. Called amatol, this mixture consisted of up to 80 per cent ammonium nitrate.

In addition, ammonium nitrate could be added to aluminium powder and TNT to produce ammanol, which had a civilian use in mining, but was adapted for use in explosive mines placed underneath German positions on the Western Front during key battles in 1918.

With a workforce heavily dependent on women, HMEF Stratton, Swindon produced up to 500 tons of ammonium nitrate a week.

Almost all of the HMEF Swindon has now been demolished, although a small building used as a store still exists on Bramble Road, along with a pair of semi-detached bungalows that began life as a hostel. ∎

Toasts to 'fellow Moonies'

Change was in the air for *The Moonies in London* in 1891 as the organisation spread its wings and found a bigger and grander venue for its annual dinner in London.

It was on March 14 that they gathered at the Bridge House Hotel, London Bridge, with the *Swindon Advertiser* report explaining:

As is well known, this idea of Wiltshiremen residing in London meeting together owes its inception to a number of former employees at the GWR Company's Works at Swindon who are now engaged at Woolwich Arsenal, and for the first three years of the movement [four, actually] it was celebrated in that district, the attendance being necessarily composed of local gentlemen. But such were the convivial and harmonious times enjoyed that their fame spread to many other "Moonies" engaged in various parts of London, and they wished to join their old friends and acquaintances in keeping up associations of "home".

The situation of Woolwich precluded this to many, and hence it was a happy thought of the committee to select the Bridge House Hotel, London, as the rendezvous – a place within easy distance from Woolwich and other parts of London as well.

The character of the occasion may have been changing, but the same

Left: the front of an 1880s menu card from the Bridge House Hotel, the venue for *The Moonies in London* dinner in 1891

atmosphere of county pride prevailed, John Templeman was still in the chair, and the wish to celebrate the achievements of fellow Moonies was as strong as ever.

'Several gentlemen present had risen to positions of importance and trust,' noted the *Advertiser*, adding:

It was very interesting to note that all these laid the credit of their success to the excellent education received at the GWR Schools under the tuition of Mr Braid, and the training under the foremen in the Works. It would have been a proud time for Mr Braid had he been enabled to be present to have heard the eulogiums of those of his old school boys in [showing] their success in life had been due to him, looking back with gratifications even on the "whacks" he had administered to them.

Over a period of several years it was always hoped that Braid's health might allow him to attend one of the dinners, but he never did.

Also unable to accept an invitation was renowned Swindon athlete James Kibblewhite, who was 'in training for a race for a fifty guinea cup at Easter', but was toasted in his absence, as was footballer Henry Offer, the Royal Arsenal star who had attended the dinner with his team-mate Richard Horsington, the year before.

Moonies also had reason to be proud of local achievements in the arts, the report said, with scenic artist 'Mr W[T] Hemsley, whose work is to be seen in

We have only the poor-quality newspaper reproduction (above) to show us the emblem that was 'suspended over the head of the Chairman at the 1891 dinner – hence the modern artist's impression of how it may have looked (below). (Courtesy of Shannon Jones)

most London theatres and the provinces,' adding that 'the promoters of the School of Art at Swindon have occasion to be proud' and 'the Council of the Mechanics' Institute were also not forgotten, and the admirable services they rendered by means of the evening classes.'

The artistic skills of WT Hemsley would be put to work on producing a moonrakers painting to be hung at future dinners, but for now there was a different arrangement:

Suspended immediately over the head of the Chairman was the "Moonies" Arms, a rough-and-ready sketch in oil by, it was understood, Mr G Tooes, a local Swindon artist and which we have produced as above. When, in course of his remarks, Mr Morris pointed to this sketch as proof positive of the origin of the term "Moonrakers", the company was fairly convulsed with laughter.

The 'Mr Morris' referred to was 1891's guest of honour, William Morris, the editor and proprietor of the *Advertiser*.

He began a long speech by saying he 'might at once say his great desire to be present at their meeting was because he saw in it a principle which was well worth the consideration of all men'. However, when he moved on to an ▸

anecdote about a visit he had made to Bowood and alluded to 'a circumstance in connection with the Marquess of Lansdowne' it caused a rare moment of disharmony in the *Moonies in London*'s proceedings.

A voice was heard to say 'No politics', an interruption that was damned in the *Advertiser*:

The gentleman who was interrupting paid neither he (the speaker) nor the company any compliment by his interruption. Wiltshiremen, as a rule, knew how to behave themselves, knew when to speak of politics, and when to leave them alone.

So there! And just in case the interruptor didn't regret the incident enough, it was compounded when one of those present, John Howcroft, felt it necessary to pen an angry letter to the *Advertiser* – with what it has to said is a brilliant rebuke. But it emphasised the otherwise extremely cordial nature of *The Moonies in London*:

SIR – Having heard that a certain person with whom subtlety is a conspicuous trait in his character, had the audacity to circulate my name amongst some of those present at the "Moonies" dinner, as being the person who so rudely interrupted you in your response to the toast of the "Moonies," allow me to contradict this false statement, and to say (and prove it necessary) that the guilty one was my accuser's relative from Swindon.

Hoping you will endeavour to stop this lie before travelling further.
I remain, yours truly,
JR Howcroft

'As Mr Howcroft requests it,' added Morris, 'we publish the above, but the circumstance does not really require it.

It was merely the petulant remark of an ill-conditioned individual who must have regretted that he had spoken when the better manners of those around him made him feel his own foolishness.'

Howcroft, a metal turner at the Royal Arsenal, was serving a second (and final) year as Honourable Secretary of *The Moonies in London*. Born in 1864, he moved to Swindon to take up an apprenticeship with the GWR and lodgings at 27 Oriel Street, where he fell in love with the landlord's daughter, Sarah Friar. The pair married and moved to Plumstead when he took his new job at the Arsenal, and Howcroft was a member of the Union Waterloo Lodge of Freemasons. By 1901 Sarah had returned to Swindon, and the marriage – unusually for those days – ended in divorce. Ten years later, Howcroft was the proprietor of a laundry business, but is listed in 1939 (seven years before his death) as 'retired engineer/turner'.

The irony of the incident involving Morris is: although he was renowned for having a dislike for certain members of the ruling classes (see page 82), he was just about to compliment Lansdowne for his pride in his Wiltshire ancestry, and his sentimentality over home, when he was rudely interrupted.

The interruption was a reminder that whatever class divisions might have existed, what bound together all those present at the dinner – namely their Wiltshire roots – always proved stronger. It was a principle that prevailed throughout the life of the Association.

Another irony is the nature of the annual dinners would shift in later years – from this early atmosphere of reunion and celebration of working men made good, to one dominated by the upper reaches of Wiltshire society and the military.

In the meantime, Morris ended his speech by returning to his previous theme, which exonerated anyone who retained a sentimental attachment to childhood and bygone Wiltshire days:

He would urge them to cultivate to the greatest possible extent of their powers their best and happiest reminiscences of home and of the scenes of their childhood. Let them never be ashamed of being called "Moonies", never take offence at any ridicule that might be attempted on the term.

When the thunderous applause for Morris's speech had died down, the company were treated to a few songs, including *The Exciseman*, which no doubt harked back to the moonrakers story, and there was a toast to "Old Swindonians".

This was answered by two old railwaymen, including Jack Harding, who had served his apprenticeship in Swindon and was now a consulting engineer. He explained how he would "look back and remember Mr Braid and the Mechanics' Institute for the means given him to get on in the world," and, the report added:

When a Swindonian applied to him [for employment], he wanted no further recommendation – not from a spirit of clannishness, but because he knew that nine hundred and ninety-nine times out of every thousand, men from the Works were good men, and had been taught their trade well.

Another engineer who was present, Mr Williams, foreman of the boilermakers at the Great Eastern Railway's works in Stratford, East London, concurred, saying he was 'very glad to have a lot of Swindonians [working for him], for he had found Mr Harding's remarks true – they did their work well.'

The entertainments that followed

Above: *The Moore and Burgess Minstrels*, in Brighton in 1888, with William Lacey in the back row, ninth from the left. (Courtesy of Jean Thomas)

included a performance by William Lacey, 'whose engagement with *The Moore and Burgess Minstrels*, St James's Hall, prevented his earlier attendance'.

Lacey, who 'is regarded as one of the finest cornet solo players in London' duly gave a recital and an encore of *The Lost Chord* 'in a manner so effective that it will not soon be forgotten by those who had the privilege of listening to it'.

Lacey is a good example of the accomplished Swindon-born musicians who appeared at *The Moonies'* dinners over the years, who would have been well known to those present, were highly esteemed, often on the national stage –

and have been somewhat forgotten in Swindon's history. Born in New Swindon in 1851, Lacey grew up in the Railway Village at 5 Reading Street, and completed his apprenticeship with the GWR as an engine fitter.

He was a long-time member of the 2nd Volunteer Battalion band of the Wiltshire Regiment, but moved to Brighton after serving his apprenticeship, where the 1871 census listed him as a 'railway engine fitter' – almost certainly with the London, Brighton and South Coast Railway.

But he was soon to become a professional musician, joining the

prestigious Moore and Burgess Minstrels in 1876, who were on their way to enjoying a residency at St James's Hall, Piccadilly, that would span four decades.

Founded in Buffalo, New York in 1843, they were originally called *The Christy Minstrels*, and had established the format and popularity of minstrel shows in the United States.

It was a style of light entertainment that spread across the Atlantic and remained popular throughout the 19th century and even well into the 20th century, despite now being considered racially offensive because it consisted mainly of white players performing in blackface. ▶

79

Although the photograph on the previous page shows the troupe not in costume, the reality is, as the poster from the touring version of their show demonstrates (left, courtesy of The Huntington Library, San Marino, California) the reality is that *The Moore and Burgess Minstrels* continued this blackface tradition.

However much this seems to be at odds with 21st century values, especially in proudly multicultural Swindon, it should not detract from Lacey's memory.

His inclusion in such a popular troupe is testament to his skill as a musician, and *The Moonies in London* would have considered his appearance at their dinner as something of a coup.

Lacey eventually moved to Lambeth, became a Professor of Music, and returned to be a very popular performer at other annual dinners, his career as a musician continuing until at least 1911. He died in London in 1918, aged 67.

The 1891 dinner had proved a roaring success and all those present – 117, to be exact, compared with only 15-20 who had attended the first dinner – were seeing *The Moonies in London* go from strength to strength.

And although those present still reflected the group's origins and purpose – including the foreman of forgers in the Gun Factory, the assistant foreman of the Royal Carriage Department and the foreman of the New Turnery – the mould had been cast for future dinners. ■

When *The Moonies in London* invited William Morris to be guest of honour at their 1891 dinner, it was a fitting tribute to a key figure in the history and development of Swindon.

It was also timely; he would be dead, just over three months later.

Although it is impossible to ignore William Morris in any history of Swindon, thanks to his founding of the *Advertiser* in 1854, it is easy to overlook the impact that his personality had on the rapidly growing town.

Fortunately, research by Swindon historian Frances Bevan has put him into proper perspective, and we are obliged to her for the following, which paints a vivid picture of a man on a mission.

Born on January 27, 1826, in Wotton-under-Edge, William was the eldest of James and Elizabeth Morris's ten children. As a young man, his father had fought in the Peninsular War and lost an arm at the Battle of Orthes in 1814. Invalided home, he set himself up as a bookseller – a career choice which would have an enormous impact on his son, William.

In 1830 the family moved to Swindon, and by the time of the 1841 census,

Cheers for Morris, man of the people

James had a bookshop and stationery business in Wood Street, in a premise later occupied by watchmaker and jeweller, HJ Deacon.

William Morris's lasting legacy, the *Swindon Advertiser*, was conceived out of the chaos resulting from legal action brought against Charles Dickens and the publishers of his magazine, *Household Words*, in 1854.

Stamp duty on newspapers made them unaffordable to the vast majority, but when Dickens, whose magazine comprised both fiction and news reports, was charged with contravening the stamp duty law, it suddenly became necessary to define what constituted a newspaper.

It was finally declared that a publication produced at an interval of 28 days or more was not a newspaper – and that was a green light for Morris.

Within days of the ruling, he had produced the first edition of his monthly penny newspaper, the first of its kind in England.

In 1855, further changes to the stamp duty law saw the *Swindon Advertiser* published weekly, and in 1861 Morris wrote that the duty had been totally repealed and "the Newspaper Press of England was thereby made absolutely free for all good and righteous purposes".

Outspoken and tenacious, Morris was a force to be reckoned with in Victorian Swindon.

He argued that one Bible equalled one Church, and chose to attend a different ▶

place of worship every Sunday, marching his large family down the aisle, and – for maximum impact – always arrived late.

Morris was a lifelong Liberal, although frequently at variance with party policy and eventually breaking away.

He stood for election in the Cricklade division in 1874, and was accused of dividing the Liberal vote by his acrimonious exchanges with other Liberal candidates.

He was a member of the Old Swindon Local Board and the Swindon School Board, and for more than 25 years was one of the Highworth and Swindon Board of Guardians, seldom missing one of its meetings, and revolutionising attitudes to the poor.

He was famous for his battles with the 'squirearchy' of the day, using the pages of the *Advertiser* to fearlessly air his views.

In the bitterly cold winter of 1861, the local gentry held a feast on the frozen reservoir at Coate, and when Morris heard that young toffs were using surplus meat as a football, he was incensed at the wanton waste of food at a time when many people were starving.

Following his attack in the *Advertiser*, a campaign was waged to destroy the newspaper. An effigy of Morris was raised in the Market Square, which led to brawls between his opponents and railwaymen, who came out to support him.

Some of his campaigns were reprinted in his important 1885 history, *Swindon: Fifty Years Ago (More or Less)*, which was sub-titled *Reminiscences, Notes and Relics of Ye Olde Wiltshire Towne*.

It recalled the infamous case of the lord of the Manor at Lydiard House who attempted to silence the Swindon Works hooter that called railwaymen to work in 1873, but had reckoned without the opposition of Morris.

Referring to the 'all-supreme interests' of the landed gentry, his book recalled: Perhaps the feeling... was best of all exemplified in recent times by Lord Bolingbroke, when he set up some sentimental personal grievance of his own against the convenience of some five or six thousands of workmen to their labours on the grounds that its noise might possibly frighten and disturb a few of his pheasants sitting on their eggs a few miles off.

He also campaigned vigorously against blood sports, and took on violent badger baiters; the latter was a lucrative business, so Morris received death threats.

But not only the criminal fraternity were challenged.

He also mounted an extended campaign against the brutal sport of backswording, which had a long tradition in Wiltshire, but which Morris saw as not only barbaric but also a loathsome source of illegal betting.

On June 20, 1891, he died peacefully in his sleep in Bournemouth, where he had gone to spend the weekend, and is buried in the family plot in Christ Church cemetery, along his wife and four of their children, who had tragically died previously.

One of his obituaries said he was 'a man whose honesty of purpose carried him above the miserable trickery of party [politics], and whose dominant desire in the conduct of the newspaper which he edited with so much ability was to redress wrong and uphold the right.'

And that was the verdict of an old adversary!

His death came just three months after his triumphant appearance at the Moonies' dinner, and the reaction to his speech there, and the indignation over the interruption gives us another important insight into his popularity and standing among his contemporaries.

Even bearing in mind that the (unnamed) reporter who recorded the proceedings at the 1891 dinner had a motive for over-hyping the reaction to his speech – Morris was his boss – the warmth with which he was greeted seems unmistakable:

As Mr Morris resumed his seat, the company, apparently without exception, sprang to their feet, and for some moments the scene witnessed was of a remarkable character, the whole company joining in according the speaker musical honours and otherwise expressing approval with the sentiments he had given utterance to.

When a Swindon Heritage blue plaque was unveiled on the former Advertiser building in Victoria Road in 2022, it was a rare recognition for a man who is one of the superstars of Swindon's history, but otherwise mostly forgotten.

Even worse: the recent naming of William Morris Way and Willam Morris Primary School in Tadpole Garden Village might appear to be a tribute to him, but are named after another William Morris, the internationally acclaimed textile designer, who owned Kelmscott Manor, near Lechlade.

But the huge impact he made on Swindon during his own lifetime is a matter of history and – just three months before he passed away – William Morris could have been left in no doubt that what would become *The Association of Wiltshiremen in London* were proud to count him as a 'fellow Moonie'. ∎

On your marks...

In a modern world where sport is never far from the media's attention, it is difficult to imagine its very different role in the years before the formation of *The Moonies in London*.

The modern Olympics were not yet founded, football was in its infancy, and 'sport' probably meant something quite different to how we define it today.

The most popular sports were the preserve of the landed gentry, public schoolboys and the Varsity crowd, such as horseracing (the so-called 'sport of kings'), rowing, rugby and various others with foundations on the playing fields of Eton and its like, which they jealously protected, with the dual purpose of keeping their hobbies amateur and stopping working-class men making a living from them.

Even what they were inclined to call 'soccer' was mostly a distraction for public schools and old boys – until the formation of the Football League in 1888, made up of clubs from the industrial heartlands of the north and midlands. This turned it into a working man's sport, especially with the rise of similar clubs in the south, led by Arsenal, (see page 46).

Or else there was the kind of 'sport' (opposed by William Morris; see page 82) that existed primarily or solely as an excuse for illegal betting, such as hare coursing, backswording and (to an extent) boxing.

And 'sport' might even refer to something that most of us in the 21st century no longer recognise as such: 'blood sports' or hunting (also opposed by William Morris).

By the time *The Moonies in London* was founded, however, the transfor- ▶

Top: James Kibblewhite (third runner from the right) on the starting line of a race in London (courtesy of Bob Townsend).
Above: an artist's impression of Kibblewhite from the *Penny Illustrated Paper* of April 1891, a month after he was toasted by *The Moonies in London* at their annual dinner.

mation of many sports into working class leisure pursuits meant local sportsman became role models.

Enter the Purton-born athlete, James Kibblewhite!

When he was toasted in his absence by *The Moonies in London* in 1891, he was as good an example of the new Victorian sportsman as you would find anywhere – and at the height of his fame.

Kibblewhite was a pioneer because he won not just fame, but also a little fortune – in a manner that would have been impossible, just a generation earlier.

He was still an amateur in the sense that he had to compete while also holding down a job as a railwayman (working five-and-a-half days a week), but his talent for winning races over a range of distances meant he was able to gather enough prize money to be able to eventually buy his own home.

Not that it was always cash that he won, as the photograph (opposite, courtesy of Bob Townsend) shows, and he was able to mount impressive displays of his prizes at the Mechanics' Institute.

He won a string of prestigious races and titles during his career, and even set a world record.

James 'Kibby' Kibblewhite was born at Purton in 1866 and, like his father and brothers, eventually worked for the GWR.

He began racing competitively in 1884 and, following a full working week in R Shop (now the home of Swindon's Steam Museum), he ran record-breaking races at events across the country, in a career that spanned 13 seasons.

Although he did not believe in rigorous training – he called it "mortifying the flesh" – he enjoyed football, cricket and cycling, and ran laps around the GWR Park as part of his preparation. Legend also has it that he would race alongside the train from his home in Purton to work in Swindon.

In August 1889 he entered the three-Mile Open Handicap Race at Stamford Bridge in London, finishing in a world record time of 14 minutes and 29.6 seconds, which earned him a gold medal (inset). The record had been set by Calne-born runner WG George (see page 148), five years earlier.

Remarkably, however, Kibby wasn't the first over the line. In those days, some races were handicapped, and this time Kibblewhite was unable to catch the winner, who started 160 yards ahead of him.

When he was unable to accept an invitation to join *The Moonies in London* in March 1891, it was said to be because he was 'in training for a race for a fifty guinea cup at Easter', but in fact he was in the middle of a programme of events that kept him busy every weekend during the season.

The previous month, the *Athletes' Journal* had said of him:

There are those who suggest that Kibblewhite will not run in the Southern [Counties Championship] this year, as he would not take the risk of being beaten by Thomas or Fowler. Those who know the Swindon runner and his many admirers can afford to treat this insinuation with contempt. I am of the opinion that there has never been an amateur so good at all distances from a mile upwards, both on the flat and across country, and should he train properly for this event, there is not a man in the south, at least, that can beat him.

The writer was right; Kibblewhite won the race, in front of an estimated 5,000 people, by 25 yards; Thomas was third and Fowler finished a poor tenth.

His next major race was for the National Cross Championship, in Cheshire. Reports gave no indication of the length of the race, but Kibble-white's winning time of just under an hour means it was some miles, and therefore a long distance race, whereas he was most renowned for middle distance running.

Reporting on the race on the very day that *The Moonies in London* toasted him at their dinner, the *Swindon Advertiser* pointed out that 'one of the sporting papers' had said: 'Gallantly he upheld his worldwide reputation, and won handsomely', adding that 'Kibblewhite's history is too well known to require any words of commendation from us.'

The upcoming race that had ▶

prevented him from accepting *The Moonies in London*'s invitation duly took place two weeks later, on Easter Saturday, March 28, 1891, at Salford.

This time over a mile, he 'won easily' against the local man, WH Morton, and 'Kibblewhite's victory made the handsome trophy his absolute property, as he had won it on the two previous occasions.'

Modern membership rules did not apply in the 19th century, allowing Kibblewhite to compete for several different clubs, and in 1892 he broke the record for the four-mile Race at Stamford Bridge, this time running for the Essex Beagles.

He won the AAA one-mile championship of England three times, took the four-mile title twice, and was the champion over 10 miles twice. At one time he held the three-mile grass record and was joint holder of the 1¼-mile record.

Yet Kibby was usually at work until the eve of a competition, and sometimes even on the day of a championship.

In 1894 he married Mary Bristow and the couple had four children together. Their three sons all ran competitively, including Claude Kibblewhite, who ran in the first race organised by the Swindon Athletic Club, in 1921.

By 1895 (the year before the first modern Olympics), Kibby's running career had ended. He sold some of his prizes, valued at more than £1,000, and with the proceeds built a home he named *Spartan Cottages*, after one of his old clubs.

In November 1941, the *Swindon Advertiser* reported his death, describing him as 'one of the greatest figures in the amateur sporting world'.

It was no exaggeration.

He is buried with his wife Mary at St Mary's Church, Purton, and Kibblewhite Close, in the village, is named in his honour. ∎

The *Penny Illustrated Paper*'s version of a race that Kibblewhite competed in at the Oval in 1892. Usually a middle-to-long distance runner but prepared to try his luck at any distance, he lost to short distance specialist EC Bredin over 1,000 yards, a distance over which the reporter said Bredin 'is bound to win every time'. The report gives no details about the policeman's involvement.

Feeling 'moon-struck'

The annual dinner of *The Moonies in London* had a new venue in 1892, but otherwise it was business as usual.

This time (but for one year only, as it turned out) the gathering was in St George's Hall, in the Champion Hotel, Aldersgate Street, a fitting venue considering they were there to *champion* everything that was good about Wiltshire.

And why not?

John Templeman was still in the chair, and he opened the proceedings by telling the assembled company of former 'Moonies' and those 'visitors' who had come up from Swindon that he believed they were "moon-struck" by the superiority of the Wiltshiremen.

It was the usual signal to celebrate the achievements of their fellows, including those who had been toasted during previous meetings.

This included William Morris, the star of the previous year's dinner, who had sadly passed away, and the former GWR teacher, Alexander Braid, who was roundly praised, as was the custom – and still too frail to attend.

Attendance was slightly down on the previous year, but it was noted that a significant proportion of those present were former Swindon GWR men employed at Stratford Works, the manufacturing facility of the Great Eastern Railway (GER).

Only five of them had attended in 1890, but now it was up to 28, giving some indication of how large the quota of Swindonians must have been at the GER at the time.

Sadly missing from their ranks was James Holden (inset), who sent his apologies.

Holden had joined the GWR in 1865, had risen to be Carriage and Wagon Works Manager in Swindon in 1873, and then Assistant Locomotive Superintendent, under William Dean, in 1878 (Dean's chief assistant).

But in 1885 he had gone one rung higher at Stratford, where he was now Locomotive Superintendent of the GER, and would remain in post until 1907.

By then he would be credited with a number of loco designs, a massive reorganisation of Stratford Works and a policy of standardisation that probably came straight out of the Swindon textbook.

So, perhaps, was his idea for providing a hostel for enginemen who arrived in London with late trains from the provinces, which had opened a couple of years earlier.

Holden's disappointing absence was probably mostly regretted because Stratford Works was in the news, which was another reason why he would have made a fascinating speaker.

The reason: just three months earlier, under the guidance of Holden, the workforce had set a new world record.

It was on December 10-11, 1891 that they assembled a complete 67-ton, six-wheel locomotive and tender in the outrageously swift time of nine hours and 47 minutes of working hours; it actually took a fraction over 24 hours altogether.

Weighing in at 67 tons, it was a Class Y14 locomotive that, despite its rapid birth, eventually ran for 40 years,

covering a total of 1,127,750 miles (1,814,940 km).

Stratford Works was like a scaled-down version of Swindon Works, with a workforce (in 1900) totalling a shade under 7,000, compared with up to 14,000 at Swindon.

The Works also followed in the footsteps of Swindon with closure in 1991. By then the Great Eastern was long gone, merged, along with other railways, into the London and North Eastern Railway (LNER) in the 1920s.

Now mostly turned into the Westfield shopping complex, some of the site of the Works became a part of the impressive Olympic park in time for London 2012. Still more is now Stratford International, which is both a National Rail station and one serving the Docklands Light Railway.

While Stratford Works, at its height, can be compared with Swindon Works, the social infrastructure around it was similar too, although with more reliance ▶

7

Gleanings from the Past.—II.

By Chas. Macallan (Chief Mechanical Engineer's Department).

Included in the G.E.R. locomotive stock of to-day, there is an engine which, at the time of its construction, attracted considerable attention—indeed, it was spoken of throughout the world. As a quarter of a century has elapsed since then, it may be interesting to recall the facts.

No. 930 was delivered from Stratford works on December 11th, 1891, and it is or should be known as the "ten hours engine" owing to the fact that it was erected in that number of hours.

Before proceeding, it is as well to mention other achievements in the direction of rapid locomotive erecting. Nearly four years previously—February, 1888—a London and North Western standard six-coupled goods engine was erected at Crewe works in 25½ working hours. A few months later—June, 1888— a similar feat was performed at the

Engine Pit at 9.0 a.m., December 10th.

severely taxed when called upon to cope with the demands for new vehicles, and during the half-year ending December, 1891, new engines and tenders were turned out of the shops at the rate of two per week. The opportunity was therefore taken to establish a new record in locomotive erecting.

The assembling of the various parts of a new engine was undertaken by one of three leading erectors or chargemen, who were paid at an agreed price for the work. These men and the staff employed under them were paid a fixed daily rate during the progress of the work, and on its completion any balance was added to their next wages payment. In regard to the tenders, two sets of men were employed under the

Engine Pit at 1.0 p.m. December 10th.

Altoona works of the Pennsylvania Railroad Company, the locomotive being of the four-coupled type with a four-wheel bogie at the leading end. The time occupied in this case in assembling the parts was 16¼ hours, but it is only fair to state that the start at Crewe was made with bare frame plates, whereas the photograph entitled "Commencement" at Altoona show the frames erected with all their cross sections, and even the cylinders fixed, motion bars set, and crosshead weighbar and other details in position. Such a "commencement" as this renders all comparison with the Crewe performance useless.

When going into the why and wherefore of our Stratford Works' achievement, it is necessary to state that our

Engine Pit at 9.0 a.m. December 11th.

---

same conditions, and the aggregate time occupied on engine and tender was approximately eighteen hours.

The united chargemen and their staff, consisting of 137 men and boys, were employed on the engine and tender respectively in the case of No. 930. In order to avoid any irritation that might otherwise have been caused by the selection of one man in preference to another. This staff was divided into four sections each section being supplied with its own tools including forge, hearth and a stow shaft actuated from the main shafting, and each man was definitely instructed both as to the portion of the work which he had to perform and the order in which it had to be done, so that every one of them was engaged in the performance and subordinated with a definite purpose, and his particular work to the general

Tender Pit at 1.0 p.m. December 10th.

The whole of the details were from the various parts of the where they were ordinarily produced were laid down in a systematic methodical way at that place in that manner as would be most convenient to the erectors. They had not been previously massed, nor had there been any attempt at fitting them.

The frames had the horn blocks and spring brackets fitted previously, but otherwise nothing had been done to them and they were simply brought into position by the overhead travelling cranes in the usual manner by the fitters. The safety valves, steam dome cover, regulator and other fittings had been attached to the boiler in the usual way prior to getting the boiler under steam, and in like manner the wood clothing of the barrel

---

painting consisted only of a single color, which was done towards the of the engine and tender which took hours thereby the world's a round

American North Western the locomotive were brought into the shops running their trips, for testing purposes, and it was said by kindly critics that the erecting had of necessity been done in such a perfunctory way, that it was necessary, before the engine could be safely trusted to perform the regular train service. In the case however, it was determined upon this point, and the fire laid was filled and the out of the shops, and after adjusted on her trial was handed over, without running department and chiefly with coal trains between Peterborough and

It is estimated that there are equipped with high-degree super

The exportation and also the and tramway rails has been pro

Including the "Brussels" the Germans, seven railway st up till now. Five others were of the war.

Another ambulance train, Company, was on view at Eust and was inspected by upwards be given to one of the benevol

The Victorian Government upon the finances and working Gazette says that if the inve apply to probably all the ra

Sir A. H. Stanley, M Railways of London, who bu of Trade is, we believe, the office in a British Governm

The Chillagoe Railway Queensland for £450,000, with the addition of the was owned by the Chilla the deal.

Altogether, this performance is one on which the whole staff of the old "Locomotive Department" deserve to be congratulated.

From a strictly economical point of view such feats as we have mentioned may be described as a mison the railway company to provide, rather than the worker-led institutions found in Swindon.

In 1876 the GER gave £2,600 to build a new Mechanics' Institute, and the following year it duly opened, with a hall and stage, library, reading and lecture rooms, mechanical and electrical laboratories, a washhouse, gymnasium, games room and rifle range.

So – as was the case of the Royal Arsenal at Greenwich – Stratford wasn't an unfamiliar set-up, compared with what former Swindon workers were accustomed to at home.

Representing the GER in Holden's absence was a Mr H Williams – they neglected to mention his first name in all the formality – a foreman at Stratford, who delighted the audience with an anecdote that gave a measure of the national fame of one of last year's heroes, James Kibblewhite (see page 85).

After continuing to win races over various distances, 'Kibby' was this year's hero, too.

'As he left Aldersgate Street Station that afternoon,' the *Advertiser* report said of Williams, 'he asked the way, and how far it was to the Champion Hotel. The reply he got was, "Well, if you're a Kibblewhite you can do it in about ten minutes."'

Not to be confused with 'Mr *H* Williams', Swindon schoolmaster John Williams (see page 30) stood up as the natural successor to the popular Alex Braid, although the school had moved out of its original home in Bristol Street and into Sanford Street in the meantime, the pupil register mushrooming in tune with Swindon's population.

Williams had an idea, which he put to the gathering, for a scholarship to be raised and presented to one of his pupils – the first signs of *The Moonies in London* turning from a merely supportive one to a charity.

And its wings were spreading in another way too, thanks to a kind of annexe or 'spin-off' back home in the Railway Village:

At this stage of the proceedings the Chairman read the following telegram, which had just been received from New Swindon: "To the Chairman of the 'Moonies' dinner, Champion Hotel, Aldersgate Street. Compliments to the 'Moonies' from the 'Moonies' of Billy Thomas's parlour. Wishing you success. Hurrah! Hurrah!!"

To this was added another hurrah by the company on their hearing the telegram read, and it was decided to send the following reply: "One hundred and twenty 'Moonies' send

their greeting to Billy Thomas's parlour. Grand success."

'Billy Thomas's parlour'? It was the affectionate name for the private bar at the back of the Gluepot, then still known as the London Stout House: Swindon's railway pub – then and now.

Billy Thomas, the pub's first landlord, happens to be the great-great-grandfather of one of the authors of this book, Noel Ponting. The pub is also where the authors' planning meetings about this book were held. So you could say these words also come from Billy Thomas's parlour! ■

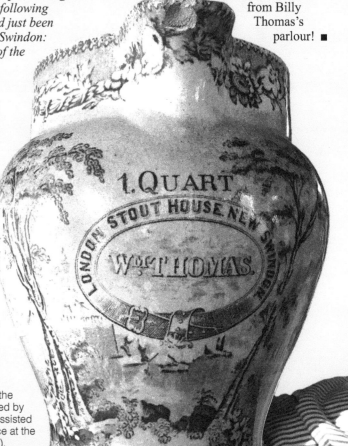

Opposite: the Great Eastern Railway Magazine looks back (from 1917) to the building of a locomotive in less than ten hours in 1891. It was masterminded by former Swindon railwayman James Holden, and he was almost certainly assisted by other GWR-trained men, who formed a large contingent of the workforce at the company's Stratford Works (courtesy of the Great Eastern Railway Society).
Right: a jug from the London Stout House (which was to become the Glue Pot), bearing William 'Billy' Thomas's name.

Inside Billy Thomas's parlour

No document addressing the social history of Swindon in its GWR age can be complete without including the Gluepot, which has stood in the Railway Village for longer than the Mechanics' Institute has existed, opposite it.

Even its name is steeped in local folklore; locals nicknamed it the Glue Pot from August 1863, and at some stage it stuck (pun intended) and became official.

It was all down to the pots of glue that upholsterers and others from the nearby Carriage and Wagon Works left simmering on the pub's stove at lunchtime; it kept the glue on their brushes fluid until they returned to work in the afternoon.

Authentic glue pots can still be found in the (now single) bar today, in a place widely accepted as Swindon's most unspoilt pub, and the one most suggestive of our railway heritage.

It now oozes history and charm, rather than glue, but it may never have become a pub at all without the arrival in New Swindon of William 'Billy' Thomas.

Born in Bristol in 1825, he was the son of millwright Edward Thomas, and was brought up in a humble community, adjacent to the city's Floating Harbour.

At the age of 12 he followed his father in working for a firm of importers, before moving to ironfounders Bush & Beddoes, makers of steam engines.

In 1841, aged just 15, Billy was already listed as an engineer, and in March the following year he moved to Swindon, attracted by engineering opportunities at the GWR's brand new Works.

However, there was promptly a recession, and by December 1846 Billy was laid off, so left Swindon – at first to be an engineer on board the steamship, *Sir Robert Peel*, before working in Southampton and Northfleet.

Meanwhile, in Swindon, on June 7, 1848, Scottish sculptor David Dunbar and his wife Arabella (nee Riddiford), trading as Dunbar & Co, opened a 'linen, draper, milener (sic) and dressmaker shop' at what was then known as 6 High Street, in Brunel's Railway Village.

Records show the business failed, shortly afterwards and, later that year, occupation passed to William and Sarah Warner (trading as Warner & Lewis), who continued with a new drapery business at the premises.

By 1857 the Warners had decided to become 'beersellers' as well, although William Warner still called himself a draper. It wasn't an unusual business tactic at the time, the growing demand from thirsty GWR employees causing a number of people to combine beer retailing with other occupations.

In the meantime, Billy had returned to Swindon and, working as an engine erector and living at 26 Oxford Street, he met and married Arabella Riddiford, a girl already resident at the future Glue Pot's address, 6 High Street.

Arabella was later to recall being in the crowd when the foundation stone for the Mechanics' Institute was laid on May 24, 1854, and later that same year she and Billy were married at St Mark's Church.

Following a short period when Billy was posted to Barnstaple, the family were soon back in Swindon for good, and on May 7, 1863, he took on the lease and ▶

Opposite: Billy Thomas, the first landlord of the Glue Pot, with his wife, Arabella (courtesy of Donald Day). Right: Swindon photographer Dennis Bird's view of the Gluepot, c1970 (courtesy of The Swindon Society).

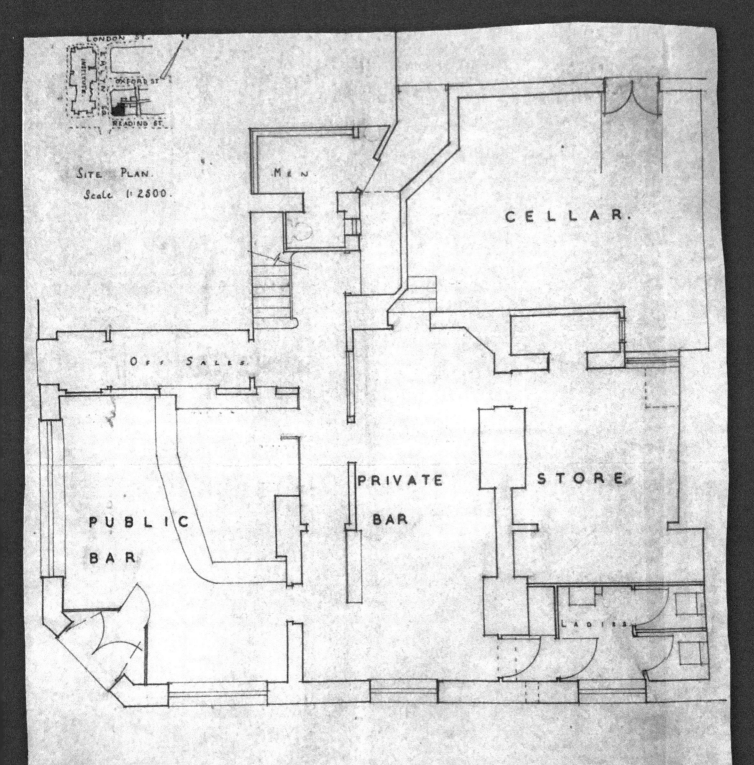

SITE PLAN.
Scale 1: 2500.

MEN

CELLAR.

OFF SALES

PRIVATE   STORE

PUBLIC   BAR

BAR

LADIES

READING STREET.

took out a licence on a pub he called the London Stout House.

It was the installation, three months later, of the pub's iron-made heating stove that gave it its nickname, as recalled by the *North Wilts Herald* in 1933:

What tales this stove could unfold, if only it were human. In the winter months it throws out a heat enough to drive the Cheltenham Flyer [see page 186], and when the company is gathered round, there is not a complaint. It is never too hot in the Glue Pot.

The stove no longer exists, although the flue does. You'll find it just in front of the bar, boxed in behind wooden panelling, now utilised as a table.

The Glue Pot must have been an instant hit because Billy went on to build what was to become The Eagle Tavern in 1867, at the corner of College Street and Regent Street.

And two years later he purchased a canalside coal wharf in Bridge Street, which he later leased to the New Town Local Board (a forerunner of the Council), for storage. Billy had other properties in Swindon, with Henry Street (1873), William Street (1878), Thomas Street (1884) and Charles Street (1884) named after him and his sons, Charles and Henry.

He succumbed to pneumonia on October 28, 1885, aged just 60, leaving his wife Arabella, three sons, three daughters and a substantial freehold property portfolio.

So, by the time telegrams were sent to *The Moonies in London* in 1892, Billy had already been dead for more than six years.

His final journey appropriately began at the Glue Pot and progressed directly to

A glue pot in the Glue Pot, in 2024

his final resting place: Radnor Street Cemetery.

A new licence was granted to HW 'Harry' Thomas (see page 94) at the Gluepot, immediately after his father's death, but he only held it for a couple of years before it passed to his mother (Billy's widow), Arabella.

Ten years later, when Arabella died, it passed to Billy's other son, Charles 'Charlie' Riddiford Thomas, and it was during his tenure in 1901 that the address formally changed from 6 High Street to 5 Emlyn Square.

Charles Riddiford 'Charlie' Thomas was born in the flat above the Glue Pot and was landlord there for just short of 50

years, from 1897 until he died in 1946. He was a property investor in his own right, a director of Swindon Town Football Club, and was a founding member of two Masonic Lodges in Swindon, including Lodge of Remembrance No 4037.

His death ended nearly a century of Riddiford/Thomas family occupation of the Glue Pot, although the Thomases continued a long association with the Swindon pub trade.

The Glue Pot is said to be haunted, and although the ghost's identity has not been confirmed, there is no doubt that the spirit of 'Billy Thomas's parlour' lives on in the Glue Pot. ∎

Opposite: a plan of the Gluepot, drawn up before alterations in the middle of the 20th century, showing the pub in its original format, including the 'private bar' that it is believed to be the specific location of 'Billy Thomas's parlour'. (Courtesy of Wiltshire & Swindon History Centre/John Stooke)

Sporting Thomases

Billy Thomas (see page 90) may not have lived to see *The Moonies in London*, but his son Harry and nephew Edwin attended several dinners between them – and when they didn't, they probably toasted them from 'Billy Thomas's parlour'.

Henry William 'Harry' Thomas (pictured, left) was born in New Swindon in 1860, and his first job was assisting his father in the family property business, which was heavily involved in the development of Even Swindon (Rodbourne).

He took over as licensee of the Glue Pot in 1885, following the death of his father, eventually switching to The Eagle in Regent Street in 1887, and remaining there until he retired from the trade in 1914.

He was elected a member of the New Swindon Local Board in 1891, was Chairman of the *New Swindon Permanent Building Society*, and a JP.

Well known for having a good tenor voice, he performed songs at the 1897, 1900 and 1901 dinners of *The Association of Wiltshiremen in London*.

Harry was appointed Honorary Treasurer of Swindon Town Football Club in October 1897, and is also credited with having saved the club from extinction on May 15, 1901, when he wrote off a significant cash advance he had previously made to the club.

His life was not without its fair share of tragedy. He lost his first wife, Amy, in 1903, at the age of 43, and his only child,

William Henry Thomas, died in 1917 while serving with the Honourable Artillery Company in the First World War.

He died at the age of 84, in 1944.

Edwin 'Eddie' Thomas (inset) was born in Wardour Street, Soho, in 1873, the same year that his father died, aged only 33.

So, at the age of three, Eddie was brought to Swindon and raised by his uncle, Billy Thomas, and his wife, Arabella.

He served his apprenticeship as a coach builder at Swindon Works, before entering the pub trade in 1895 at the age of 22 – initially at The Artillery Arms, then The Rolleston Arms, and finally The Eagle, where he remained as licensee from 1914 until 1945.

He became a celebrated host and performer at the many 'smoking concerts' he staged in support of local sporting associations; he was a director and Treasurer of Swindon Town for 25 years, President of the Swindon and District Football League, President of Swindon Rugby Football Club, and took an interest in swimming, boxing and gymnastics.

His grandson (also Eddie Thomas) played in goal for Southampton.

In 1902 he survived a major gas explosion at his home, 12 Sanford Street.

He was well known for singing his party piece, *The Deathless Army*, which he occasionally did at dinners of *The Association of Wiltshiremen in London*.

Eddie died in May 1952. ∎

All together now...

Reports of the meetings of *The Moonies in London/The Association of Wiltshiremen in London* alert us to lots of forgotten local heroes – and never more so than in 1893.

On March 18 of that year, the company returned to the Bridge House Hotel, London Bridge, with the numbers as high as previous years, but apparently this time with more 'old friends' travelling up from Swindon to join the celebrations.

It was part of a trend away from the gatherings' original intention, the annual dinner increasingly becoming a reason for the great and the good of Swindon to hop on the train for an evening out.

Back home, 'Billy Thomas's parlour' had already offered an alternative for those who were priced out by the fare to Paddington, and there was a cloud hanging over proceedings in London, too, with mention of short time working and a recognition that the 'absence of some was no doubt due to depression in trade and other causes'. Even Swindon Works was not immune to the rise and fall of national economic fortunes.

For now the redoubtable John Templeman still headed the committee, which now included former footballer Richard Horsington (see page 46). He had been listed as a member of the committee, a year earlier; now he was down as Honorary Treasurer.

If we needed an example of Wiltshiremen's achievements, 1893 provided a perfect example, *The Moonies in London*'s annals containing information that has otherwise been forgotten by history.

It came with musical entertainment from two esteemed Swindon-born musi-cians, Edwin 'Fred' James and his younger brother Frank; a third brother, Wilfred, who wasn't present, was also a very highly regarded musician (see page 96).

Edwin had been mentioned after the 1891 dinner, a speaker referring to 'Messrs James and Mr WJ Lacey (see page 79), who occupy honoured positions, and enjoy a distinguished repute in the great world of London.'

If he was present at any of the procee-dings in previous years, it is not recorded, but he was certainly there in 1893. First he 'favoured with a bassoon solo, "Lucy Long," which was received with great delight and rapturously encored'; it would become a favourite over the years. Then, later:

By this time Mr WJ Lacey, of the Moore and Burgess Minstrels, had arrived, and he played a cornet solo, a fantasia on Beethoven's themes, being accompanied by Mr F[red] James on the bassoon, his brother [Frank] presiding at the piano... Mr Frank James also gave a well rendered cornet solo, "Love's old sweet song," which was loudly encored, and the same responded to.

Not for the first time, it was something of a coup for *The Moonies in London* to be entertained by a leading professional musician, and it is clear that both James's and Lacey's reputations were well known to those present. Despite remarkable achievements in their lifetimes, the James brothers' story has been left untold for decades in Swindon... ■

The Moonies in London loved a sing-song, and in 1893 'Mr C Spratt [see page 28] rendered a comic song, in character [typically adopting West Country vernacular], entitled "Wiltshire Jack," which was vociferously encored' – and made reference to the recently built (1891) GWR Medical Fund baths in Milton Road (pictured on pages 36-37) and the new Town Hall:

In Swindon what a change there's been
Sin' our young Jack were born!
When I looks round about the town
It gives I quite a turn,
And I takes our Mary out at night,
Such funny sights we see;
We wanders all about, and darn'd
If we knows where we be.
We've got a Regent Circus, steam roller,
clock, and bells,
And Public Offices, where we finds berths
for they thur swells.

*Chorus: For I can plough and I can sow
And I can reap and I can mow*

And I goes to market with father's hay
And I earns me nine pence everyday.

Our new swimming baths ain't pretty,
But inside they takes the bun –
It doos I good to see 'em
Splash about and ha'e such fun.
Our new Institution's rising
Like a mushroom from the ground,
And now it's finished it will be
A credit to the town.
We're going to buy the gasworks, the
water and the air;
Mister Hinton's gwine to be the
Corporation and the Mayor.
Chorus ■

You have to take your hat off to *The Moonies in London*; in an age without television, the internet or even radio, they managed to keep their fingers on the pulse of what was happening in the country.

For men who were more accustomed to being at the cutting edge of industry, and could have been excused for focusing on that sphere of life, they seemed remarkably up-to-date on *what was what* and – more importantly – *who was whom*.

Ever-ready to honour the achievements of all fellow Wiltshiremen, after the 1892 dinner they toasted a hero of literature, noting 'the honour which the late Mr Richard Jefferies, a Swindonian, had gained, and to the fact that only the previous Wednesday his bust was unveiled in Salisbury Cathedral'.

And the following year they turned their attention to Swindon's prowess in the world of music.

To persuade bassoonist Edwin 'Fred' James to play for them in 1893, and bring along his brother, Frank (who was also making a name for himself, on the cornet), looks like something of a coup, even if Edwin's greatest achievements were still ahead of him.

To his credit (and perhaps as a measure of his pride in being a Wiltshireman), Edwin kept accepting invitations to come back, even at a time when he was in huge demand, and even after becoming the Chairman of the London Symphony Orchestra.

In all, he would perform at 13 dinners over a period of 15 years, sometimes accompanied by his brother Frank, although their younger brother, Wilfred, another bassoonist, never made it.

All three James brothers were ex-railwaymen – and all three were destined for greatness in the world of classical music...

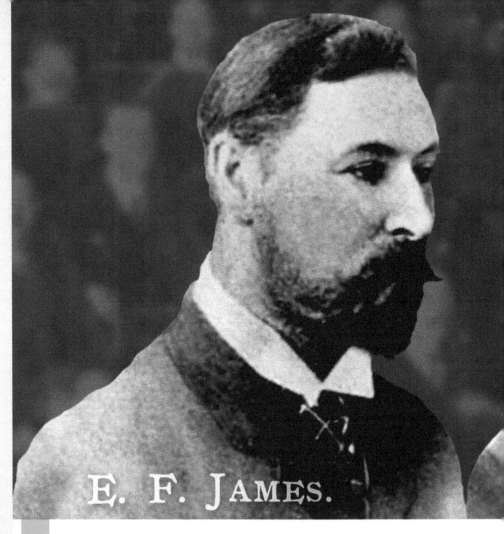

E. F. JAMES.

Band of brothers

It is June 22, 1911, and three Swindon-born brothers are on a mission.

Edwin 'Fred' James, aged 50, Frank Greenland James, 48, and Wilfred George Turner James, 39, all have an appointment to keep in Westminster Abbey; they have been selected to play in the orchestra at the coronation of King George V and Queen Mary – Edwin and Wilfred on bassoon, Frank playing trumpet.

It is the culmination of the remarkable careers of three men who at first had all followed their father into Swindon Railway Works to start apprenticeships, only to leave them uncompleted when their talents opened up opportunities as professsional musicians.

The 1911 coronation was only one highlight in a remarkable story of a musical dynasty; indeed, two of the three –

RANK G. JAMES.

WILFRED JAMES.

Edwin and Wilfred – had already played at the coronation of King Edward VII in 1902.

They are arguably the most accomplished of all Swindon-born musicians, and certainly the greatest musical family from the town – and their story is made all the more surprising by the fact that these three men have slipped through the net of local history research.

Until now.

Their father, a GWR engine fitter who was originally from Brecon, was called William, and their mother was Mary, a policeman's daughter from Pilton in Somerset. But the musical influence didn't come from their parents.

It came from their mother's brother, William Hawkins, who was bandmaster of the 2nd Battalion Wilts Volunteers, musical director of the Mechanics' Institute, and the choirmaster at St Mark's Church.

Edwin Frederick James was born in Swindon on February 16, 1861 – probably at the family home, 7 Bristol Street. He was baptised at St Mark's, a stone's throw from home, and was edu-

cated even closer – at the GWR School. Ten years later the census found him at 2 Henry Street, now with a new brother Frank (born September 30, 1862).

Edwin was indentured as an apprentice fitter in Swindon Railway Works on May 16, 1876, but just over three years into a term that should have lasted five years and nine months, he left.

The record book states: 'Allowed three months' leave during summer of 1879. Did not return.'

Younger brother Frank (whose indenture as a fitter and turner began on his ▶

14th birthday in 1876) has exactly the same note against his record, and the *North Wilts Herald* had an explanation on July 26, 1879 (referring to Edwin by his middle name of Fred):

Many of our musical readers will feel an interest in knowing Mr Fred James and his brother Mr Frank James, who were well known as prominent members of the XI Wilts RVC band, and other bands – notably that of the Choral Class – in connection with the town, have left Swindon and accepted a permanent engagement with Miss Sarah Thorne, a talented provincial actress, who has on several occasions pleased numerous Swindon audiences. On Monday night this lady commenced her usual season at Margate Theatre [Royal], on which occasion the young men made their debut in the orchestra and most satisfactorily acquitted themselves, a cornet solo by Mr Frank James being rapturously greeted. His brother, we should add, manipulates the double bass. At the conclusion of the season at Margate, which will last two months, the Messrs James will accompany Miss Sarah Thorne on her annual tour through the provinces.

Both are young men, not yet out of their teens, and this fact says something for the patient perseverance, combined with natural ability, which, under the supervision and instruction of their uncle, Mr W Hawkins, the efficient band master of the XI Wilts band, have enabled them, at an age so comparatively early, to

start in life in a profession in which we are sure the many friends of the young fellows wish them every success.

In December 1879 they were back on home soil and appearing together in a concert at Winterbourne Bassett, with Frank on cornet, and Edwin playing 'contra basse' (probably a contrabass clarinet).

Then, in March 1880, they performed on consecutive nights at the Mechanics' Institute, Swindon, with Sarah Thorne's company, the second night ironically 'for the benefit of Mr WT Hemsley, scenic artist and a native of Swindon' (whom we will meet again, shortly).

The *North Wilts Herald* gave a lukewarm review of a show that clearly did not reflect where the Jameses' careers would later go, but noted: 'Messrs FG and F James, brothers, also born in

Swindon, gave respectively solos upon cornet and clarionet [sic]'.

By September 1880 their short-lived variety theatre careers appear to have petered out as Edwin placed an advertisement in the theatrical newspaper, *The Era*, seeking work with either the double bass or the bassoon, which he is believed to have taught himself to play.

At this stage the brothers were both living at 2 Guinea-lane, Bath; it was the address Edwin gave in the advertisement, and where Frank would still be living at the time of the 1881 census, six months later.

His move to Bath was also mentioned in the review when Frank made a guest appearance (to cover for illness) in a concert in Hereford, given by *The New Swindon Amateur Minstrels*, in which *Moonies in London* co-founder Harry Batten (see page 26) was a leading light.

(593)

	Date of					
Ref. No.	Indenture.	Commencement of Term.	Name of Apprentice.	Trade.	Premium. £	Years bound for
99 1	16 6 75		Mutlow Benj.	Fitting, Turning & Erecting	100	4
2	2 11 74		Dulin Wm Thos	do do	£50	5
2a	1 74	1 74	Walker Wm D	do do	£50	5
3	9 75	1 7 75	Wyatt Chas	do do		3
4	3 4 76		Davis Wm	Moulding		7
5	18 4 76		Walters Wm Jno	Boilermaking		
6	18 4 76		Walker Francis Isaac	"		
7	2 5 76		Dean Geo H.	Carr Finishing		6
8	11 5 76	23 10 75	Rigg Harry	Boilermaking		
9	16 5 76		James Edwin Fk	Fitting		5
100 0	18 5 76		Blake Albert	Boilermaking		6
1	19 5 76		Hemsley Henry	Fitting		

Great Western Railway.—Loco. and Carriage Department.

The report, published in the *North Wilts Herald* on Christmas Day 1880, revealed that Frank had formerly been a member of the troupe. An earlier report (in June 1879) had found him playing in a trio with the boys' oldest brother, William (see below) on violin, and Henry Batten on harp.

Soon after, Edwin and Frank seem to have gone their separate ways.

Edwin's advertisement apparently did the trick for him as he took up a post in the orchestra at the Brighton Aquarium, a curious venue that – as well as the obvious attractions – had a reading room, restaurant, roof terrace, roller skating rink and music conservatory.

The 1881 census shows Edwin living in Brighton, boarding with a fellow musician.

But we lose Frank's trail for the next decade, until he rejoins his brother in London in the mid-1890s. There is some indication he was living and occasionally performing in the Southampton area, and he is known to have played trumpet at the wedding of Major-General Charles Pleydell Calley, of Burderop Park, in 1883.

By that time, Edwin had moved to London and stepped into the classical musical spotlight. By 1885 he was playing in the prestigious Hans Richter concerts, at St James's Hall (the same venue where Swindon musician William Lacey was resident with *The Moore and Burgess Minstrels* (see page 79)).

Opened in 1858, St James's was the main concert venue in central London for half a century, so Edwin was now developing a formidable reputation in the capital.

He briefly returned home in May 1890, to play bassoon (along with his brother Wilfred) in a production of *The Messiah* at the Mechanics' Institute.

By the spring of 1893 – when *The Moonies in London* showed perfect timing in persuading him to perform for them – this particular Wiltshireman was heading for even greater heights.

Ten months after entertaining *The Moonies*, the musical tide began to turn in the capital with the opening of a new venue, taking Edwin with it.

It was on November 25, 1893 that the Queen's Hall opened in Langham Place, and within months it had superseded St James's as London's premier venue, becoming the new home of *The Philharmonic Society of London* and the *London Ballad Concerts* (which had previously been fixtures at St James's Hall) – and Edwin James was installed as the Queen's Hall Orchestra's first bassoon.

So he was almost certainly involved in a concert performed there by *The Royal Amateur Orchestral Society*, in its first week of opening. That was attended by the Prince of Wales (the future King Edward VII), who watched from an armchair in the front of the stalls because there was no royal box.

Even greater things were coming to the Queen's Hall, however, and on August 10, 1895, the first of the legendary *Promenade* concerts took place there.

Organised to tempt London audiences to listen to classical music in the heat of the summer, when many stayed away, and with tickets at knockdown prices, the 'Proms' would, of course, become an institution.

Edwin James not only performed in the first-ever *Prom*, but was one of only two musicians asked to perform solos that night, under legendary conductor Sir Henry Wood, with whom Edwin would have a long association. ▶

Register of Apprentices' Indentures.

STATION.	Wages each Year, in Rate per Day.							Given up.		REMARKS.
	1st.	2nd.	3rd.	4th.	5th.	6th.	7th.	Date.	To whom.	
ndon Loco	1/-	1/4	1/8	3/-					Indenture out to Mr Apple	18/8/77 See A 1075 transferred to New Milford 24/6/78
" "	1/4	1/6	1/8	1/10	2/-				Indenture cancelled Oct 23 1878	
" "	1/-	1/4	1/6	1/8	2/-					Not bound by Indenture
" "	1/-	1/4	1/10							
" "	10	1/2	1/6	4/10	2/-	2/6	3/-		Indenture cancelled apprentice going abroad	apprentice going abroad ch 8/4/80
" "	10	1/2	1/6	1/10	7/2	7/6	3/-	21 4 83	B Kennedy	
" "	10	1/2	1/6	1/10	7/2	7/6	3/-	21 4 83	B Kennedy	
" Car	10	1/1	1/4	1/8	2/-	2/6	-	5 5 82	Pratt	
" Loco	10	1/2	1/6	3/-	2/6	-	-	23 10 80	B Kennedy	
" "	10	1/2	1/6	1/10	2/4	2/0 (9mo)				allowed 3 months leave during Summer of 1879. – Did not return –
" "	10	1/2	1/6	1/10	7/2	7/6	3/-	26 2 83	B Kennedy	
" "	10	1/2	1/6	1/10	7/2	2/6	3/-	2 6 83	B Kennedy	

THE ILLUSTRATED LONDON NEWS

REGISTERED AT THE GENERAL POST OFFICE FOR TRANSMISSION ABROAD.

No. 2850.—VOL. CIII.　　SATURDAY, DECEMBER 2, 1893.　　TWO WHOLE SHEETS　SIXPENCE. By Post, 6½d.

THE FIRST CONCERT AT THE NEW QUEEN'S HALL, LANGHAM PLACE, IN THE PRESENCE OF THE PRINCE OF WALES, DUKE ALFRED OF SAXE-COBURG, AND THE DUKE OF CONNAUGHT.

And Edwin would go on to perform in all of the *Proms'* first ten seasons, often appearing in multiple concerts. Brothers Frank and Wilfred would also play in a string of concerts across multiple *Proms* seasons.

The year 1895 was to be a particularly auspicious one for Edwin. He also married, and became a Musician-in-Ordinary to Queen Victoria. This ancient title was bestowed on those selected to form a state orchestra for performing at coronations, although they would also play private concerts for the royal family as part of the 24-piece Private Band.

Edwin is known to have played for Victoria at Buckingham Palace and Windsor Castle, each time with his brother, Wilfred; they also both played in a private concert for Kaiser Wilhelm II at Lowther Castle, in the Lake District, on August 11, 1895, the day after Edwin's appearance in the first *Prom*.

By this time, Edwin's brother, Frank, had also become a prominent musician in

THE MORNING LE...

'ENTERTAINMENTS.

MOORE and BURGESS MINSTRELS. —ST. JAMES'S HALL, PICCADILLY, W.— BRILLIANT SUCCESS.—Redecorated, reupholstered and reseated. NIGHTLY, at 8　MATINEES MONDAYS, WEDNESDAYS, and SATURDAYS, at 3. Prices, 5s., 3s., 2s., 1s. Bookings at True's. Manager, Mr. LAWRENCE BROUGH.

PROMENADE CONCERTS.—QUEEN'S HALL. COMMENCE TO-NIGHT (SATURDAY), 10 AUG. And EVERY EVENING, at 8. Admission ONE SHILLING. Madame Marie Duma, Mrs. Vander Veer-Green ; Messrs. Iver McKay, Ffrangcon Davies, W. A. Peterkin. Flute, A. Fransella. Bassoon, E. F. James. Cornet, Howard Reynolds. Full Orchestra. Leader, W. Frye Parker. Accompanist, H. Lane Wilson. Conductor, Henry J. Wood. Promenade or Balcony, 1s. ; Grand Circle (reserved), 2s. 6d. ; Season Tickets, 21s. ; of the usual agents, and at Robert Newman's Box Office, Queen's Hall, Langham-place, W.

COMPANIES' NOTICES.

The LIST of APPLICATIONS will OPEN on TUES...

W. Whiteley Ltd Photographers   LONDON.

London, and in 1896 he was appointed principal trumpeter at the Royal Opera House in Covent Garden, where he remained until 1932. He played for Queen Victoria at Windsor and Balmoral, and must have made an impression, because she presented him with a travelling rug (of all things) and a framed photograph of one of his pupils: the Queen's grandson, Prince Maurice of Battenburg.

Like his brothers, Frank was also

Musician-in-Ordinary to the royal family.

In late 1900, tragedy struck when Frank, who was then living in Kilburn, lost his wife, Lilian, perhaps in childbirth. It left him with four daughters, aged 12, eight, five and three.

After the death of Queen Victoria in 1901 and the ascension of King Edward VII, all three brothers retained their royal connections, and both Edwin and ▶

Opposite: the *Illustrated London News*'s view of the concert at the Queen's Hall on November 25, 1893, in which Edwin James performed while Prince Edward watched from the stalls. Contrary to the caption, the concert was held two days after the official opening. Opposite: an advertisement in the *Morning Leader*, announcing the first *Promenade* concert, featuring Edwin James. Note *The Moore and Burgess Minstrels* show, above it, which included William Lacey. Above: the Queen's Hall Wind Quintet (courtesy of the London Symphony Orchestra archive).

Wilfred played bassoon at the new king's coronation in August 1902 (it would be nine years later when all three James brothers played at the coronation of King George V).

Also in 1902, Edwin joined Henry Wood's prestigious Queen's Hall Wind Quartet.

But a revolution was coming that would see Henry Wood and Edwin James on opposing sides of a musical schism.

In effect, the Queen's Hall Orchestra became a victim of its own success, because the musicians it relied on to fulfill its increasingly busy diary often took other work to supplement their incomes, especially at the opera and in provincial festivals.

The Queen's Hall Orchestra generally paid less for musicians' services than most musical halls and opera houses, and when they got better offers, the musicians would send 'deputies' to take their place in the orchestra.

So Robert Newman, the entrepreneur who ran the orchestra, demanded 'exclusive service', and when he told the musicians "Gentlemen, from now on there will be no deputies," it did not go down well.

Things came to a head in May 1904, when a plot to break away was hatched on board a train to Manchester, while the orchestra were heading for a festival in Kendal.

There were four original conspirators: three horn players and a trumpeter – or as *The Musical Times* cleverly put it: 'No strings, no wood-wind, no percussion, only bold brass.'

Three quarters of the orchestra were persuaded to resign, and the proposal was to not only to form a new orchestra, but a

MR. EDWIN F. JAMES.
Chairman and 1st Bassoon.

new kind of orchestra. It would be run as a co-operative, with a constitution, some even referring to it as a 'musical republic'. And the players would choose the conductors – not the other way round.

A managing committee was elected,

comprising the quartet of brass plotters, along with a viola player called Alfred Hobday – and Edwin James.

And so the London Symphony Orchestra (LSO) was born, and gave its inaugural concert at the Queen's Hall on June 9, 1904, with Hans Richter as conductor and, of course, Edwin James on bassoon.

Ironically, many of the players were already booked to play at the Royal Opera House in the evening, so it had to take place in the afternoon.

'Success was immediate', according to *The Musical Times*, and the LSO could soon be compared with 'the best Continental orchestras'.

Part of its success was attributed to rejecting 'the one conductor system... [which] has the disadvantage of stereotyping one view of the music performed'.

The orchestra was unique in Britain in that the musicians were all required to hold shares to the value of £10 (and no more), and were paid no fee for concerts, relying on the payment of a dividend at the end of the season.

The foundation of the LSO created different opportunities for Edwin's younger brothers.

Frank quickly became one of the orchestra's trumpeters, while the vacancy created by Edwin's resignation from the

Opposite: Edwin James, pictured by *The Musical Times* in 1911. Above: the London Symphony Orchestra featured in the same edition of the journal, with Sir Edward Elgar conducting. Although shown here as exclusively male, in fact the LSO's principal harpist was Mrs M Timothy, and she was absent on the day.

Queen's Orchestra was filled by Wilfred, who had been 2nd bassoon for the past three years.

Wilfred's path to classical musical stardom had been rather different to his brother's, although he, too, had started an apprenticeship as a fitter – on his 14th birthday, May 5, 1886.

That ended in March 1890 when he was awarded the first-ever bassoon scholar-ship at the Royal College of Music, and soon after qualifying he became first bassoon in the recently

created Scottish Orchestra in Glasgow (now called the Royal Scottish National Orchestra).

In September 1917 he was involved in a Zeppelin bombing raid while playing in a *Proms* concert at the Queen's Hall.

An eyewitness said:

Carmen Hill was singing, when we heard ominous sounds outside, but we all sat tight. The next item was a bassoon solo. In the middle of it there was a crash, and then a cracking sound, and a shower of plaster began

to fall from the roof...

One or two of the orchestra disappeared from their seats. Even Sir Henry Wood himself glanced rather anxiously up at the roof, though still wielding his baton. The bassoonist, however, kept merrily on... The soloist got a rousing encore and treated us to "We won't go home till morning", amidst cheers and laughter.

The piece Wilfred was performing at the time of the raid was *Lucy Long*, a ▶

bassoon standard that was performed more than once by his brother at *Moonies in London* dinners.

Ironically, the Queen's Hall was eventually destroyed in a bombing raid, during the Blitz in 1941.

Back at the new LSO in 1904, it was clear that Edwin James was highly

TO MR. EDWIN F. JAMES.

ROMANCE

FOR

BASSOON AND ORCHESTRA

COMPOSED BY

EDWARD ELGAR.
(Op. 62.)

FULL SCORE.

FIVE SHILLINGS NET.

LONDON: NOVELLO AND COMPANY, LIMITED.
NEW YORK: THE H. W. GRAY CO., SOLE AGENTS FOR THE U.S.A.

Copyright, 1912, by Novello and Company, Limited.
The right of Public Representation and Performance is reserved.

respected as a man, as much as a musician, and his status may be even more surprising, given that the bassoonists sit towards the back of the orchestra, behind the massed ranks of strings.

Indeed, it was a violinist, Ellis Roberts, who was elected as the first Chairman, but James became the second when he was unanimously elected in 1909 – a post he held for the rest of his life.

There is some evidence from his tenure that he was something of a radical.

During one season, the orchestra briefly took the controversial step of eliminating 'chestnuts' (experimental new pieces) from its repertoire, and when the LSO supported a concert called *Women Suffragists' Celebration*, in 1918, the orchestra shared the stage with activists in the women's suffrage movement.

It probably said much about the orchestra's (and maybe the Chairman's) philosophy.

Meanwhile, Edwin's long association with Sir Edward Elgar led to him being honoured by the great composer.

Their paths had crossed through Hans Richter, a champion of Elgar's work, then at the Queen's Hall, where Elgar conducted some of his own compositions, and also through the LSO, for whom Elgar conducted during its first season.

And they must have been naturally drawn to each other because Elgar played bassoon in a wind quintet, and the instrument features strongly in many of his works.

In 1910 Edwin James's playing directly inspired Elgar to write *Romance Op 62* (sometimes referred to as *Romance for Bassoon*). Said to be written on a single day (January 11, 1910), it was dedicated to Edwin, and he was naturally given the honour of performing it first – in a *Herefordshire Orchestral Society* concert, at Hereford, on February 16, 1911, which Elgar conducted.

Although primarily a piece for solo bassoon, it also incorporates flutes, oboes, clarinets, horns, trombones, timpani and strings, as well as two other bassoons.

Edwin was not just renowned as a performer, but also as an authority on his instrument. Described as 'the greatest bassoonist of his age', in 1911 he edited a manual on the instrument, called *Bassoon School*, and became a prominent Professor of Music, teaching (as did brother Wilfred) at the Royal Academy of Music, the Royal College of Music, the Royal Military School of Music and the Guildhall School of Music.

He was renowned for always playing 'French-type' bassoons, starting with the sharp-pitched Savary, but later, more famously, a low-pitch Morton; he could also play the tenor version of the instrument, sometimes called a tenoroon.

He died in February 1921, six days before his 60th birthday, and the following month he was honoured with a memorial concert by the LSO, appropriately at the Queen's Hall.

His brother Frank died in 1934, aged 72, while living at 130 Victoria Road, Kilburn; younger brother Wilfred, who lived yards away at number 126, died seven years later. Ironically, their oldest brother, William, also died in Victoria Road, but in Swindon (in 1914).

That wasn't to be the end of the musical family. Wilfred's son, Leslie James, who was born in 1909, won a bassoon scholarship to the Royal Academy of Music in 1926, but took his own life in 1930, shooting himself because of an unhappy love affair.

However, a younger son of Wilfred, Cecil James, who was born in 1913, went on to be another highly acclaimed bassoon player until his death in 1999.

And there ends the story of the three Swindon-born musicians, but like other three-brother acts, there was a fourth who never quite achieved a similar fame.

In this case it is the boys' oldest brother, William. He played the trombone in the 2nd Wilts Volunteer band, but was mostly renowned as a violinist. Indeed, in his obituary, the *North Wilts Herald* said 'there were few more accomplished violinists in the West of England, and there is little doubt that, had he chosen, he would have made his mark, as his brothers have done'.

Well known as a violinist and sometime conductor in *The New Swindon Amateur Minstrels*, he probably gave professional musicianship a try because (at an unknown date) he was first violin at the Brighton Aquarium, the same venue where brother Edwin played in the early 1880s.

However, 'family considerations induced him to return to Swindon, and he took up his old position as a clerk in the Locomotive Department at the Great Western Works', and he became a much-respected local figure.

He was first violin for the *Swindon Choral Society* and the *Cirencester Choral Union*, and the *North Wilts Herald* said, 'he conducted an excellent orchestra of his own'. This probably refers to the band he ran for playing the music at 'quadrilles' or square dances.

All the Jameses were Freemasons, but William was the most prominent, rising to become Worshipful Master of Swindon's Gooch Lodge. He died in 1914, aged just 55, following a stroke, and is buried in Radnor Street Cemetery.

Compared with his younger brothers, William's life might sound like a case of what might have been, but it is notable that his death led to longer obituaries in the local press than his brothers.

And he gained another rare accolade: invitations to perform at *The Moonies in London*'s dinners, which he accepted in 1897, 1900 and 1902, each time performing with his brother, Edwin. ■

Hope amid the Depression

For students of history, the reports of the annual gatherings of *The Moonies in London/The Association of Wiltshire-men in London* provide priceless insights into various aspects of life in those times – but sometimes you have to look for hints.

This was true as the proceedings of the 1894 dinner got underway with the Chairman, John Templeman, carrying out the usual check on who was absent, and why.

This included the now customary communication from retired schoolmaster Alexander Braid, confirming that his infirmity would, as usual, prevent him from attending.

But ill health was not the only reason for absence; there was also what the Chairman called 'dullness of trade'.

The economic realities of the times were not often discussed by *The Moonies in London* – it was, after all, a happy occasion for rejoicing, congratulation, nostalgia, optimism, thanksgiving and hope – but even they couldn't ignore the elephant in the room this time.

'Trade during the past year had been very slack,' remarked the Chairman, 'and as short time was still in force at the GER Works at Stratford, it had this result: that whereas they had 34 "Moonies" present at their annual dinner last year from Stratford, there were only six that evening.'

It reminds us of why *The Moonies in London* was formed in the first place, which was to give support to former Swindon railwaymen now trying to make a living in London. If we look more closely at the economic situation that existed at the time, it becomes clear that their motive was not just fraternal, but also a response to genuine economic hardship; throughout the first decade of the annual dinners, there was a recession.

The idea that our fathers and grand-fathers could be assured of 'a job for life' was as much of a myth, then, as it is for anybody, today, when no-one beginning work would expect any sort of guarantee of continous employment.

Back then, as we have seen, it started with apprentices having no assurance of a job at the end of their indenture, to the extent that most of them expected and prepared for the opposite.

And they also couldn't fail to realise the enormous extent to which railwaymen were vulnerable to two other factors, neither of which were under their control.

The first was the volatility of the railway trade – and in the living memory of most of those present at the annual dinners there was plenty of evidence of that.

Many of them were old enough to remember the instability of the very earliest days of Swindon Works, in the late 1840s, and even those who were too young had only to think back to a catastrophic loss of confidence in railway investment generally (to which the GWR wasn't immune) between 1864 and 1868, in order to be reminded of the inherent uncertainty that came with being employed by a railway company.

They were always more interested in looking after shareholders than workers.

On top of this, there was a national recession, which had started long before the foundation of *The Moonies in London* – and still persisted.

Most people today have heard about the *Great Depression* of the 1930s, but it wasn't the first; the term was coined to describe another deep recession that came half a century earlier.

Starting in about 1873 – the exact date is a matter of debate – this first *Great Depression* was still having an impact in 1894.

It was not a gradual decline that produced smooth lines on the graph, but a general downturn in which there

were several short spells when its effects were even more acute.

One of these periods had clearly arrived in 1894, but for *The Moonies in London* that was only half the story.

Notice how the Chairman pointed out the problems of the ex-Swindon men working for the Great Eastern Railway at Stratford; but didn't mention Swindon.

Wasn't the downturn also being felt at home?

Although the answer is inevitably yes, Swindon's troubles were, in comparison, of less concern.

The definitive history of Swindon Works, written by Alan S Peck in 1983, tells us why – and probably goes some way to explaining why the comparatively secure workers in Swindon felt the need to support their counterparts in London by forming *The Moonies in London*, in 1886.

That was less than three years after a false boom, followed by a rapid collapse in trade, had sent shockwaves through the industry.

But here's the crucial point: those shockwaves were often much easier to ride in Swindon.

Peck's book, *The Great Western at Swindon Works*, points out:

If one expects to find a period of extended gloom in the town, nothing is further from the truth, although this cannot be said of the GWR as a company. This strange situation has intrigued some historians of our economic development, who have advanced various theories and reasons for the comparative stability of the Works during this time.

The short answer is Swindon benefited from the immense legacy of Joseph Armstrong, who was Chief Mechanical Engineer until 1877. He instilled a 'high level of efficiency', while the financial acumen of the then Chairman, Sir Daniel Gooch, helped too.

So Swindon possessed some immunity to the worst economic ups and downs that other industries and – more importantly – other ▶

Nostalgia – sometimes to the point of outright sentimentality – was a theme of *The Moonies in London*'s dinners.

That was certainly the case in 1895, when a Mr Harding recalled *The Great Exhibition* of 1851, where the Swindon-built locomotive, the Lord of the Isles (pictured) was prominently displayed.

He had been told 'that the "Lord of the Isles" ran 385,000 miles without requiring anything done to it, and that was a record worth preserving'.

The locomotive was an Iron Duke Class engine that was capable of the then breathtaking speed of 78.2mph (126kph), and had been withdrawn from service in 1884.

Although *The Moonies in London* made no mention of it, the GWR's whole network was converted over a single weekend in May 1892 – as a result of the abandonment of broad gauge (7 ft, 1/4 in) in favour of narrow gauge (4 ft, 8 1/2 in).

Harding's reference to 'preserving' is apt because hundreds of broad gauge engines had been scrapped at Swindon, but *Lord of the Isles* was preserved in the Works – probably because of its role in *The Great Exhibition*.

It proved to be only a stay of execution as lack of storage space was given as the reason for scrapping this historic engine in 1906. Only its driving wheels and name plates have survived, and these are on display in the lobby of the Steam Museum in Swindon.

However, a replica Iron Duke Class engine was built in 1985, and is on long-term loan to Didcot Railway Centre. ■

WILTSHIRE GAZETTE

railway companies, could not rely on. This probably explains why *The Moonies in London* were not inclined to dwell on the state of the economy for long, and is perhaps also the reason why their gatherings seem so full of joy and hope.

It could even be said that they thought themselves as somehow blessed with a kind of untouchability.

Add to this everything else that had been achieved by Swindondians – the Mechanics' Institute, the GWR Medical Fund, a successful school system and more. And then also consider all those high achievers *The Moonies in London* delighted in highlighting, every year, by inviting them to their dinners – and we can understand why they must have thought they were capable of achieving anything!

There is possibly direct evidence of this in the rest of the report from 1894, which was attended by about 90 people.

'As soon as the Wiltshire meal was over,' reported the Advertiser, 'the toast list was started, and pipe and glass, with plenty of song, was the order of the evening'.

The Chairman mentioned various successful Moonies by name, but:

There were many others he could name who had received their training in their youth at Swindon, and who had now risen to positions of importance and trust. He considered they owed much to the tuition they received in connnection with the Mechanics' Institute, New Swindon, and also at the hand of their old schoolmaster, Mr Alexander Braid (cheers), and also that more modern institution, the Swindon School

Board, *represented that night by Mr J Williams (hear, hear).*

Mr Miles, who responded to the toast:

...said he looked forward to this annual gathering as one of the greatest pleasures of the year. He alluded to the fact that Swindonians were to be found holding their own in all parts of the world, and he believed that should anyone present that night visit the North Pole, they would most probably discover a Swindonian already there (laughter and applause).'

This was followed by two comic songs, one by WT Hemsley, whom (the report of the 1895 dinner later revealed) had made *The Moonies in London* a promise to those present that he would return with a special gift, the following year.

Sure enough, 12 months later, he obliged as they convened for what would be the tenth annual dinner, and the final one at the Bridge House Hotel.

The *Advertiser*'s report suggests it was the first dinner to be held under electric lights, pointing out that 'the large dining room in which the company assembled was brilliantly lit up with electric light, and the table decorated with exotic and other plants'. However:

The gem of the decorations was a picture hanging at one end of the room, and representing the "Moonies at Home". It was a painting by that famous scenic artist who obtained his tuition in his early days at Swindon, Mr WT Hemsley, who now redeemed his promise of last year and presented the painting for the occasion. The picture was greatly admired by all, and to add ▶

Left: the reading room of the Mechanics' Institute in 1916, with WT Hemsley's Moonies painting on the far wall, second from the left. A postcard version of the painting can be found on page 113. Attempts, in recent years, to find the current whereabouts of the painting have sadly failed.

amusement to the scene a large rake was made in a rough fashion, and hung below the picture... needless to say the picture is very cleverly done.

Ironically, WT Hemsley couldn't be there to present the painting in person, but sent a telegram from Brighton, saying: 'Regret enforced absence, kindly accept picture, and may the smuggled spirits not make you "Mooney"'.

The Chairman said the drop in the number of people attending – 70, compared with the previous year's 90 – was due to 'a variety of causes. One was the tendency amongst "Moonies" to move about the globe to gain knowledge which should enable them to fulfil high positions in life. Another cause was the continued depression in trade... Another reason for absentees was the prevailing epidemic of influenza.'

A Mr Fairlie rose to respond to the various toasts, telling 'Brother Swindonians' that he 'gloried in the name [of *Moonie*] for the reason that in all his experiences in travelling in the world, wherever he had met a Swindonian, he was generally to be found at the top of the tree (applause)'. And, he recalled:

He went to Swindon in 1847, and was there brought up to the bar – a bar of iron (laughter), for he was a smith. At that time the staff employed at the GWR Works consisted of about 500 men. In 1849, when there was a great depression in the financial world, the number was reduced to 150, and the days of work reduced from six to four...

It was in 1849 that he and two or three of his colleagues thought they might improve the occasion by starting a fife and drum band, and he well recollected the ocassion of the making of the big drum; he had the honour of holding the candle whilst

they riveted the head on... When the drum was completed, and they ventured out for the first time to show what they could do... their big drummer got so excited in playing "The girl I left behind me" that he knocked the head of the drum in... and then said that somebody had thrown a stone... Swindon was, to his mind, the greatest place in the world... [it] was then a little village of some 900 inhabitants all told, and everybody knew their neighbour...

There was no idea of strikes and trades unions, but all were a simple, loving band; and he would be glad to see to-day the same good feeling existing between employer and employed as existed then.

If he wanted good men to send out to important positions abroad, as he often had to do, he wrote to his friend at Swindon, Mr [Samuel] Carlton [who had been Locomotive Works Manager since 1864], "Send me a good man," and he never made a mistake when he had a Swindon workman.

Before their next meeting, the Great Depression would at last be in its death throes, and *The Moonies* would make a tradition of taking Hemsley's moonraker painting with them, every time they boarded the train to London for the annual dinner.

For years afterwards it would hang in the reading room of the Mechanics' Institute for 364 days a year, but be removed so it could be placed over the main table at *The Moonies*' dinners.

It reminded them not just of their roots, but of the achievements of all those who were proud to call themselves *Moonies* – and in 1895 there was no better example than the rise to fame of former Swindon railwaymen than the remarkable WT Hemsley. ∎

William Thompson (often known simply as 'WT') Hemsley, was born in Gateshead in 1850, the son of George Hemsley, an engine fitter who came to New Swindon in the very early years of its new Railway Works.

William began a five-year apprenticeship as a fitter in 1866, where a workmate was John Templeman, the first Chairman of *The Moonies in London*.

He enrolled for evening art classes in the Mechanics' Institute, earning a teaching certificate and a First Class Certificate from the Society of Arts, and he painted scenery for productions in the Mechanics' theatre.

In 1875 he was still in Swindon, where he briefly worked in a photographic studio at 47 Regent Street, but by the end of the decade he, his wife and their family moved to Margate, where he worked at the Theatre Royal for Sarah Thorne (who also features in the story of the musical James family, see page 98).

His big break came when he was introduced to scenery painter William Beverly, who produced pantomime sets at Drury Lane, but was soon working in his own purpose-built studio in Lambeth (pictured, opposite).

Hemsley produced sets for every major theatre in London, and was renowned for highly technical special effects – no doubt a legacy of the technical training he received in his youth as a railwayman.

Notices in the *Swindon Advertiser* in January 1886 announced that Sarah Thorne's 17th annual pantomime, *Zac and the King of the Mannakins* or *The Pig Race of Pigminutia* included 'New and Magnificent Scenery with Novel Effects by WT Hemsley'.

And in 1900 he designed the set for

Hemsley's scenic route

the melodrama, *A Dark Street*, at the New Queen's Theatre in Groundwell Road, Swindon (later renamed *The Empire*).

This ambitious production required a river of water on the stage, where one of the characters drowned.

He would go on to work for virtually all the theatrical greats of the era, at every major theatre in London, designing sets for all kinds of productions. They ranged from music hall variety shows in the *Tivoli* and the *Pavilion*, to Shakespeare's *A Midsummer Night's Dream* at the Globe Theatre.

The list of people William worked with reads like an entry in the *Who's Who* of theatre royalty.

It includes Sir Henry Irving, actor/ ▶

manager at the Lyceum, and Sir Herbert Beerbohm Tree, actor/manager of the Haymarket and His Majesty's Theatre, and the founder of the Royal Academy of Dramatic Art.

William and his family lived at several London addresses, including 1 Comyn Road, Battersea, but their long-time home was 158 Lambeth Road, which was convenient for his studio in Felix Street, near Westminster Bridge.

In partnership with theatre proprietor Charles Wilmot, he first opened a scene-painting factory in Belvedere Road, but it was his purpose-built studios at Felix Street that became one of the most up-to-date premises in London.

It was here that William installed a bridge contraption that could be raised and lowered by means of a windlass.

This allowed for the backdrop to be tacked on to a suspended wooden frame, and saved the artist from the usual method: bending over to paint it on the floor with a long brush.

He remained at the top of his profession until the end of his life, as this entry in the 1914 edition of *The Stage Year Book* reveals:

His many famous productions have covered nearly the whole range of Shakespeare's plays; he has painted Greek scenes for the University plays at Cambridge, and Roman scenes for the far-famed 'Quo Vadis'; indeed, he has covered nearly every sort of ground in historical and modern settings.

We are glad to be able to add that his present activity shows no sign of declining, and he is now at work on some remarkable new scenic effects for a forthcoming Horse Show.

William died on February 8, 1918, at his home at 34 The Chase, Clapham Common, following a short illness.

Not only the talented designer but also the man was mourned.

An obituary published in the *Newcastle Daily Telegraph* recorded how his long career in the theatre provided him with an inexhaustible fund of good stories, and described him as being reliable in an emergency "always to be counted upon, never considering the trouble to which he might put himself in order to assist a friend or even a casual client".

He attended half a dozen dinners organised by *The Moonies in London*, apparently immensely proud of his Wiltshire roots and his Swindon upbringing.

His moonrakers painting, which was completed in 1895, was reproduced countless times on postcards, so that it became the definitive image of the Wiltshire legend.

The painting hung in the Mechanics' Institute reading room for at least 35 years, and although a photograph of it remains (see page 24), the whereabouts of the original artwork is unknown.

However, two examples of William's theatrical work survive.

A year after he delivered his painting to *The Moonies in London*, he was commissioned by Spencer Cavendish, 8th Duke of Devonshire, to transform the Chatsworth House ballroom into a theatre.

It has a permanent stage, a painted proscenium with a drop curtain, and a number of seats (pictured, left).

The estate's account book for 1896 reveals that William was paid £121 5s 2d for completing the work, the equivalent of around £30,000 today.

Between 1898 and 1907, the Prince and Princess of Wales (later Edward VII and Queen Alexandra) were such frequent guests to performances on the Chatsworth House stage that it became known colloquially as the *Theatre Royal*.

Three of William's sets at Chatsworth – a French country house interior; the interior of a cottage, set in woodland, with a baronial hall; and a desert island, complete with Palm tree – were discovered in 2006, during restoration work.

Meanwhile, the *Gaiety Theatre*, at Douglas, Isle of Man, features an act drop (a curtain lowered between acts in a play) that was painted by William as part of a reconstruction in 1893, and was restored in 1992.

Made of wood and canvas and depicting "an Eastern Sultan being amused by dancing girls", it is one of only four historic act drops still in existence in British theatres, and the only one by him.

And he left another legacy of sorts: his son, Harry, who joined him at several of the annual dinners and went on to be just as famous as his father (see page 125). ∎

Above: a typical 20th century picture postcard relating the legend of the moonrakers. It features a cropped version of WT Hemsley's painting, which was presented to *The Moonies in London* in 1895, and appears to be an artificially colourised version, but we do not know whether its creators referenced the original painting, which used to hang in the Mechanics' Institute in Swindon (see page 24).

A long way from Plumstead

WT Hemsley's painting based on the legend of the moonrakers was dusted down and taken back up to London on March 21, 1896, as *The Moonies in London* met for their annual dinner – this time at a new venue: the Horse Shoe Hotel, Tottenham Court Road.

There was a good attendance, reckoned to be more than 100, and the Chairman had good news: the idea for a scholarship for a pupil at Sanford Street School, mooted by headmaster John Williams, at a previous dinner, had borne fruit.

He (the Chairman) was glad to know that Mr Williams had persevered with the object he had in view, the result being the formation of a Union at Swindon, called the GWR and Sanford-street Old Boys' Union,' inaugurated the previous October. 'The Union was formed with two objects, first, for providing scholarships, and secondly for convening a social gathering of the "Old Boys" once a year.

Later in the meeting it was revealed that WT Hemsley had given ten shillings to the fund.

Hemsley's painting was the subject of some debate, and it was at this meeting that they agreed that it should be put on display in the Mechanics' Institute, when not on its annual journey to London for the dinner. A Mr Bowker 'said he would give an undertaking on behalf of the Council of the Institute that the picture should be taken great care of, and should be returned for the next annual dinner.'

This caused a Mr Harris to joke: "I hope they won't lose it like the Aston Villa Cup was lost" – a reference to the recent burglary in Birmingham in which the FA Cup was stolen (and was never recovered), with one wag suggesting, "Get a deposit of £50."

The Chairman insisted 'it would be taken great care of and be appreciated as a memento of the "Moonie's Dinner"', which is ironic since although it would be displayed in the Mechanics' Institute for at least 35 years, its whereabouts is now unknown.

The same is true of an item that was presented to the Chairman on behalf of a Swindon inventor:

Mr Williams observed that they had been seeing and hearing, that evening, men who had made their mark in different spheres. Now he was going to present the Chairman with a pipe which he had bought from Mr Charles Fouracre, of New Swindon, who had made his mark as a patentee. Messrs Fouracre and Moore had discovered that the pipes which had been smoked for the last 100 years were all made wrong, and they had patented a pipe, the principal advantages of which were that it was always cool and non-fouling. He had much pleasure in handing one of these pipes to the Chairman... The pipe had the "Mooney" Arms engraved upon it.'

Fouracre, a GWR engine fitter, seems to have been busy in his spare time: as a steam engine model maker and a concertina player, as well as an inventor. And the pipe wasn't his only patent. In 1890 he had patented a device for 'improvements in clack boxes, for supplying water to steam boilers', and two years later the *Wilts and Gloucestershire Standard* reported:

The Parisian Academy of Science had awarded Mr Charles Fouracre of Fairland House, The Park, New Swindon, the great gold medal and first class diploma for his patent clack box and safety valve. The recipient has also been awarded several first class prizes and certificates for steam and other models at exhibitions held at Bristol and Cheltenham.

It was a measure of the technical ability and engineering vision prevalent in Swindon at the time, where the highly skilled nature of the workforce meant there were hundreds of potential inventors.

The 1896 dinner also seems to embody everything that *The Moonies in London* had set out to be.

But times were changing.

There was yet another new venue for the 1897 dinner: the 'Council Chamber' in the Holborn Restaurant.

The Holborn was regarded as one of the grandest restaurants in London, and was billed as 'a spice of poetry to the dull prose of everyday life'.

It contained a range of banqueting spaces, including the sumptuous Royal Venetian Chamber and King's Hall, both of which would host future annual dinners organised by *The Moonies in London*, who would hire it more than 30 times in future years.

Its official address was 129 Kingsway, and just 11 years after the inaugural dinner – and in more ways than one – it was a very long way from the Prince

Alfred Hotel, Raglan Road, Plumstead. *The Moonies in London* were moving onwards, upwards and (geographically speaking) outwards, as the traditional *Advertiser* report pointed out: 'Mr Templeman and all the Committee decided to endeavour to make the gathering more a County affair than simply a meeting of Swindonians' – and, in toasting the Chairman, a Mr G Moore 'strongly supported making this affair a County gathering'.

In the meantime, two local MPs were approached with invitations to chair the proceedings, but both were unavailable, so it fell to a Swindonian, after all, to preside: *Advertiser* editor William E Morris, apparently with little or no prior warning.

There was less emphasis on speeches, this year, but 'one of the hits of the evening' was 'Mr C Spratt [see page 28], a well known Swindonian comic, singing a new specially written song for the occasion', which contained the chorus:

You'll have a job to beat them,
though you search the world around.
For wherever you may wander
there is a Mooney to be found:
To each walk of life you'll find him,
and although he likes his fling,
Yet he wouldn't feel offended if they
tried to make him King.

It was archetypal *Moonies*, but when Mr Morris stood up to lead the toasts and remarked on the changing nature of the organisation, it seemed incongruous:

At the commencement [of the organisation] it had been looked upon rather as a gathering of Swindonians, but from the faces he could see in the room, it was evident that that impression was dispelled, for he saw "Moonies" from the neighbourhood of Salisbury, numbering a dozen, and from the neighbourhood of Devizes, Pewsey and Marlborough, 40, all taking an interest in the movement.

There was no denying that the dinner ▶

EXTERIOR VIEW

HOLBORN Restaurant

was going from strength to strength in terms of attendance, Morris estimating there were about 200 present, although another estimate put it at 160. And perhaps because it was already outgrowing itself, a bigger venue was necessary. One could even argue that the glitz of the new venue was no more than the *Moonies'* growing prestige deserved.

But there was an unmistakable shift in the nature of the event, which Morris must have sensed when he 'suggested to the committee… that they should secure as their chairman some man of standing', the names he suggested largely being those of MPs, members of the aristocracy and senior military men.

The event already seemed to be organised now as much for the great and the good visiting from Wiltshire as the London-based ex-GWR railwaymen of yesteryears.

And just in case anyone hadn't realised the full opulence of the occasion, the *Advertiser* report decided it was necessary to report, in full, the 'bill of fare':

Soups – Sicillienne, Clear Mock Turtle. Fish – Supreme of Sole Joinville, Whitebait. Entree – Bouches à l'Imperatrice, Mutton Cutlets Renaissance, Removes – Ribs of Beef and Horseradish, Spinach, Plain Potatoes, Braised York Ham and Madeira, Roast Turkey. Sweet – Victorian Pudding, Mirlitons de

Above: one of the medals that were presented to distinguished visitors to the Holborn Restaurant – this one in 1895, two years before *The Moonies in London* first used it as a venue for its annual dinner. Previous page: a postcard from the same era. Opened in 1874 in fashionable Kingsway, the restaurant would go on to host banquets for participating athletes at the London Olympics of 1908. It was also where the British Chess Federation was founded in 1904. Even Sherlock Holmes dined there. After the Second World War, it became a white elephant, and was demolished in 1955. In recent years the site has been occupied by a branch of Sainsbury's.

Rouen, Macedoine Jelly, Ice Pudding. Dessert – Cheese, Celery.

Those attending could even take away a souvenir of the dinner, as the conclusion of the *Advertiser*'s report revealed: 'During the evening, by arrangement, a photograph of the company was taken, and the reproductions are now on sale, and can be obtained through the Committee.'

There are no known surviving copies of this photograph, but the co-authors of this book remain hopeful that one day, it will surface again.

For some it must have seemed like they were entering a new era, but *The Association of Wiltshiremen in London* (as they would soon become) had reached the end of an era. And for a while they could be forgiven for thinking they had reached the end of the road.

Despite the record attendance of 1897, despite the swelling of the ranks caused by opening it up to be a countywide event, and despite suggestions for a new Chairman to be appointed who was 'some man of standing', in 1898 no dinner was held.

When the annual dinners resumed in 1899, no explanation was given for the previous year, and, indeed, *The Moonies in London* simply carried on where they had left off, but with a new chairman: Thomas Hooper Deacon. ∎

Over to you, Mr Deacon...

If the Holborn Restaurant was a long way from Plumstead, then the new Chairman of *The Moonies* was also a very different man to John Templeman, who co-founded the organisation in 1886.

Thomas Hooper Deacon (pictured) – not to be confused with the local jeweller, George Deacon – lived at Kingshill House and was a leading figure in Swindon.

He was born in Faringdon, Berkshire, the son of Cornelious and Ann Deacon, and by 1861 was working as a saddler in Highworth.

Widowed in 1866, he remarried Elizabeth Kempster Sainsbury, two years later, eventually moving to Swindon at around the same time.

Along with his business partner, Thomas Edmund Liddiard, Thomas Hooper Deacon established the Vale of the White Horse (also known as Messrs Deacon & Liddiard's) Horse & Carriage Repository in 1871, located opposite The Market Square in High Street, Old Town.

Following improvements to the site access, their very first auction sale took place in February 1872, and included 'upwards of 40 horses'.

Over the next three years they bought up a considerable amount of adjacent land and property, extending their facilities and expanding the business.

This culminated, in 1874, with the pair signing a lease on the three-story Georgian mansion house at 30 High Street, that had once been the home of brewer and landowner, John Henry Harding Sheppard, along with the garden, yards and stables.

According to historian Frances Bevan, 'under the same agreement, they also acquired various other properties in the area behind High Street and Newport Street, further extending the Repository premises. The business flourished and in 1879, 1,872 horses were entered for sale across the year.'

The premises became particularly well known for the auction of horses and saddlery, and later for the sale of wool, cattle, cheese, horticultural plants and even cars and motorcycles.

Deacon's death in 1915 produced a fulsome obituary in the *North Wilts Herald*, which underlined how active he had always been, and where his sympathies were:

A familiar figure has been removed by the death, at the age of 79 years, of Capt Thomas Hooper Deacon, an alderman and ex-Mayor of the borough of Swindon...

Born at Faringdon [in 1837], he ▶

117

MEET OF THE V.W.H. HOUNDS, CORN EXCHANGE, SWINDON

A postcard showing the hunt that Thomas Hooper Deacon brought to the Market Square in Old Town annually, from around the time that he became Chairman of *The Moonies*. It is shown setting off from the south-east corner to what would have been open fields. (Courtesy of the Swindon Society)

came to Swindon from Highworth in 1868, and three years later opened the VWH Repository. At first there was stabling for only a dozen horses, but, in conjunction with his partner, Mr TE Liddiard, the deceased gentleman soon built up a flourishing business, and in time the Repository became one of the largest, most convenient and best-equipped places of the kind in the country...

Among his clientele were many noblemen and even Royalty, and there was no man better known or more highly esteemed in the West of England... and in his capacity as a purchaser and seller of horses there was none in the kingdom whose judg-ment commanded greater respect... For some years the deceased gentleman also followed the pursuit of agriculture. Formerly he occupied the Manor Farm at Purton, and until quite recently kept up the Park Farm at Swindon...

The fact that he was so popular with all classes may be attributed to his strong affection for many forms of manly sport...

Mr Deacon's... 33 years of active participation in the town's affairs met with an appropriate reward when, in November 1908, he was elected Mayor of Swindon...

He fought some half dozen elections, and was returned at the head of the poll on every occasion... He was a man of moderate views and a great advocate of the policy that municipal affairs should be run on strictly business lines, and it will be remembered that he strongly opposed the Corporation Tramway scheme...

Although not a Wiltshireman, Mr Deacon formerly identified himself very closely with the objects of the Association of Wiltshiremen in London, and... presided at the annual dinner at the Holborn Restaurant... He was connected with Freemasonry through being a very old member of the Royal Sussex Lodge of Emulation, and was a vice-president of the Swindon Victoria Hospital... In politics the deceased gentleman was an ardent Conservative...

Mr Deacon was a thorough sportsman, and it was in hunting circles that he was best known. His association with hunting dates back as far as 1887 when he started a pack of harriers, and next year he took over the Mastership of the Savernake Stag Hounds... In 1895, on the death of Mr H Fox Townsend, Mr Deacon took over the secretaryship of the VWH (Cricklade) Hunt... For many years the opening meet of the season was held at the VWH Repository...

As a follower of hounds the deceased gentleman was known all over the West of England, and in other branches of sport he evinced an almost equally keen interest... in years gone by he participated in many a hard and exciting polo match at Burderop.

No sketch of Mr Deacon's interesting career would be complete without some reference to his connection with the Royal Wiltshire Yeomanry, for it was largely through his efforts that the Swindon troop was revived. He joined the Yeomanry about 1870... in August, 1900, he received his commission... and in October of the following year was promoted to the rank of Captain.

The year after Deacon's death, the VWH Repository was put up for auction at the Goddard Arms Hotel. A number of bids were submitted, but it was eventually withdrawn, presumably because it had failed to reach its reserve. However, it was subsequently sold privately, to an undisclosed buyer.

By September 1916, auctioneer Edward Ferris was holding the '44th Annual Colt Sale' at the former VWH Repository 'kindly lent by FHW Cundell', a local vet, horse breeder and farmer.

However, in December, Edward Ferris held a poultry auction there 'by the kindness of Mr JL Chappell' – the proprietor of the Swindon Motor Company.

In late 1918, the premises were lent to Swindon Chamber of Commerce for storage purposes, until they were 'taken over by the military authorities for motor transport workshops'.

However, by March 1922, Skurray's Garage were operating from their new premises at the site, having already sold their former garage business in Princes Street to HC Preater Ltd. ∎

A supporter of *The Moonies in London* at the turn of the century was James Protheroe – although it is a wonder he ever found time.

When he died in 1929, the *North Wilts Herald* called him 'Swindon's busiest man'.

He moved to Swindon from Swansea in the late 1870s, and established his photographic studio at 30 Regent Street, later moving to 96 Victoria Road.

His obituary explained that 'he did a tremendous amount of work for the public weal and... in all the work he undertook, he showed devotion and a great deal of ability'. Even when he was appointed tax collector for Swindon, he 'carried out difficult duties in the most pleasant and affable manner possible'.

As well as being a prominent Freemason, Protheroe was Chairman of the Swindon and Highworth Board of Guardians for over 30 years; Secretary to the Swindon Chamber of Commerce, for 26 years after its inception; the first secretary of the Swindon branch of the National Farmers' Union; a Justice of the Peace; Secretary to two Educational Associations; a member of the old Swindon Urban District Council and the Wilts County Council; a director of the Swindon Permanent Building Society; a member of the management committee of the Victoria Hospital; a member of the New Town Board; a member of the Swindon branch of the Workers' Educational Association; Chairman of the Wilts Joint Vagrancy Committee; a member of the Wilts County Mental Hospital committee; President of the Swindon Town Gardens Bowling Club; leader of the Baptist Tabernacle Choir; a director of the Swindon United Gas Company; a director of the Swindon Market Company; and he represented East Ward on the Wilts County Council for many years. ∎

Richard Horsington and Henry Offer (see page 46) weren't the only London-based football stars to attend The Moonies' dinners in the 1890s.

In 1897, another guest was Albert 'Albie' Edwards (pictured). This 'well-known footballer, late of Swindon, now of Thames Ditton', was then on the books of Thames Ironworks FC.

Like Arsenal, Thames Ironworks were originally a (ship-building) works team, and would eventually be called West Ham United; it's why they are nicknamed The Hammers (or sometimes The Irons).

Albie was born at Southbroom, Devizes, and was listed in the 1891 census as a full-time engine turner, aged just 13.

He began his senior football career with Trowbridge Town, but joined Swindon Town as a winger in 1895, and stayed for two seasons before moving to Thames Ditton – almost certainly for work-related reasons.

He later had two spells with Queens Park Rangers, before returning to Swindon in 1900, playing his last game for them in 1906.

On Boxing Day 1901 he was picked to play for Town in an away match at Portsmouth – but failed to turn up.

He later explained to secretary Len Dodson that he had 'informed the club of his unavailability by postcard', but it must have been delayed in the Christmas post!

Somewhat handicapped by only being able to field ten players, Town lost 1-5. ∎

The Moonies' return

'I was afraid that your annual festivals had ended,' wrote former school-master Alexander Braid to those attending the 1899 dinner of The Moonies, 'but am glad to find that you together have revived them, as I quite think they have a good tendency'.

It was part of Braid's now-traditional letter of apology for absence caused by old age, and refers to The Moonies' failure to hold an annual dinner, the previous year.

No explanation was given (or can be found) for the sojourn, but any lingering doubts were extinguished by the Advertiser's report:

On Saturday evening last, the 12th annual dinner of "Moonies" or "Moonrakers" took place at the Holborn Restaurant – one of the finest buildings of its kind in London, and the increased attendance showed that the interest in this annual re-union was on the increase rather than the decrease. Woolwich saw the gathering started thirteen years ago in a very small way and it has grown each year by leaps and bounds. Last year no dinner was held.

Tribute was paid to co-founder and long-time Chairman, John Templeman, who had stepped aside in favour of Thomas Hooper Deacon, but remained on the committee. However, the report seemed to damn him with faint praise. 'As is well known,' continued the Advertiser, 'up till the last dinner that good old "Moonie" Mr John Templeman had filled the chair, but it has been decided to endeavour to make it a more county affair than merely a gathering of old Swindonians.'

Held in the opulent surroundings of the Royal Venetian Chamber of the restaurant, it had a strong military theme.

Mr WH Waister referred to the 'recent achievements of the army in Soudan [sic],' a reference to the recent colonial dispute in Egypt and Sudan, which had seen the French forced to withdraw. Waister suggested it 'had made all nations admire [the British], in fact, almost to fear them. But they did not want to be feared, for they wished to live at peace with all men.'

Surgeon Capt G Rodway Swinhoe brought the discussion closer to home (in more ways than one) by saying the Forces would be of little good if not for the railway companies.

Some discussion about volunteer forces followed. References to the military would become a feature of Moonies' dinners in future years, starting with the Second Boer War, which began later that year.

The military theme was another sign of the changing nature of the dinners, although the usual telegram arrived from 'Billy Thomas's parlour', offering 'hearty greetings and congratulations, and best wishes for a jolly evening.'

Other absent friends were toasted, as they always had been, but William Hogarth, who had been high on the invitation list for years but never attended, had missed his last chance... ∎

A gentle giant of the stage

THE LATE WILLIAM HOGARTH.

William Hogarth was one of those people whom *The Moonies* liked to point to as evidence of what Wiltshiremen could achieve in the wider world, especially when it came to the arts.

His chosen field was not painting, like his 18th century namesake, but comic musical theatre. And, like many others featured in this book, he was admired as much for his genial nature as his many talents.

William, whose brother, Thomas, attended several annual dinners, needed no introduction to the assembled *Moonies*, and was first mentioned at the 1891 dinner, when he was said to be a professional vocalist 'of repute' who owed his success 'to the early musical training received at St Mark's Church and the choral and vocal classes of the town'.

He sent an apology for his absence in 1894, and again from the Nottingham Opera House in 1897, saying he had to perform elsewhere. But his fellow *Moonies* never gave up hope of finding a rare gap in his diary – until his unexpected death at the age of just 55 in 1899. The theatre newspaper, *The Era*, printed a long obituary, which included the only known picture of him (left).

Although William Hogarth was born in South Shields, County Durham (in 1844), he moved to Swindon when he was about four years old. His father (also William) was the first foreman of the smiths' shop in the Railway Works.

By 1861 William junior was an apprentice engine fitter in the Works, but by the time of his marriage in 1865, aged 21, he was in Brighton.

At least some of his time since leaving Swindon was spent working ▶

for Maudslay, Sons & Field, a Lambeth-based firm of marine engineers, founded in 1798 by the great engineer Henry Maudslay, who was born in Woolwich and worked in the Royal Arsenal at Woolwich (see page 64).

Hogarth became the choirmaster at a Brighton church, and was known to play the trombone in a theatre orchestra, but was still having to supplement his income as a performer, the 1871 census still finding him in Brighton, listed as 'musician and insurance agent'.

During the 1870s he joined a minstrel company that toured India, and (according to his obituary in *The Era*): 'While on this tour he visited Peshawur, going up the Himalayas as far as the Khyber Pass. He also went to Hyderabad, Agra and Cawnpore; *The Moonies'* often-made claim that Wiltshiremen could be found all over the world was true!

Back in England, Hogarth took singing parts, joined an opera company as a baritone and was even 'lecturing in a panorama', before his breakthrough came in 1879.

He was engaged by Richard D'Oyly Carte's Comedy Opera Company to play Captain Corcoran, one of the lead parts in Gilbert and Sullivan's *HMS Pinafore*.

It had flopped when it was first staged, the previous year, but after a revamp Hogarth joined a touring version, performing for much of 1879 and 1880.

His performances were extremely well received, *The Stage* saying 'Mr Hogarth

Public Notices.

MECHANICS' INSTITUTE, NEW SWINDON.

MESSRS. SHIEL BARRY and WM. HOGARTH'S Celebrated Comic Opera Company.

FOR TWO NIGHTS ONLY—FRIDAY AND SATURDAY, DEC. 3rd and 4th.

POWERFUL COMPANY OF THIRTY ARTISTES.
CONDUCTOR: MR. W. F. GLOVER.

FRIDAY, DECEMBER, 3rd, the Celebrated Comic Opera in three acts,

"LA MASCOTTE,"

As played at the Comedy and Strand Theatres, London, for 800 nights (first time in Swindon).

SATURDAY, DECEMBER 4th, the enormously successful Comic Opera,

'LES CLOCHES DE CORNEVILLE,"

With MR. SHIEL BARRY in his original part of "Gaspard, the Miser," as played by him over 1,600 times at the Folly and Globe Theatres, London.

This is the only Company that has the right of performing the Operas as produced in London; has been appearing with enormous success at all the provincial theatres; and had the honour of singing to HER MAJESTY THE QUEEN at Liverpool May 11th and 12th, 1886.

Prices of Admission: 3s., 2s., 1s., and a few seats at 6d.

Doors open at 7·0 p.m; performance to commence at 7·30; carriages at 10·30.

Plan of the room, and seats booked, at Miss Woodham's Library, Swindon; Mr Birch, Mechanics' Institute, New Swindon.

MECHANICS' INSTITUTE, NEW SWINDON

A *Swindon Advertiser* notice for the visit of Hogarth's comic opera company's production of *Les Cloches de Corneville* in 1886

But Hogarth found the perfect vehicle for his talents in another comic opera, *Les Cloches de Corneville*, playing the hero. He would eventually buy the rights to the show and form his own company, with a fellow singer called Shiel Barry, so they could tour it – which they did to 'overflowing houses' for nearly two decades.

One performance, at the Theatre Royal in Edinburgh in May 1881, received a particularly glowing review in *The Stage*:

Mr W Hogarth (who was a great favourite during the run in the pantomime, in which he took a prominent part last Christmas) as the Marquis Henri, received a very cordial reception on his reappearance. His impersonation of this character is, without doubt, the finest we have seen in Edinburgh. Gifted with a remarkably powerful yet pleasant voice, he sang his music with an amount of spirit that won for him several encores; his acting was marked by a degree of refinement and easy self-possession, while his excellent stage presence was well in keeping with the character.

as the "right good captain" was immense' in Aberdeen in March 1880.

Hogarth's contract coincided with a volatile chapter in the Gilbert and Sullivan story, which eventually led to producer Richard D'Oyly Carte obtaining exclusive rights to G&S performances.

After another appearance, six months later, *The Stage* said 'his experience as a musician and his versatile abilities as an actor will eventually place him in the foremost rank of English artists on the stage'.

By 1887, Barry and Hogarth were

looking for new material, so Hogarth co-wrote the words for their own comic opera, called *Gipsy Gabriel*.

But Les Cloches de Corneville remained a favourite, and he was reckoned to have appeared in more than 3,000 performances of the show, making it and him well-known to theatregoers all over Britain.

In later years, when he outgrew the role and passed it to a younger actor, he sometimes took over as the conductor of the orchestra.

In the meantime he produced several pantomimes – at Crystal Palace, Leicester and (providing another link between *Moonies* and the south coast theatre (see above)) the Brighton Aquarium.

Hogarth played at the Mechanics' Institute on several occasions – the last time in 1893, when 'his songs, rendered in fine style, were rapturously applauded'. And he was arranging autumn and spring tours, including a visit to the *Queen's Theatre* in Swindon (later called *The Empire*) when he fell ill.

Hogarth's death – he died from blood poisoning at his home in Brighton on June 4, 1899 – was widely reported in provincial newspapers, the *Newcastle Daily Chronicle* saying he was 'one of the kindliest of men, and extremely well-liked in the profession'.

His popularity with his peers led to him being elected to the council of the Actors' Association, and *The Stage* said: 'Physically a splendid man – he stood considerably over 6ft in height – Mr Hogarth had a most genial and attractive nature and a cheery word for everyone.' ■

The clouds of war

When *The Moonies* reconvened for the first annual dinner of the 20th century, there were clouds hanging over proceedings.

War had been declared in the previous October – the Second Boer War – and a gathering so often filled with joy and hope in previous years, naturally had a preoccupation, this time, with the conflict.

The Moonies provide us with lots of insights into life in their era, so although it is beyond the scope of this book to look closely at colonial wars and the British Empire, we must take a brief look at their reaction to the war in South Africa.

For the second year running, Thomas Hooper Deacon was Chairman, and he was a man with a vested interest in the war, on account of his equestrian expertise and his military background, especially his backing for volunteer forces and their recruitment in Wiltshire (see page 117).

For one thing, according to the *Advertiser*'s report, Deacon 'remarked with pleasure on the decision of the War Office to establish a great military centre on Salisbury Plain'.

This is a timely reminder to us that while we might think Wiltshire has a close relationship with the Army built up over centuries (and in some respects it has), it wasn't until 1897 that land was first purchased for military use on Salisbury Plain.

The previous year there had been references to another colonial campaign, in Egypt and Sudan, where – although they did not see it quite this way – a major factor was the challenge of raising sufficient forces to stop the sun setting on the British Empire. A modern conclusion that historians have drawn from that conflict is the British were lucky they came up against French armies that were experiencing even more acute manpower challenges.

So it is not difficult to see how similar challenges might apply to the British efforts to keep control in South Africa, and how volunteers would probably be the difference between success and failure.

However, nothing said by Deacon and other *Moonies* in 1900 tells us whether or not the public thought the Boer War was a colonial war too many.

The recent changes in the make-up and aspirations of those present – of which the new Chairman was the best example – suggest they might have had a different view on the war to Joe Public, and the enthusiasm the diners had for the war in the opulent surroundings of the Holborn Restaurant's Royal Venetian Chamber were not necessarily the same as the man in the street. Or, indeed, in Billy Thomas's parlour.

The first toast was to the Forces, and this 'which would, two months ago, have been quietly honoured, was to-day received with a shout of triumph... Englishmen ought to be proud that they belonged to a country which produced such gallant men'. And:

They were well aware of what had been done in Wiltshire in connection with the Imperial Yeomanry: 300 men had volunteered to do duty for their country, and two units were already on their way to the Cape (applause). ▸

He believed the Wiltshiremen were bursting for a chance of getting at the Boers.

He added that although he had personally been unable to fight, 'he had a son in South Africa, and he had had good news from him.' The Chairman had been involved with mustering volunteers since 1868, 'had been brought into close touch with "Tommy," and he knew what a really good fellow he was.'

And the Chairman, who was an expert on horses (but clearly not on the development of mechanised warfare), added that, 'in future, mounted troops would have to figure more prominently in the constitution of the Army.'

Finally, 'he trusted that the war would be brought to a conclusion with as little bloodshed as possible, but only when the supremacy of this country had been established.'

The war talk over for now, the Chairman then turned to the usual business of the dinner, which this year had attracted 150 diners, presumably with a large contingent who had taken the train from Swindon, 'the majority of whom made the journey in a comfortable saloon provided by the GWR.'

There was bad news about former schoolmaster Alexander Braid: he had finally 'gone to his long rest'.

Twelve months later they were back at the Holborn Restaurant, with someone else to mourn: Queen Victoria, who had died seven weeks earlier.

The 1901 dinner was described as 'a monster gathering' by the *Advertiser*, with 177 present, now under the Chairmanship of George Jackson Churchward (pictured).

His presence underlined the status of *The Association of Wiltshiremen in London* (as it was about to become), since Churchward was currently Mayor of Swindon (the first to hold the title since the unification of Old Town and New Swindon, the previous year) and was also the *de-facto* Chief Mechanical Engineer of the GWR, much of William Dean's work having been delegated to him; he officially took over the post in 1902.

This year's Boer War talk was led by a senior railwayman, Lieut FG Wright of the F and G Companies (Swindon) of the 2nd Wilts Volunteers, and he spoke for some time about its progress, and his thoughts on modernisation. This included a hint about the inefficiency of British Forces, and how it might become more of a meritocracy, stating: 'It was interesting to note that officers in the army would in the future obtain to their position by reason of their ability.'

The irony of Churchward's chairmanship is that – like Deacon before him – he was not born in Wiltshire, as the *Advertiser* explained: 'Although not born in the county, he pitched his tent there, 23 or 24 years ago, and he had been, and was, very happy there, and had no desire to change (applause).'

The evening was concluded with the usual entertainment, which included a turn by Harry Hemsley, the son of WT Hemsley. He had first attended as an 18-year-old in 1895, first entertaining with a song, two years later. This year:

Mr Harry Hemsley gave a... highly pleasing performance on his part was his sketch, a novel and humourous entertainment in itself. He faithfully reproduced in voice and gesture children from the age of one to six years, giving selections from their quaint sayings and peculiarities, their manner of singing, reciting, etc.'

What they were seeing was a very early preview of an act that would earn the Swindon-born man a national reputation, and even a footnote in the history of advertising and product placement. ∎

Voices from the future

While *The Moonies*' annual dinners are a good barometer of what was fashionable and popular at the time, when Harry Hemsley entertained them in 1901, it was a rather different story.

He was 'loudly encored', but all they could have known about him at the time was that Harry was the son of top-rated set designer WT Hemsley (see page 110), and he would probably follow his father – one way or another – into the theatre.

The report of his turn at *The Moonies* dinner tells us that his trademark child impersonation routine had been established by then, but it would be decades before it would bring him the national stardom he enjoyed in his later career.

Harry was born in Regent Street, Swindon, on December 14, 1877, the third oldest of seven children, but the family soon left town because of his father's job: first to Margate in about 1881, then to Battersea, London, four years later.

As a child he was both an actor and a designer of posters, costumes, ornaments and even lampshades; it wasn't yet clear whether his future would be on stage or, like his father, behind the scenes.

His first stage appearance was in 1885 at the *Grand Theatre*, Islington, and on January 31, 1891, aged 13, he performed at the opening of the *Royal English Opera House* (now the Palace Theatre) in London. ▶

Radio Pictorial   HARRY HEMSLEY   Photo. Navana

Photo Card

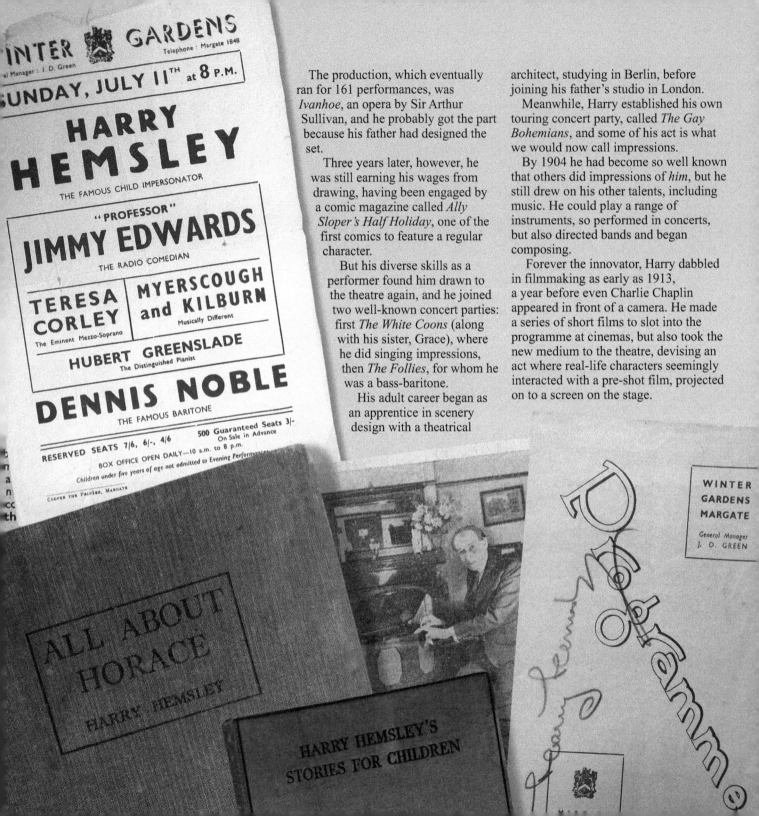

The production, which eventually ran for 161 performances, was *Ivanhoe*, an opera by Sir Arthur Sullivan, and he probably got the part because his father had designed the set.

Three years later, however, he was still earning his wages from drawing, having been engaged by a comic magazine called *Ally Sloper's Half Holiday*, one of the first comics to feature a regular character.

But his diverse skills as a performer found him drawn to the theatre again, and he joined two well-known concert parties: first *The White Coons* (along with his sister, Grace), where he did singing impressions, then *The Follies*, for whom he was a bass-baritone.

His adult career began as an apprentice in scenery design with a theatrical architect, studying in Berlin, before joining his father's studio in London.

Meanwhile, Harry established his own touring concert party, called *The Gay Bohemians*, and some of his act is what we would now call impressions.

By 1904 he had become so well known that others did impressions of *him*, but he still drew on his other talents, including music. He could play a range of instruments, so performed in concerts, but also directed bands and began composing.

Forever the innovator, Harry dabbled in filmmaking as early as 1913, a year before even Charlie Chaplin appeared in front of a camera. He made a series of short films to slot into the programme at cinemas, but also took the new medium to the theatre, devising an act where real-life characters seemingly interacted with a pre-shot film, projected on to a screen on the stage.

ALL ABOUT HORACE

HARRY HEMSLEY

HARRY HEMSLEY'S STORIES FOR CHILDREN

Programme

WINTER GARDENS MARGATE

General Manager J. D. GREEN

But it was the advent of radio and the foundation of the BBC (in 1922) that produced the opportunity for his child impersonation routines – previewed to *The Moonies*, more than two decades earlier – to make him a star.

Radio was just what he needed because he was no ventriloquist; on stage he raised his hand to his mouth or covered it with his book while voicing his characters.

His radio debut came when *The White Coons* appeared on the BBC in 1923, but his first documented appearance as a solo performer was not until January 6, 1927, when Harry, now aged 39, performed his child impersonations on a variety show.

But his biggest break was still years away.

It was in December 1934 that the makers of Ovaltine, a hugely popular milky bedtime drink, sponsored a weekly half-hour Sunday evening programme on Radio Luxembourg, Britain's first commercial station, called *The Ovaltineys' Concert Party*.

Harry's already well-established fictional family of children (called Winnie, Johnny, Elsie and baby Horace) were the obvious choice to play the starring roles in what became a pioneering sponsorship and spin-off phenomenon.

Harry wrote the signature tune and provided the voices for *The Ovaltineys*, and by 1939 no fewer than five million British children were members of the *League of Ovaltineys*.

A series of spin-off books were written and illustrated by Harry (pictured, along with various Harry Hemsley/ *Ovaltineys* memorabilia, courtesy of Swindon Libraries/Local Studies and Mike Atwell). ▶

Harry made countless appearances on stage, radio and even television – he took part in experimental broadcasts between 1932 and 1936 – right up until the year of his death.

Between 1923 and 1934 he also released nearly 50 records, almost all of which he wrote and recorded himself.

It made him a household name in Britain, but his characters were just as well known, and even found themselves introduced into everyday language.

Because Winnie often used to interpret the garbled sounds made by baby Horace, "What did Horace say, Winnie?" became a catchphrase.

It was often quoted when anyone failed to catch what someone else had said in a conversation, and was still heard often enough for it to be used by Mr Humphries in the 1970s sitcom, *Are You Being Served?*

Harry Hemsley is best remembered today as the voice behind *The Ovaltineys*, but he was a consummate entertainer, immensely versatile and willing to embrace new ideas.

Sadly, he suffered a heart attack while making a television series called *For the Children*, and died on April 8, 1951, in Wimbledon, aged 73.

Not even *The Moonies* could have envisaged the invention of radio and how it would transform the career of Harry Hemsley, all those years after they cheered his performance in 1901. Indeed, it would even be another eight years before Ovaltine was introduced to the UK.

Ironically, despite his great fame, there is no record of Harry Hemsley performing solo in Swindon, making the routine he served up to at the Holborn Restaurant in 1901 even more of a treat for *The Moonies*. ■

Making it official

One consequence of the annual dinner in 1901 was the creation of an official organisation.

Until then known by their nickname of *The Moonies in London*, and sometimes referred to 'Swindonians in London' (for want of an official title), henceforth they would be known as *The Association of Wiltshiremen in London*.

It has been seen how the nature of the annual dinners progressed from humble beginnings in Plumstead to a prestigious (and no doubt expensive) venue in central London, now with high-ranking people chairing, and a more serious and formal (although still quite jovial) air.

So when he addressed those attending in 1901, Chairman George Jackson Churchward proposed to make it more than just a sociable annual gathering of like-minded men, and give it a specific purpose.

Churchward used his knowledge of a similar association in Devon (his home county) to propose an idea that had clearly been discussed with the committee beforehand:

It had been suggested that this annual dinner should partake of a more comprehensive nature, similar, for instance, to that which had existed amongst the Devonians in London. It would be an excellent opportunity for any young man to have some place to go to, when he arrived in London, where he might refer to some one in case of any difficulty or obtain any information he might require (hear, hear).

It seemed very probable if the idea should "hook on" that it would form

the nucleus of an Association of Wiltshiremen in London.

If such an Association were formed it would bring in members from all parts of the county of Wilts, who had left their native place, and in the course of time they would get quite as large and influential Society of Wiltshiremen in London as the Devonians could claim in regard to their county at the present time.

Sure enough, a meeting was arranged for a couple of weeks later, and another quickly followed. Then, in May 1901, the *Wiltshire Times and Trowbridge Advertiser* reported:

A well-attended meeting of Wiltshiremen in London was held on Monday evening at the Salisbury Hotel, Camomile Street, to give effect to a proposal made at the 14th annual dinner of Wiltshiremen in London by Mr GJ Churchward JP, Mayor of Swindon.

They listed all those present – Messrs G Avenall [sic], S Brown, JA Fulton, W Haggard, GH Leonard, T Palmer, FH Spencer, FS Wallington, GB Moore, Clack, G Davis, SG Huntley, W Jones, Seaplehorn and Drewitt – and said the Association's rules, based on those set down by their Devonian counterparts, were approved 'with a single dissentient'.

Along with his account of the following year's dinner, the *Advertiser*'s reporter reviewed the story so far, which was rather dismissive of the efforts of the founders of the now-defunct *Moonies in London*:

Time has wrought a great many changes in the short space of 15

Par for the course

years, and nowhere could this be more forcibly illustrated than at the 15th annual dinner of Wiltshiremen in London, which was held last Saturday evening. Started on a very small scale at Woolwich, amongst a few Moonies who had gone there to work, the annual re-union has grown year by year, increased in popularity, and extended its useful purpose. Hitherto the annual gathering had been managed by a Committee of Moonies, and the objects were mainly to meet for social and convivial purposes. But last year it was decided to launch out on more ambitious lines, and an Association of Wiltshiremen in London was formed, which has for its object the assistance of any member at a time when help is needed, and, on the social side, to bring Wiltshiremen in London together once a year for a few hours at the festive board.

The first President of the Association is Mr Richard Burbidge, a native of Melksham, who has now been resident in London 40 years. There is a strong representative committee, and already during the first year of its work, the Association has justified its existence by rendering help in time of need to one of its members, whose lines have not fallen in pleasant places. As the Secretary announced on Saturday evening, the minimum subscription is 1s per annum, and the maximum 20 guineas, which sum the President has handsomely contributed to the funds. ■

There was a potentially awkward moment during the long speeches at *The Association of Wiltshiremen in London*'s 1902 dinner, held in the lavish surroundings of the Royal Venetian Chamber of the Holborn Restaurant.

It occurred when proceedings were halted for a presentation to one of the co-founders of *The Moonies in London* (and apparently the only one of the original attendees present), Frank Wallington (see page 27).

He was getting a special gift because he had 'so ably discharged the duties of Secretary' for many years, but was now stepping down.

The Chairman gave him an illuminated address and 'a splendid silver hunting watch', though it is difficult to imagine what opportunities an engine fitter who worked a five-and-a-half-day week at the Royal Arsenal in Woolwich had to use it in its intended context.

If a symbol was needed to show that the gentrification of the organisation from a humble reunion to one of the highlights of the social calendar was complete, then this was it.

The gathering was now frequented by many upper class characters, some of the richest men in the country and senior military figures – but the now-record attendance figures apparently seemed to rely, as much as anything, on a large contingent turning up on the train, each year, from Swindon, for a jolly night out.

At the head of the table, this year, a curious character had been chosen as the Presiding Chairman: Sir John Tankerville Goldney (pictured).

Born at Corsham in 1846, Goldney was a barrister who had been Chief Justice of Trinidad and Tobago, and would also become High Sheriff of Wiltshire in 1910.

But history mostly remembers him for his strange claim to fame: he was the man who brought golf to Singapore.

Visiting there in 1891, he had taken his clubs with him, but there was no course. So he proposed that land belonging to the Singapore Sporting Club could be used, and they set out a nine-hole ▶

1902

course. Goldney became the first president of the club, and he got to drive the first ball.

The *Advertiser*'s report, that year, would be the longest so far; there were long speeches, often concerning the military, sometimes returning to the theme of Wiltshire's superiority over other counties, and although jovial at times, was often serious and – dare we say? – dull.

That's not to say that the proceedings give us any less of an insight into life in Wiltshire, or how the other half lived in 1902; or that there weren't highlights; or that it was all in a worthy cause. But as he looked at his hunting watch, we can only guess what Frank Wallington thought of it all.

The *Advertiser* looked on in awe, noting:

> It was expected that the attendance at the annual dinner this year would be a record one, and the expectation was realised, albeit there were many notable absentees through illness and other causes. For instance, the Right

Hon [Colonel] WH Long, MP, had been announced to preside, but was prevented doing so by illness, and for the same reason Lord Edmond Fitzmaurice MP, and other leading Wiltshiremen were absent.

Also absent was George Jackson Churchward, who was 'taking care of the King while travelling on the GWR in the West country'.

The Chairman's first job of the evening was 'to congratulate the Dinner Committee on their happy selection of the date for that annual gathering' adding:

> It enabled them to express how grateful they were to the Prince and Princess of Wales for their visit to Wiltshire that week. He (the Chairman) had the honour to be on the platform at Chippenham Station to welcome their Royal Highnesses. He was also at that grand meet of the hounds at Badminton, and those who were there would agree with him that it was a most wonderful sight to see

> the hounds going up the Long Walk, three miles long, followed by the Prince and Princess. It was truly a magnificent picture. There were thousands of people present from Wiltshire and Gloucestershire – some on horseback, some on foot, some on bicycles, and some even on motor cars.

It is not clear how many of Chippenham's *hoi polloi* (let alone colonists) had been consulted by the Chairman, but he told the diners:

> People from all parts gathered to show their loyalty, as it was perhaps the only chance they would have in their lives of showing what they would do for the Prince and Princess of Wales in some acknowledgement for what they had done for our Empire. He (the Chairman) had lived nearly a quarter a century abroad – in Greater Britain, across the seas – and he could recognise what good their Royal Highnesses had done. By their trip to the colonies they had placed another link in that chain of affection which bound us to our

SWINDON. Hooper.

SOUTHERN LAUNDRY Co L

colonies, and which would never be broken. It was the aim of their Royal Highnesses to do what they could for the welfare of the people, who owed them a debt of gratitude.

There followed news of the Boer War, delivered at great length by Thomas Hooper Deacon, the former Chairman, who reeled off a long list of upper class Wiltshire colonels and their sons who had been fighting in South Africa. It included Col Calley who 'was welcomed home to Swindon some months ago with the greatest cordiality, and he would be again if he returned twenty times'.

Not that the upper ranks were afforded any privileges in Britain's modern army, Deacon noting that every man had to tend his own horse, and clean his own tackle, like any other soldier'.

He also made reference to his son:

He had received a letter from him that morning, in which he said he had had his horse shot under him, and he himself was shot through the waistcoat. He said he intended to have that waistcoat darned, and to wear it in the hunting field when he returned.

Next up was Capt Fred Wright, who seemed anxious to underline the new status of industrial Swindon (pictured, below, in a composite image, based on William Hooper's photographs from the first decade of the 20th century, courtesy of Paul Williams).

The town was the new heart of the county, or as Capt Wright cheekily put it: 'He had been living in the new Capital of Wiltshire (Swindon), for 20 years, while sitting on his right was the Mayor of the old Capital (Salisbury).' And he noted: 'The population of Swindon was now more than all the other Boroughs in the County put together'

He then spoke at length about the value of Wiltshire's volunteer forces, and how the government ought to do more to encourage them, including allowing a week's holiday for them to attend an annual 'camp'.

Mr R Burbidge, the new President, later responded with a short speech, and a promise:

Speaking, in conclusion, as one who employed 2,000 or 3,000 hands, he said his firm [Harrods] *would give their employees a week's holiday in*

the year to enable them to attend the drills and camp if they joined the Volunteers, and would pay them their week's wage at the same time (applause).

More military talk followed, the Presiding Chairman first recalling an incident in the Crimean War in which 'Wiltshiremen taught a very distinct object lesson to the Russians', then how Wiltshire was 'a good hunting county'; how he had heard Lord Lansdowne once explain that 'while he was in India, the Regiment which had the best record in every way was the Wiltshire Regiment'.

At last he asked:

Could any other County with a similar population to Wiltshire boast of having three men of their County as Cabinet ministers? They had Lord Lansdowne, Sir Michael Hicks-Beach, and the Right Hon Walter H Long (applause).

In the circumstances, the choice of guest speaker was an interesting one.

It was Trowbridge-born wit and raconteur Spencer Leigh Hughes, or (as he was better known to readers of ▶

the radical *Morning Leader*): Sub Rosa. Hughes would eventually become a Liberal MP – and he was another coup for the *Moonies*, being famous as an after-dinner speaker.

No wonder he was also back for the following year's dinner, in 1903, when he again delivered a speech extolling the virtues of Wiltshire.

Also back was Sir John Goldney, along with another long report in the *Advertiser* on the long speeches, of which the favourite subject, once again, was war and the military.

But there was a big difference this year, as the Chairman pointed out. Something had happened 'of which they were all glad': the end of the Boer War:

He need not mention the names of those Wiltshiremen who had bravely done their duty in that great war. Many had come back with honours, and some were laid to rest out there. What more glorious death could there be than for a man to die fighting for his country?

Captain Deacon said local men had done their duty and:

They would be pleased and proud to know that the Metropolis of Wiltshire, Swindon, turned out a whole Squadron of Yeomanry [in the war]. As for showing the growth and the contrast with former years, he could remember driving to the annual training at Devizes in a gig, only a few going. Now they went out 200 strong, and no other town in England could put such a Squadron in the field as they sent on to Salisbury Plain (applause). He advised Wiltshiremen in London to take a holiday during the training season, and go down on Salisbury Plain and witness the men do their

work. It was real military duty, and very different to what he had seen in the old days of the Yeomanry.

There was no mention of (which history now has evidence of) the cost of the war to the British people (£211m, equivalent to about £20bn now) nor the British tactic of using concentration camps that led to the deaths of more than 26,000 women and children, and at least 20,000 others.

When the subject of the speeches changed, they turned to other national issues, even including the Licensing Act 1902 and the Education Act 1902.

About the former, the Chairman said: 'According to statistics that were most closely watched by temperance societies, Wiltshire stood first, as being the most sober County in England (applause).'

The latter was a controversial subject because it abolished local school boards, which were heavily influenced by non-conformists, in favour of a national system that supported Church of England and Catholic-run schools.

However, it did allow for the creation of hundreds of new secondary schools, and, as the Chairman put it, that night:

there should not be a single boy or girl who would not get a thorough education in the future, fitting them to wrestle with the problems of modern life, and to compete, in educational matters, with Germany and those other countries which had made a special feature of higher education.

At least the long speeches 'were interspersed with songs, etc, a splendid programme having been arranged by Mr EF James, an old Swindonian, who was an efficient musical director. He delighted the company with his masterly performance on the bassoon' while 'Mr HM Hemsley gave a pleasing sketch, imitation

of children's songs and sayings.' The meeting also took time for the usual self-praise of Wiltshire and every man in it, but they seemed to be trying too hard to keep the mood light:

The modesty of Wiltshiremen was proverbial, and the keenness of the intelligence of women of Wiltshire was also proverbial. A poet had "dropped into poetry" over a woman of Wiltshire. He would just quote them five lines:

There was a young lady in Wilts, Who walked up to Scotland on stilts. When they said, "Oh how shocking, You show so much stocking," She replied, "What about you and your kilts?"

But there could be no denying that the new format of the dinners since the formation of the Association was a winning formula, and Mr GB Moore got up to say:

He was pleased to say the Association was gaining rapidly in numbers. They had uphill work at first, but they made 100 members in one year, and they had more than doubled the number during the past year. Within the last month about 30 had joined.

And he couldn't deny the significance of the 'large number of gentlemen who had that day come from North Wilts, and especially from Swindon'. The town was now an undoubted powerhouse, compared with the rest of the county.

At one stage during the proceedings, Swindon was described as 'the Chicago of the West of England', and another speaker said 'Swindon was a most unique town, with a population of nearly 50,000, and all a working class population.'

Many attending the dinner these days may have represented the old order, but there was no doubt that Swindon had arrived, and there was no stopping it. ■

Wiltshire's after-dinner wit

He was (according to *Encyclopaedia Britannica*) the cleverest after-dinner speaker of his time – and he was a Wiltshireman.

Spencer Leigh Hughes was the perfect choice to add some wit to the proceedings of *The Association of Wiltshiremen in London* when he first attended an annual dinner in 1902 – and, like the original *Moonies in London*, he even had an engineering background.

The son of a Wesleyan minister, Hughes was born in Trowbridge on April 21, 1858.

He trained as an engineer with Ransomes, Sims & Jefferies, an Ipswich-based firm that produced agricultural machinery, but also traction engines and trolleybuses.

'It was while there that he did his first journalistic work,' the *Wiltshire Times* later revealed, 'and a weekly article in a Suffolk paper resulted in his being invited to take up regular journalism in London.'

He wrote professionally under the pen name 'Sub-Rosa', specialising in light and witty commentaries on current affairs, and was a familiar figure in the Parliamentary press gallery.

His nonconformist religion and association with the radical publication the *Morning Leader* (described as 'the only radical morning paper in London in 1901') and later the *Daily News,* had reinforced his already strong Liberal leanings.

It all gave him a heightened interest in politics, and he aspired to a Parliamentary career.

He first stood for parliament in Jarrow in 1907, and again in Bermondsey in 1909, finally tasting electoral success in the 1910 General Election, winning one of the two Stockport seats for the Liberal Party, and he held the seat for the rest of his life.

Sir Henry Campbell-Bannerman (when he was Prime Minister) wrote of Hughes: 'I owe him many a hearty laugh and jocund moment in the enjoyment of humour so light, so refined and so good-natured.'

And a matter of a few days before Hughes died, the then-Prime Minister, Lloyd George, wrote to him to say: 'I am very sorry to hear of your illness, which, as I understand, involves your being laid up for some time. Your cheerful and friendly companionship is greatly missed at the House. As one of your old friends, I send you my best wishes for a speedy recovery and an early return to our midst in Parliament.'

It was once written that 'his stock of telling anecdotes and amusing experiences' was 'practically inexhaustible'.

A fervent, popular and enthusiastic supporter of *The Association of Wiltshiremen in London* dinners, he attended almost every one during the period 1902 to 1911.

He died aged 61, from heart failure, and was laid to rest in Ipswich. His obituary in the *Wiltshire Times*, dated February 28, 1920, said:

Mr Spencer Leigh Hughes was one of the best-known and best-liked personalities in the House of Commons. A witty and convincing speaker, he was in much request at Liberal and social gatherings, also at the annual dinner of Wiltshiremen in London.

He was most widely known, however, as a journalist, having for many years written Parliamentary sketches, as well as chatty articles under the title of "Sub Rosa"... He was also a regular contributor of an unfailingly humorous article to "Reynolds' Newspaper". ∎

Burbidge, the hero of Harrods

When *The Association of Wiltshire-men in London* appointed Richard Burbidge (pictured, opposite, courtesy of Harrods Company Archive) as its first President in 1901 – a post he held until his death – he was already a man with a towering reputation. And he left a legacy that lasts even to today.

According to the archivist at Harrods, arguably the most famous department store in the world: "His contribution to the development of the store was enormous. He was the man who made Harrods the great department store it became in the early twentieth century."

Born in South Wraxall, near Bradford-on-Avon, of relatively wealthy farming stock, Richard Burbidge went to school in Devizes and Melksham, and first went to London in 1861.

His period as President of *The Association of Wiltshiremen in London* is marked by his tenacity and commitment, and he is remembered as much for generosity, compassion towards staff and efforts to minimise working hours as he is for his radical, innovative and at times visionary approach to managing the store.

Following his death, on June 8, 1917, the *North Wilts Herald* printed a heartfelt obituary: an extraordinary account of the life of an extraordinary man:

Sir Richard Burbidge, head of Harrods Stores, chairman of the Association of Wiltshiremen in London, one of whom not merely Wilts but the nation is proud and will greatly miss, died suddenly at his home at 51, Hans Mansions, SW...

After a busy day at the great stores... he retired to bed early – shortly after eight – and less than two hours later called to say he felt faint. For a long time Sir Richard's heart was known to be weak, and now he was found to be in a precarious position. He sat by the open window that he might have the full benefit of the air, but death occurred shortly afterwards.

No better monument could be erected to the memory of a man than that which Sir Richard built for himself in Harrods stores. As all the world knows, he was managing director of that immense undertaking since 1891, and under his direction its growth has been phenomenal.

Outside these business activities Sir Richard found time to serve the State in many valuable capacities and to help out, by service and gift, many philanthropic movements. As to the secret of his success, his power in business amounted almost to genius. It was multiple, and some will think one factor greater than another. He had seemingly illimitable energy, power of concentration and application. He won by hard work.

He abstained from all intoxicants and did not smoke. He was also, and first and last, a firm believer in advertising... He was the first, one believes, to take a full newspaper page advertisement, and the first to issue the artistic fashion catalogues now frequently met with.

He had the imagination which enabled him quickly to seize the possibilities of new methods, and in the working out of details he had remarkably good judgement. He was a keen reader of character – no small accomplishment to a leader of men – and was able invariably to choose the right men for the right posts.

He was appreciative of good work, and at the same time that he was building a business whose scope and character was as different from that in which he had his early training as the farm he left at South Wraxall to go to London. He was a pioneer in shortening the hours of labour for employees, improving their conditions and providing them with facilities for recreation.

Businesses are built in the mornings, said an observer once. Sir Richard was a life-long early riser... He had trite sayings as finger-posts to success in business for others. His own earliest motto, he said, was "Stick it." His golden rules for success included: Be persevering; be moderate; be prompt and punctual; be courteous; don't shift from one firm to another; don't look down on anyone and make your employer's interest your own.

Sir Richard knew the business methods of another generation. At the age of 13 he went to London to be apprenticed to another Wilts man – Mr Jonathan Puckridge, who carried on a well-established and reputable business as provisioner, grocer and wine merchant in Oxford Street...

Sir Richard would smile as he spoke, but he would betray the fact that he retained vivid impressions of

his own early struggles, the long hours and the lack of recreation. He had been "through the mill," and it was this experience that made him a great as well as a lovable man among those who worked under him.

"Terrible hours," he once said when referring to his apprenticeship. "We were supposed to be down at half-past six in the morning, and to start business at seven. We never closed before nine at night, and were never out of the shop until half-past nine or twenty to ten. On Fridays and Saturdays it was later still, ten being the hour of closing on Fridays and eleven on Saturdays, and it always meant half an hour more to get the shop straight.

"Good Friday and Christmas Day were the only days off during the year. There was no Boxing Day. The Bank Holiday Act had not been passed." In those days apparently summer holidays were not the rule in the grocery trade. But Sir Richard would tell how, after 20 months' service, Mr Puckridge, as a favour, allowed him "a week off".

One great thing Sir Richard retained all through that period of hard toil – his sense of humour... which helped in a large manner to make up his charming personality, and was a priceless help to him at all times.

He won the respect and esteem of his employees as well as his peers. His tact and mental alertness were invaluable on committees, and it was because of these powers and of his extensive experience in business and ▶

organisation on a large scale that he was able to be of considerable service to the Government in connection with the [First World] war. He knew he had heart trouble, but his pleasure in life was his work, and he "stuck it"...

Chief dates in Sir Richard's life are: Born, 1847; goes to London, 1860 [actually: 1861]; sets up in business, 1866; becomes general superintendent Army and Navy Auxiliary, 1880; general manager Whiteley's, 1882; manager West Kensington Stores, 1889; head of Harrods, 1891.

The baronetcy came to Sir Richard in the New Year's honours list of 1916. Special mention was made of his public work and of his invaluable services to the military. He filled numerous public positions of an important character, and performed many services of a philanthropic and charitable nature.

He was a member of the Commission appointed to inquire into the wages of Post Office employees, of the General Purposes and Executive Committees of the Board of Control of Regimental Institutes. He was acting chairman of the Executive and War Emergency Committees for the provision of invalid kitchens, and was also prominently associated with Queen Alexandra's Field Force Fund, King Albert's

Civilian Hospital Fund, and the Anglo-Russian Hospital. He had a seat on the Advisory Board of the Ministry of Munitions, and was chairman of the Royal Aircraft Factory Committee. All these duties did not exhaust his great energies, for he was trustee of the Crystal Palace, hon treasurer of the Tariff Commission, chairman of the Decimal Association, and a JP for the County of London.

That Sir Richard retained always the liveliest affection for his native county – no Wiltshireman needs reminding.

Probably no position that he held was more pleasurable to him than to be president and take the chair at the annual meetings of the Association of Wiltshiremen in London. It was a memorable gathering at which he was honoured by more than five hundred fellow county-men in 1911, when he celebrated his business golden jubilee.

At this gathering there was given some idea of the rise of this firm from the small business founded by Henry Charles Harrod in 1849. It had been converted into a company just before Sir Richard Burbidge became general manager in 1891; but he, it may be said, laid the foundations for the phenomenal growth of the business, which has led to the erection of the magnificent buildings containing the stores, and covering acres in Brompton Road.

When he became manager the firm employed 200 hands; to-day there are 6,600, and this apart from the 2,000 employees who are serving in various ways in the war. Under his care Harrods has become world-famous as a shopping centre. In March last, when he completed 25 years' association with the company, Sir Richard, who had been created a baronet in the New Year, was entertained at the Albert Hall by 6,000 employees.

A hard worker himself, Sir Richard appreciated the value of a loyal and contented staff, in order to secure great results, and he did much to improve the working conditions of his employees, by shortening the working hours, promoting recreative and educational facilities, and in other ways...

But the valuable influence of his direction was not confined to Harrods in London; he took a keen interest in the branch of the business in Buenos Ayres [sic], and he was also a director of the Hudson Bay Company, and as a member of the board concentrated his attention upon the development of the stores of that company in Canada. He was also the chairman of the directors of Dickins and Jones (Limited).

Another service performed for the nation by Sir Richard was the preservation of the Crystal Palace. Before the outbreak of war its demolition appeared imminent. Sir Richard wrote to the "Times" and initiated the fund which saved the situation, subscribing himself £32,000. With a later donation he recollected the first holiday he had in London and which he spent in the Palace, and also said he made it as a thank-offering for a successful business career.

Sir Richard was elected President of the Association of Wiltshiremen in London on its formation in May 1901, and has been re-elected annually since that date. The success of the association has been mainly due to his generosity. A busy man, he could not give much time to executive work, but in his own words to the Secretary: "I cannot attend your meetings regularly, but when you want any financial assistance, appeal to me." And the appeal was never in vain. He was the recipient of many applications for relief, and as an instance of his kindliness of heart it may be mentioned that when the Secretary has felt compelled to advise that no assistance be given, Sir Richard has said in his quiet way, "Give him a little, and I'll send you a cheque."

Of a retiring disposition, it was a difficult matter to induce Sir Richard to preside at the annual dinners, and it was not until 1911 (his 50th year in London) that the committee persuaded him to occupy the chair. On that occasion, the association presented him with an illuminated address.

Shortly before his death, he inquired what the association was doing in the matter of the Prisoners of War Fund and visiting the wounded in hospitals in London, and sent a handsome donation to the fund.

The association was represented at the memorial service at St Saviour's, Chelsea, on Tuesday, by many officers and members, including Messrs SA Giddings, G Davis, E Harrison, SG Huntley, WG Howard, HM Piper, EW Palmer (assistant hon secretary), T Palmer (hon secretary), E Thomas (Swindon), JH Willis, W Viney, and GB Moore (hon secretary). The Rev Mills Robbins (hon chaplain) assisted at the funeral service at Shepperton. ∎

The importance of Ernest Skurray

Ernest Skurray's Swindon Town Flour Mills, pictured in 1905 by William Hooper (courtesy of Paul Williams/The Swindon Society)

In the first years of the 20th century, *The Association of Wiltshiremen in London* counted among its supporters Ernest Clement Skurray, a man with a personality as big as the five-storey mill he owned in Princes Street.

When he died in 1940, the *North Wilts Herald* tried to sum up the life of an extraordinary man, as follows:

Pioneer of the English motoring industry, and until recently prominent figure in local public life and politics, Mr EC Skurray, who rose from the bottom to the top rung of the ladder of success through his own initiative and perseverance, died on Monday evening at his home, West Lodge, Swindon, at the age of 74...

His life story is a romance of industry, for although his father was a successful business man, Mr Skurray... made his own way through life.

Ernest Clement Skurray was born in Swindon on 20th September, 1865 according to his birth certificate, but he always said he was born on 19th September. He always celebrated his birthday on that day...

At the age of 17 he was apprenticed to a firm of engineers in Birmingham district and eventually entered the flour milling business, on the mechanical side. He began business as a corn dealer and started with a capital of only £33 which he had saved...

At the end of five or six years he decided to have a mill of his own, and the Town Mill, Swindon, was built... He was miller and motor engineer at the same time for many years. On 27 November, 1899, he bought his first motor-car and made a contract with a firm to purchase at least six and not more than 12 cars within a year at £170 each.

This contract was the first officially stamped contract made in England for the sale of cars...

Motoring was a slow business, and a novelty then, but he saw there was a future for it, although people told him he was mad. But he proved otherwise...

For many years he was chairman of Swindon Conservative Association and latterly he was the president. As a member of Swindon Town Council for a number of years he served on the Electricity and Tramways Committee and was its chairman. He was instrumental in getting trams for Swindon and was a street lighting pioneer. Before street lighting came he demonstrated its possibilities with an arc lamp outside his Princes-street premises, lighted from a dynamo in his mill...

Borough and County magistrate, he was also a founder member and past president of Swindon Rotary Club. An early member of Swindon Town FC, he was chairman of the directors in the days when it had its headquarters on the Croft ground....

During the last war he had important work in control of food production tractors and was awarded the OBE.

He loved Wiltshire and delighted in motoring in the country, while he was also a great garden lover. He was a Commissioner for Income Tax. ∎

Then God created Wiltshirewomen

1904

Just when it seemed the annual dinner of *The Association of Wiltshiremen in London* couldn't get any grander or bigger, it did.

In 1904 the *Advertiser* reported that it 'was held on Saturday last [March 5], as usual, in the King's Hall of Holborn Restaurant' (pictured, left).

The attendance proved to be the largest on record, '276 gentlemen sitting down to the dinner'.

In fact, it was to be the first time (if previous reports were correct) that it had been held in the King's Hall, specifically, one of the more opulent rooms in the Holborn Restaurant – apparently even a step up from the Royal Venetian Chamber.

Even then, as one speaker pointed out:

Never before, since the establishment of the Association, had it been necessary for the Committee to have to put in fresh seats, at the last moment, and even then find it difficult to accommodate the large number of Wiltshiremen assembled from all parts.

Presiding this year was the Marquess of Bath, from Longleat, and once the now customary review of the military situation (especially the ongoing enthusiasm of Wiltshiremen to volunteer to do their bit for the Empire) was done, he delivered 'an eloquent speech'.

The main toast was 'Wilts, our county,' while the evening's main theme was 'local patriotism'.

Sir John Goldney told the diners:

He believed the quiet strength of the Wiltshire Downs, and the bracing air which came from them, and the beautiful streams that ran near them, affected the character of Wiltshiremen. One of the great characteristics of Wiltshire was this, that with the exception of Swindon and Salisbury, there were no large manufacturing towns in the County.

Not that Swindon wasn't a cause for Wiltshire pride. Sir John said he 'was proud as a Wiltshireman that they [the GWR] could turn out such work at Swindon (applause)'.

The entertainment was of the usual high quality – 'This was arranged by an old Swindonian, Mr EF James, Musician-in-Ordinary to the King' – but with a difference:

An innovation was made this year in the introduction of lady vocalists, and these were from Wiltshire – Miss Pollie Finn and Miss Olive Batten (both of Swindon). They contributed some pleasing songs, which gained hearty encores.

This is the first time the presence of any women at any of the dinners was reported. Indeed, it was effectively the first admission of the existence of females. To say that it was a man's world in 1904 would be an understatement.

At least it was fitting that one of the first two Wiltshire*women* allowed in by ▶

the Wiltshire*men* was Olive Batten, who was the 16-year-old daughter of the late Harry Batten, who had sung at many of the *Moonies in London*'s dinners.

It was back to the King's Hall again, in 1905, where the attendance was slightly down on the previous year, but another member of the aristocracy was presiding: Lord Methuen (pictured, below).

Otherwise it was business as usual, starting with a toast to 'imperial forces', proposed, as in the previous year, by Charles Awdry of *The Wiltshire Society*.

Even he had to admit it put him in difficulty:

> *When he received the invite to again be present, the Secretary forwarded to him a complete and accurate report of all that was said at last year's dinner. He found that having said so much about the Imperial Forces then, what was there new to be said to-day?*

He was probably somewhat upstaged by what came next.

> *After this speech, Mr W Pennington, the veteran actor, recited "The Charge of the Light Brigade,"* [by Lord Tennyson] *which was loudly encored. Additional interest was given to this from the fact that Mr Pennington is one of the survivors of that famous charge at Balaclava.*

William Pennington, a former Shakespearian actor and one-time manager of the Sadler's Wells Theatre, whom the *Daily Mirror* claimed was [the Prime Minister] Mr Gladstone's favourite actor', had been performing the poem at theatres and benefits for at least the previous 26 years – often in the uniform of the 11th Hussars.

Pennington (pictured, right) had ridden with them in the Charge of the Light Brigade in 1854, which was part of the Battle of Balaclava in the Crimean War.

According to the *Daily Telegraph* in an article in 1900, 'In this last desperate onslaught, Mr Pennington had his horse shot beneath him, and was himself wounded [in the leg], but a comrade pulled him up on to a riderless steed, which was passing, and thus he escaped.'

His injury caused him to spend a month in hospital in 1855 – at Scutari, where he briefly became Camp Cook before returning home; this would have led to him knowing the nurse who was managing the care of the soldiers at the hospital: Florence Nightingale.

Pennington was still performing the poem in 1911, 67 years after the battle, and died in 1923, aged 90.

It would be pleasing to say his appearance at the annual dinner of *The Association of Wiltshiremen in London* was because of some connection with the county, but in fact he was born in

Middlesex. But it was yet another example of the sometimes curious but always interesting entertainment provided between the long speeches.

One of those speeches was about education, Sir John Goldney telling the diners:

> *They had in Swindon some of the greatest engineering works in the world (hear, hear). The importance of education was this, that, as Lord Methuen had stated, every boy in Wiltshire should be so educated that he would be enabled to enter those works and learn something about engineering, if that was his bent in life.*

It was noted that the musical entertainment again included two female singers, 'Miss Pollie Finn, of Swindon (soprano); Miss Gertrude Pryce Crewe, formerly of Swindon (soprano)'. And William Pennington got up again, to sing *The Bonnie Banks of Loch Lomond*.

The 1906 dinner, which was attended by 230 people, began with a review of the gathering's origins, exactly 20 years ago, with a reminder of its now-charitable nature:

In addition to arranging the annual dinner and concert, and a dance once a year, the Association has its benevolent side, and many men and women in the great city who have hailed from Wiltshire have had reason to be grateful to the Committee for most generous help rendered in times of need, as was instanced by the Secretary in his speech on Saturday evening.

The *Advertiser*'s report again made a record of what was on the menu, including 'thick and clear soup'.

With Earl Radnor presiding, there were the usual toasts and speeches about 'imperial forces' and Wiltshire volunteers, followed by a potentially controversial response from a Mr EP Hillier:

He was sorry to see there was a tendency – he was not going to speak politically, because one party was as bad as the other in this matter – to "coddle" the men. Why not leave them to their officers, who knew the men best, and who would never "bully" or badly serve them. When we heard of questions being put in Parliament as to whether our soldiers had enough to eat, whether they were flogged, etc, it was going too far. No one was the worse for a flogging (laughter), but the men very much felt the degradation of imprisonment.

Again, he said, leave the men to their officers… Boys should be taught how to use the rifle. If something was not done in this direction, conscription must come, or we should "go under."

The entertainment included the usual witty speech by Spencer Leigh Hughes, bassoon solos by Edwin James and, for the third year running, songs including two ladies: Madame Effie Thomas and Miss Winifred Dereham.

'Hitherto the Association has had a successful career,' said the *Advertiser*'s report of the 1907 dinner, 'though for some reason or other the attendance at Saturday night's function was not nearly so large as on some previous occasions.'

It was down to 150.

The honour of presiding fell to the Marquess of Ailesbury.

At the last minute, a family bereavement prevented the President, Sir Richard Burbidge, from attending, but he had arranged for each guest to receive a gift of cigars and cigarettes – even though he was not a smoker himself.

It wasn't the only freebie:

During the evening the booklet which has been issued by the Association was distributed for the first time. The little work consists of some 36 pages, and contains a well-written article on "Our County," by the proprietor and editor of the "Devizes and Wiltshire Gazette," while the hon Press correspondent of the Association (Mr D Clack, formerly of Swindon), contributes a brief history of the Society. The booklet is beautifully illustrated and nicely printed on art paper, and, in addition, gives the rules of the Association, together with its officers and members.

Unfortunately, no copy of this booklet is known to survive.

In a nod to the past, Mr J Templeman, one of the founders of the old Moonies'

dinner, and a vice-president of the Association, submitted the next toast, that of "The Visitors".

A notable aspect of this year's dinner, compared with normal, was the dearth of military talk – and what talk there was was quite negative.

Thomas Hooper Deacon, who traditionally spoke about the state of volunteer forces, took exception to what became known as *The Haldane Reforms*, begun in 1906 by Sir Richard Haldane.

These would include the formation of an expeditionary force to respond to major wars, and the reformation of the historic Volunteer Force and Yeomanry into Territorial Force and Special Reserve – which did not go down well with the conservative Mr Deacon. He said:

He had had the honour of belonging to the Wilts Yeomanry for 40 years (cheers), and he could assure his hearers that he viewed with a great deal of suspicion the Army scheme just thrown out by Mr Haldane. At present time the Yeomanry numbered 10,000 or 12,000 men, and he could not see how they were going to maintain that force and make themselves efficient on a less grant than they now received. At the present time the men received "a fiver" for their 18 days' training, and it was proposed to reduce the grant to 18s, and seeing that the class of men now in the Yeomanry was not the same as it used to be, and were not now so well able to bear the expenses – it could not possibly be done, and the result would be that the Yeomanry would be broken up.

From our modern perspective, Deacon's attitude seems to typify how ▶

political the annual dinner had become.

It appears to have become a bastion for old military and aristocratic powers and personalities who were trying to cling to their declining power in the face of modernisation and the inevitability of their eventually losing grip.

Britain was inching towards the First World War, which would change everything, and in hindsight, resistance to change was useless.

And there was a hint, in the *Advertiser*'s report, of other, further-reaching changes in the pipeline, to which even *The Association of Wiltshiremen in London* could not be immune to:

A number of ladies were present in the balcony during the speech-making and concert. By the way, it is possible that on future occasions the representatives of the fair sex will be partakers of the dinner, and not on-lookers merely.

The ladies didn't have much longer to wait; just a year, in fact, as the report of the 1908 dinner explained:

There was a very large assembly at the 21st annual dinner of Wiltshire-men in London, which was held last Saturday evening in the Venetian Chamber, Holborn Restaurant. A new feature about the gathering this year was the presence of ladies, who are now admitted as members of the Association, and consequently many availed themselves of the opportunity of attending the dinner for the first time.

There was even a toast to 'the ladies':

This ... was entrusted to Mr George Avenell, who said he rose to try and do justice to what was, after all, the toast of the evening. Formerly, one could speak to this toast without risk, but now-a-days ladies, like the birds in spring, had become vocal ... They welcomed the ladies that evening as all Wiltshiremen should do, and they were especially glad that the ladies had been promoted from the gallery where they used to sit as outlaws to "this floor of this House" (laughter). It was a promotion which they thoroughly deserved.

Ladies may have been welcomed, but they still weren't allowed to speak, and it was left to Spencer Leigh Hughes to respond to the toast on their behalf:

Mr Hughes remarked how pleased they were to have the ladies with them on that occasion. He asked a lady before he came into the dining hall that evening, what she would say in responding to this toast, and she replied with that kindness which marked the sex, "I should say how pleased we are to be here." Speaking for the men, he could say how pleased they were to have the company of the ladies. If the ladies enjoyed being there, the men enjoyed their presence far more, and hoped to see them there repeatedly for many years to come (applause).

Presiding was Lord Fitzmaurice of Bradford-on-Avon (pictured, left), the Under Secretary of State for Foreign Affairs.

One of his duties was to present a gold watch to Mr S Bown, 'who had served them most nobly and faithfully for a long period as the Treasurer of the Association but who had now removed from London to Peterborough.'

In acknowledging the present, and as well as saying he 'was glad to see the ladies present with them that evening':

Mr Bown mentioned that he was one of the oldest members of the Association, which was few in numbers when it started. It was a great pleasure to see such a large gathering [240, to be precise] that evening ... He thanked the subscribers most heartily. It had been a pleasure to see the Society advance as it had done.

It was the end of an era in another respect, too; no members of the James family (see page 96) were on hand to lead the entertainment.

But it did contain a new novelty: a banjo solo by George F Mathews.

Not only women, but a banjo, too!

The Association was on the up again, and 1909 saw another record-breaking turnout.

Around 300 were present in the 'magnificent' King's Hall of the Holborn Restaurant on March 13, with Col CEHA Colston, of Roundway Park, Devizes,

144

H.M. KING EDWARD VII.
SPECIAL TRAIN G.W.R.
PHOTOGRAPHED PASSING SWINDON.
AT 50 MILES PER HOUR.
HOOPER. SWINDON.

Although the speeches at the 1910 dinner recognised that Wiltshire had had 'the honour, both in North Wilts and South Wilts, in recent years, of visits from their Majesties, and [the Chairman] did not think that they could have received a heartier welcome in any part of the world,' they seemed reluctant to come to Swindon. Edward VII visited Calne, Chippenham and Bowood House in July 1907, then Salisbury in 1909, but despite being the largest town in the county, Swindon was overlooked by reigning monarchs until the visit of George V and Queen Mary in 1924. To rub salt into the wounds, the Railway Works produced carriages for the Royal Train, and townsfolk were given a tantalising glimpse of the King as his train rushed through in 1909, captured by Swindon photographer William Hooper (above). (Courtesy of Swindon Libraries/Local Studies and Paul Williams)

presiding, 'and a large number came from that district to support him'.

The first toast of the evening was to 'The Houses of Parliament', the Chairman noting there was talk of abolishing (or at least reforming) the House of Lords, but:

He was sure they would all feel proud as Englishmen of the Wiltshire representatives in the House of Lords [and although]... they did not enter into politics at that dinner... if he might express his own simple wish, it was that that House might endure for a very long time to come.

The presence of the ladies was still on everyone's mind, and Spencer Leigh Hughes said he was relieved to be proposing the toast to them, this year, rather than responding to the toast, which was the job of Thomas Hooper Deacon.

'It was a much more difficult thing to reply to it than to propose it,' said Hughes, 'because he... had to speak in ▶

their name at a time when ladies were saying all over the country that they could speak very well for themselves (laughter).'

Deacon said: 'The admission of ladies during the last two years had been one of the finest things inaugurated by the Association', before turning to the more pressing question of unemployment in Swindon:

He was perfectly certain they would be glad to hear that although one of that morning's papers gave a very depressed account of affairs at Swindon, things were not so bad as they were painted (hear, hear)... They all knew that in a manufacturing town like Swindon there was a certain amount of ups and downs. He had lived at Swindon, and had seen it quite as bad some 15, 16 or 17 years ago as now. Let them hope it would rally now as it did then... He would be sorry for Wiltshiremen and Wiltshire ladies to see their town of Swindon, with 50,000 inhabitants, go down in any way.

On a topical note, Honorary Secretary, GB Moore, 'said he would like to call attention to the relief granted last year, and this by the Society':

Last year they gave away £30 out of the funds of the Association for the relief of distressed Wiltshiremen in London. This year, up to that day, it was £30. It might be news to some that one of the objects of the Society was to assist distressed men of their County in London who were in that position through no fault of their own. ■

Football fantasies

The Moonies in London and its later incarnation, *The Association of Wiltshiremen in London*, had an uncanny knack of setting the date of their annual dinners to clash with big cup ties taking place in the capital on the same day.

We have already seen (see page 46) how they managed to be in the city for the appearance of two former Swindon Town players in a cup final involving Royal Arsenal in 1890.

Part of the reason was the football season finished much earlier than it does now – often in March, which was when the annual dinners were invariably arranged.

In 1905 it was noted that the 'English Cup Tie Final' (what we would now call the FA Cup final) coincided with the dinner, suggesting this would be an extra incentive for *Moonies* to travel up to London on the day – and reminding us there was a time when you could just turn up for a cup final and expect to get in!

Then, between 1910 and 1912, the dinners coincided with Swindon Town's greatest ever runs in the FA Cup.

In proposing a toast to the ladies at the 1910 dinner, Mr B Howard Cunnington:

pointed out the good effect of the presence of ladies at football matches. Not only had it a restraining influence on the men, but he hoped and believed that it was the presence of the ladies on the football ground at Swindon that had spurred the team on to win the English Cup.

He was getting carried away.

Exactly a week earlier they had won through to the semi-finals for the first time with a famous 2-0 win over Manchester City, and although George Avenell said: 'It was probable that if Swindon won the Cup, Wiltshiremen in London would hold a dinner on the night of the victory,' they were beaten 2-0 by Newcastle United at White Hart Lane.

But the Town came storming back the next season, and on March 11, 1911 (the very day of the Association's dinner), they faced Chelsea in the quarter-final (programme pictured, opposite).

This was thought to be one of the reasons for the record attendance at the dinner that year, 'for quite a large number of the County's sons who made the journey to Town to see the game very appropriately combined with it the pleasure of attending the "Moonies'" dinner in the evening'.

Sadly, Town lost again – 1-3, in front of 77,952 at Stamford Bridge, an attendance that underlined how huge football had become in the last couple of decades.

A year later, Town were back in the quarter-finals, and when the Association met for dinner on March 9, 1912, Mr RC Lambert MP said:

they had heard... that their County was prominent in military and naval matters and in public affairs, and might he be allowed to say in football also (hear, hear). He would draw their attention to the splendid victory which Swindon had won that day over Everton (loud applause).

They won 2-1 at home, so for the second time in three years (but also the last time in their history so far) they had reached the semi-finals of the FA Cup, where they would face Barnsley.

But there was to be no special Moonies dinner organised for winning the cup that year, either; Town drew 0-0, and lost the replay 0-1. ■

The CHELSEA F.C. Chronicle

OFFICIAL PROGRAMME

of The Chelsea Football & Athletic Company, Limited.

(Edited by " McW." of " The Wisdom Shop.")

[ENTERED AT STATIONERS' HALL.]

The Football League (Division 2). MEMBERS OF

South Eastern League (Division 1).

London League (Premier Division).

VOL. VI. No. 34.   Saturday, March 11th, 1911.   [ONE PENNY. POST FREE 1½D.

THE TRAGEDY OF THE FOURTH ROUND.

Both (aside): "It's a dirty trick to do, but it must be done."

Wiltshire sporting legends

Once a Moonie, always a Moonie – and once a sporting legend, always a sporting legend. Because one thing *The Association of Wiltshiremen in London* never forgot was the success of men born in the county.

So Walter George and Sir Kynaston Studd, who both wrote themselves into the sporting record books (and were both born in 1858), were welcomed to the Association's annual dinner, years after they had made the headlines.

We have already met Walter

George briefly – he lost one of his records to James Kibblewhite (see page 83) – but it is worth finding out more about an athlete who rewrote the record books on his favourite training diet of 'a glass of beer with bread and cheese'.

Walter was born in Calne, where his father Frederick was a chemist with premises on The Strand.

By 1881, he had moved to London and was working as an assistant chemist, having already established himself as a formidable amateur athlete. Over a period of six years he won a dozen AAA Championships – said to be the highest number ever to have been gained by one man.

He first secured the amateur World Mile record in 1880, in a time of four minutes, 23.2 seconds, then lowered it by nearly four seconds in 1882, before resetting it again, to four minutes, 18.4 seconds, in 1884. This record held until it was beaten by Irish runner, Thomas Conneff, in 1893.

It is claimed that, at the age of 26, George had set records for all distances from 1,500 yards to 12 miles. He also won the national cross country titles in 1882 and 1884, the year before he turned professional.

By the time he was a guest for the *Moonies* in 1910, his running career was over, but some of his records still stood.

He is best remembered for breaking the world mile record on August 23, 1886, in a professional challenge race against holder William Cummings at Fulham, in front of 20,000 spectators; his time: four minutes, 12.75 seconds. This record was not surpassed by anyone until 1915.

Opposite (left): three famous Studd brothers, with Kynaston far left. Opposite (right): Kynaston Studd carrying the Union Jack at the 1908 Olympics in London. Right: two artist's impressions of athlete Walter George.

The winner of 'over a thousand cups and medals', his training regime, called "100-up" involved running in place with high knee lifts, springing, and taking baths in brine.

He went on to have a second career in the retail chemist trade and as a chemical manufacturer, eventually passing away at his home in Mitcham, Surrey, aged 84.

He was inducted into the English Athletics Hall of Fame in 2010, and plaques recording his world record are to be found on Calne's Town Hall and at The Recreation Ground.

Kynaston Studd, who attended two annual dinners in the 1930s, was the first man to carry the Union Jack at the opening ceremony of the Olympics – in London, in 1908.

Born in Netheravon, he spent part of his childhood at Tedworth House in

Tidworth, which was leased to his father, Edward Studd, a wealthy indigo planter/manufacturer and racehorse owner, from 1871 to 1876.

He went to Eton and Trinity College, Cambridge, where he became well-known as one of the three Studd brothers who captained the university cricket team over consecutive seasons.

In 1882 all three brothers were in the Cambridge University side that beat the great Australian touring team by six wickets.

Kynaston was a cricket 'Blue' from 1881 to 1884, and captain in 1884.

He was also a businessman, became Chairman of Regent Street Polytechnic (now the University of Westminster), and was closely involved with volunteer soldiers, which earned him an OBE.

He was knighted in 1923, and became Baronet of Netheravon in the County of Wiltshire in 1929.

He was Sheriff for London (1922-3), Lord Mayor of London (1928-9), and was elected President of the MCC (which he said was his best achievement) in 1930. ■

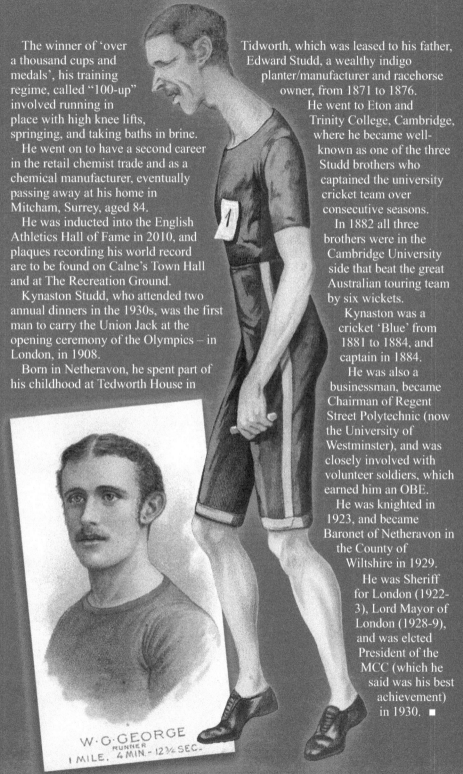

W·G·GEORGE
RUNNER
1 MILE, 4 MIN. - 12¾ SEC.

These troublous times...

In 1910, the annual dinner was once again held in the King's Hall of the Holborn Restaurant, and although no official attendance figure was given, it was 'a gratifying advance of popularity on previous years'.

It was also noted that:

The percentage of ladies appeared to be larger than ever and added much to the brilliance of the occasion, whilst it was pleasing to have the presence in person of Mr R Burbidge (president of the association), who made his customary gifts to the guests – chocolate to the ladies, and cigars and cigarettes to the gentlemen.

In the chair was the Earl of Pembroke (pictured, above), and as if to underline the exalted status of the top table, the list of those present read like a *Who's Who*, including the High Sheriff of Wilts, not one but two mayors (of Swindon and Devizes), and Thornton Lawes, Secretary of *The Wiltshire Society*. It had become the place to be seen.

However, for an organisation that was supposed to be apolitical, the annual dinners seemed to be preoccupied with the Houses of Parliament. They had been the subject of speeches for several years, and in 1910 were toasted for the fourth year in a row.

Speakers, often including chairmen who had a seat in the House of Lords, and other speakers who were Members of Parliament, used the platform to push their opinions.

The Mayor of Devizes, Capt Thompson, said 'they were told… the House of Lords was to go on the scrap heap,' adding that, there, he was 'quite certain that anybody would acknowledge that nowhere in the world would they find a class of man more patriotic or more loyal to their country'.

If it had all become rather conservative and sycophantic, at least they had the musical entertainment to look forward to, or 'the harmony of the evening' as it was called in 1910.

And – true to form – the lady singers were a hit again, namely 'Miss Mary Jarvis Finn (who sang Elgar's "Land of Hope and Glory," the company joining in the refrain), Miss Nellie Viveash, Miss Doris Elton and Miss Eugenie Boland.'

In 1911, the man of the moment was the President, Richard Burbidge, who was celebrating half a century in the capital, and this apparently modest and shy man was at last persuaded to 'occupy the chair'.

As usual, he was generous with his gifts to all those attending – 'handsome silver trinket boxes being handed to the ladies [pictured opposite, courtesy of Harrods Company Archive], and dainty boxes of cigars and cigarettes to the gentlemen'.

Getting up to reply to the toast of 'Houses of Parliament', Mr G Terrell MP 'said he had strict orders not to talk about politics (laughter)'. But he was too late.

The man who had raised the toast, Daniel Long, had already taken up the theme of recent dinners, saying 'a good deal of controversy raged about' the House of Lords, but took the opportunity for a swipe at the House of Commons as he 'referred to the previous Thursday evening's scenes in the Lower House, and said the members appeared to have acted like a lot of schoolboys'.

The good news was this controversy of the last couple of years was coming to an end. It would be resolved in the following August, with the Parliament Act 1911, which ended the Upper Chamber's right to permanently veto the Supply Bills that set taxation and government spending, also reducing the maximum term of a government from seven years to five.

It was a crucial moment in the modernisation of British democracy, marked another erosion of the powers of the upper class – and underlined how much of a microcosm of society and political debate *The Association of Wiltshiremen in London* had become over the last 20 years.

Onlookers might have been excused for

concluding that what had started as a humble movement among honest working men had been 'hijacked' by the privileged and the wealthy, and that their usurping of the Association showed how desperate they were to hang on to the influence they enjoyed in a terminally declining British Empire.

But for all of the (what might seem to us) tiresome debates over Parliamentary power and military strength, this was a period when attendances at the annual dinners were increasing.

This year

there would be a new record attendance set –and one that would never be equalled: a staggering 530 men and women that must have seen even the King's Hall bursting at the seams.

As was now customary, there was a toast to 'the ladies', but the Association clearly still didn't think it was appropriate to let them reply to it themselves.

The year's entertainment was novel:

Some first-class musical talent was engaged for the evening, and an excellent programme was provided. Particularly enjoyable were the contributions by the Greek Male Choir, who have lately been appearing at the Coliseum. Resplendent in their brightly-coloured native dress, they sang most delightfully with the accompaniment of mandolins, and so charmed the audience by their sweetness of tone... that they were enthusiastically encored. ▶

The Chairman of the 1912 dinner was Walter H Long MP (pictured, below).

Although born in Bath, Long was descended from Wiltshire gentry, and would become Viscount Long of Wraxall (Wiltshire) in 1921.

In a political career spanning five decades, he would serve as President of the Board of Agriculture, President of the Local Government Board, Chief Secretary for Ireland, Secretary of State for the Colonies, and First Lord of the Admiralty. He was also the leader of the Irish Unionist Party in the House of Commons between 1906 and 1910.

Long was something of the prodigal son to *The Association of Wiltshiremen in London*. They had been keen to get him to chair one of their annual dinners for years. He declined invitations in 1897 and 1899 because he was too busy, and in 1902, when he had been billed as the Presiding Chairman, he had to pull out because of illness.

He was often praised in his absence, and clearly revered by many of those present at dinners over a number of years, both for his Parliamentary prowess and as an officer in the Royal Wiltshire Yeomanry – a Major from 1890, and Lieutenant-Colonel in command from 1898 to 1906.

He was finally able to attend a dinner in 1911, but as Richard Burbidge was in the chair then, he had to wait until 1912 before finally becoming Chairman.

The first business of the day were the apologies for absence, and as if to emphasis the odd juxtaposition of upper and working class *Moonies*, they included letters from five Lords who were unable to attend, and 'a telegram from the Devizes Working Men's Club'.

The gathering clouds of war were evident for the first time, or – as Sir John Goldney put it:

In troublous times such as we were now in, the toast of the Forces of our great Empire must necessarily be an important one. The whole world seemed to be in a state of unrest, like a troubled sea, which could not rest – from China to the Mediterranean. In China, the oldest Empire in the world, they were suffering from a great upheaval. Coming nearer home, there were the three kingdoms of Spain, France and Italy, all in a state of unrest. Italy was already at war, and the other countries were grumbling... At any moment a war might break out, in which our own great Empire would inevitably be compelled to take part.

Also, Sir John assured them:

He had no hesitation in saying that no better Colonel of the Wiltshire Yeomanry ever existed than their present Chairman, Mr Walter Long (loud cheers). He was a born leader of men. There were very few men, not in Wiltshire only, but throughout England, who did not believe that that great Wiltshireman was the right man to lead our country... back to a position of prosperity (applause).

When the Chairman got up to speak, he insisted 'the gathering was strictly a non-political one (hear, hear)', and spoke of national and local patriotism instead, telling everyone of the beauty of Wiltshire, but also: 'if it did not contain London, it contained Swindon (applause). They could not only boast of Swindon, but boast of Devizes.'

Mr BH Cunnington responded with a humorous speech in which he claimed 'Wiltshire is the centre of the universe, and… the Garden of Eden was located there.' And he spoke for 'those miserable outcasts, 'Wiltshiremen in London':

This vast city now has come to be a city of smoke and taxicabs and underground rabbit burrows and mole runs, and I sympathise with those who are forced to live here by the necessity, I suppose, of getting their bread and cheese (laughter).

What a contrast it is to us Wiltshiremen in Wilts, who can just run out of our back doors and get to the top of the Wiltshire Downs. I assure you gentlemen who are banished from the County that you have a warm place in our hearts, and if ever you get to a warmer place, then Heaven help you!! (loud laughter).

They were brought back down to earth by the Chairman, who said the President 'was right when he said that a change had come over the scene in our old land. He hoped that change would work its own way out, and our country come safely through the struggle in which it was now engaged, and not be materially worse'.

And a change had come over the Association too, although nobody noticed during the evening – or at least the report of the dinner failed to mention it. For the first time, none of the four founders of *The Moonies in London* were present at the annual dinner (although Frank Wallington would return, one last time, to the dinner of 1913).

'The King's Hall, the largest and the most beautifully-appointed hall of the Holborn Restaurant, London,' said the *North Wilts Herald* in March 1913, 'was the scene on Saturday of a notable assembly. The occasion was the 26th annual dinner of the Society of Wiltshiremen in London [sic] – a Society which keeps green the memory of cherished associations in the worthiest manner – and the function may be written down as one of the most successful ever held.'

Colonel Calley was presiding, and the 460 in attendance were informed it was the second largest function of its kind 'in the metropolis', and 'he hoped that soon even the Holborn Restaurant would not be big enough and that they would have to take the Crystal Palace to hold their annual dinner (laughter)'.

Nevertheless:

The hall, which is well lit by electricity, presented a brilliant appearance, and the bright uniforms of Karoly Klay's Red Band, which occupied the balcony, gave a pleasing touch of colour to the scene.

Other musical entertainment was provided with solos and 'capital songs', while 'The Seth Weeks Trio of Coon Singers also contributed some pleasing items to the programme.'

Whether Seth Weeks (pictured, below) self-styled his trio as 'Coon Singers' is doubtful, but the authors' research has shown no other similar reference during his career, and we can only assume that it is an unfortunate reflection of attitudes in that era to black people and particularly black entertainers.

But we can be quite sure that Seth Weeks and his colleagues were the first non-white people to attend a dinner of *The Moonies in London/The Association of Wiltshiremen in London*. Born in Washington, USA, Weeks went on several tours of Europe, and in 1913 was living in London.

It was not the first time the annual dinner was blessed with a musician of international renown, although it was as one of the greatest mandolin players of his era (in what was known as the 'golden age' of the mandolin) that Weeks was revered, and he was also a composer. So it seems probable that he was playing mandolin that night, even though the report somehow failed to mention it.

This year's dinner revealed how many had made the journey up from Swindon, when the Honorary Secretary, GB Moore, talked about the work of the committee:

At Swindon, this function was discharged by Mr Eddie Thomas, Mr EJ Randell, and Mr JW Haggard, and their efforts in inducing the GWR to run an excursion train was much appreciated by those who availed themselves of the facility. A party of about forty ladies and gentlemen made the journey from Swindon.

President Richard Burbidge, who had missed the previous year's dinner and was again prevented from attending 'by doctor's orders', nevertheless felt obliged to send 'handsome' gifts to everyone attending:

Each gentleman was provided with "smokes" (cigars and cigarettes enclosed in a neat and nicely-inscribed cardboard box), and each lady was the recipient of a valuable and handsomely embossed trinket box, containing a bottle of scent.

The *Advertiser*'s report of the dinner included a curious remark: 'The speeches which were built round the conventional toasts, did not quite reach the excellence of former years', although the reporter did not elaborate on which speaker(s) caused his displeasure.

Perhaps it was the controversial figure of Mr JH (Jimmy) Thomas MP, who began by saying he had attended the 1907 annual dinner (which is not confirmed by the report of the dinner in that year), but was speaking for the first time in 1913.

It would be the first of many.

The *Advertiser* quoted him as saying: ▶

153

He was an engine-driver stationed at Swindon, and, moreover, he was proud of the fact (applause). He was not there that evening to apologise for the class he represented, because he believed he was expressing the sentiments of every one present when he said it would be a bad day for this country when the working-classes failed to have a voice in the govern-ment of this country (applause).

Thomas then said:

He need hardly say how delighted he was to know that the crisis through which they had passed during the last fortnight was now happily at an end (hear, hear).

It is not clear which crisis, in particular, Thomas was referring to, but there were indications in the speech that he was referring to ever-worsening industrial relations, which often involved railway workers.

But in these 'troublous times' there were plenty of other crises: not least the spectre of European war on the horizon, but also Britain's dwindling influence on the world stage, the increasingly irresistible drive for Home Rule in Ireland, and the women's suffrage movement.

On March 7, 1914, less than five months before the outbreak of the First World War, *The Association of Wiltshire-men in London* sat down for what would be their final pre-war dinner, with between 400 and 500 attending.

The Earl of Kerry was in the chair, and he told the diners:

Only a few months ago he had the honour of presiding at the annual dinner of The Wiltshire Society, and although that society could give points to the Society of Wiltshiremen in London, the latter society had a strong lead in the matter of

attendance, as that assembly testified. The societies were in no sense competitive; there was plenty of room for both, and as there was no reason to suppose that there would be any falling off in the birth rate, he hoped that as time went on, both societies would continue their excellent work.

Any historians looking back to the evening and expecting the 1914 diners to be gearing up for the increasingly likely catastrophic war ahead would be mistaken. They seem more distracted by old themes than ever, including reviving 'Houses of Parliament' as a subject they thought was worthy of a toast and lengthy debate. The Mayor of Devizes (Mr H Sainsbury) gave them a history lesson on the subject, along with various Wiltshiremen's roles in it over the years. This was the signal for Mr Bathurst MP to enter into a very long discourse on the Second Chamber.

Despite all of Britain's prob-lems, and although they were now less than half a year away from world war, the power struggle between the two chambers in Westminster was still pre-occupying the Association.

It was left to Sir John Goldney to bring them down to earth. He:

remarked that all were aware that the country was passing through a most grave and serious crisis. "The

eyes of our country and the eyes of our county," he declared, "are fixed upon one man and that man is a Wiltshireman – Lord Lansdowne" (applause).

Never in his (the speaker's) lifetime, nor in the history of the country, had such a responsibility been placed upon the shoulders of one man, but he believed that man – Lord Kerry's father – was competent and able to bear that responsibility. It would be fitting if Lord Kerry would convey to Lord Lansdowne the sympathy which Wiltshiremen had with him in his onerous and respon-sible position (hear, hear).

"I personally have no doubt," he said, "that this Wiltshireman will be able to keep his hand to the helm of the vessel of State and bring her through this storm... to harbour in calmer waters."

Goldney spoke as if Lansdowne (pictured, left) was Prime Minister; in fact he was leader of the Conservative Party in the Lords, at a time when there was a Liberal government.

War could not be prevented by one man now, and certainly not by him; he would become infamous for *The Lansdowne Letter*, which he wrote to the *Daily Telegraph* in November 1917, calling for a negotiated peace with Germany. ■

Edith, Queen of the 'window smashers'

Despite it being a big issue of the times, *The Association of Wiltshiremen in London* didn't have much to say about the women's suffrage movement – and (with one exception) it was negative.

In 1912, Chairman Walter H Long MP told diners that 'he might say his wife was not a window smasher'.

She was never mentioned by name, but this appears to refer to Swindon-born suffragette Edith New, who was given two months in Holloway Prison for throwing stones through the windows of 10 Downing Street in 1908.

A year after's Long's comment, senior railwayman and respected voluntary military man, Captain Frederick Wright, joined in, the *Advertiser* reporting:

he could not help feeling what an excellent idea it was when the Committee started inviting ladies to the function. "If we took the ladies out to dine more often than we do, we should hear the last of the Suffragettes," observed the speaker, amid laughter.

At the same dinner, Basil Peto MP appeared to refer to suffragettes when he said: 'The ladies of England were worthy of their admiration and esteem, and it was only the rare exceptions who were running the great risk of diminishing that respect and esteem.'

Then, later in the evening, Jimmy Thomas MP, gave a different perspective when he was required to respond to a toast of 'the ladies':

"And now," proceeded Mr Thomas, "I cease to be a man; I am called upon to reply to the toast on behalf of my sex, the ladies (loud laughter)... We don't want anything from the men. Give us our rights, and we will return those of our own sex to British Parliament, and then we will stop some of your all-night sittings... The way you have treated us is simply monstrous, and we are not going to be hoodwinked by mere words at a dinner of this description. You invited us here because you knew we were coming, whether you liked it or no (laughter), and not even the nice present from our worthy President is going to prevent us from carrying on our agitation in favour of equal rights of citizenship with the male sex" (laughter and applause). ∎

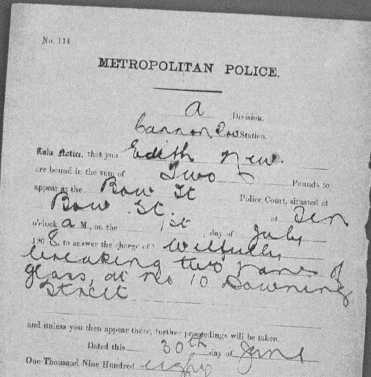

Left: the charge sheet raised when Swindon-born suffragette Edith New (pictured, above) was arrested for throwing stones through the windows of 10 Downing Street. It followed a Women's Day rally in Hyde Park, London, on June 21, 1908, where Edith was a key speaker, and which attracted an estimated 250,000 visitors. (Courtesy of Swindon Libraries/Local Studies)

Wiltshiremen and women at war

'For the present, all social gatherings have been abandoned'.

It was November 1914, four months after the outbreak of the First World War, and the committee of *The Association of Wiltshiremen in London* were meeting to discuss its response.

There would be no more annual dinners for more than five years, but that didn't stop the work of the organisation going on, with the focus on relieving distress at home in Wiltshire and in London.

Although no minutes or other documents survive from the Association's wartime meetings, sporadic press reports of those meetings, which were held at the Holborn Restaurant, give us snapshots of their activities.

There was a new Chairman: Edward Hillier, who was originally from Avebury, but had moved to Wimbledon by 1911, where he was the manager of a steel plate manufacturers.

The war years would be a torrid time for Hillier as his wife Edith, who was one of the first lady members of the Association, died in 1917, aged 46.

It appears that money was drawn off the Association's holdings during the war, while a separate fund was created for donations, and although social gatherings for their own sake were banned, the *Moonies* did, for example, organise a whist drive to generate more money, and probably other fundraisers.

They became early supporters of *The Prince of Wales Fund*, an appeal for relief for families experiencing difficulties because the male breadwinner was on active service.

They would also consider and sometimes grant money to individual cases:

A somewhat sad case of distress was reported by the hon treasurer, Mr T Palmer, and it was unanimously decided to make a grant of £2.6d per week for 26 weeks.

But they also became part of a gigantic national initiative on the 'Home Front', which saw various projects launched, many of which were led and run by women, such as one in Swindon and district that provided food for prisoners of war, and eventually earned its leader, Mary Slade, the MBE.

The Association supported a similar scheme that was initially led by Lady Heytesbury, quickly donating five guineas to the cause.

And when she had to retire from the project, they continued to send money to Mrs AR Steward, the wife of a colonel, who took it over, based at The Depot, Devizes.

In October 1915, she took time to write to the committee with her thanks:

We send away large numbers of parcels every week to the Prisoners of War of the Wiltshire Regiment, and from all the German camps where Wiltshires are interned we have very grateful letters, and in many of them they specially ask that their thanks may be conveyed to the kind friends whose liberal support of this fund has enabled us to send such supplies of food and comforts.

We send extra comforts of all kinds to the fighting battalions; there are now 4 battalions at the front, 1st,

2nd, 6th in Flanders, and the 5th at the Dardanelles. So you see we are very grateful for help, as we like to do as much as possible for all.

It is splendid work visiting the wounded in hospital, for one feels that they have all done their best, and held up the honour of the regiment.

In December 1915, after receiving a cheque for £65, Mrs Steward wrote to say that each man had been sent 'a pair of socks, a shirt, a plum pudding, a cake, a tin of beef, 200 cigarettes and a little tobacco.'

She also helped the Association locate men who were recovering from injuries in hospitals in London.

In February 1915, committee member HJ Tydeman visited Wilts Regiment solider Pte H Carter at Princess Alexandrda's Hospital in London, and found wounded soldiers wanted for little, although the committee did decide to present him with a walking stick, engraved with the words: 'Presented to Pte H Carter, of the 1st Wilts Regiment, by the Wiltshiremen in London, as a memento of the Great War – February 1915.'

It seems it was this visit that persuaded the committee to begin morale-boosting visits to wounded Wiltshiremen in London. There was a strong belief in the idea that soldiers in hospital were especially boosted by visits from people from their home town or county.

An update in January 1916, stated:

Members of the committee reported on their visits to the wounded of the Wiltshire Regiment in the London hospitals. All appreciated the good treatment they were receiving in the hospitals, and their only requests were for walking sticks, pipes, cigarettes and fruit. It was decided to continue the work.

It seems Wiltshire's was one of the first in what became a national movement among county associations and other local groups, as the committee were told in August 1917:

There are over 100 hospitals for the wounded in London. At each there is a lady commissioner who daily makes a return to the central offices of the men admitted. Post-cards giving hospital, number of ward, hours of visiting, man's name, regiment and native town and county, are then sent to the Secretary of the County Society, who forwards the card to the member of his Committee who is visiting that particular hospital, so that in two days a visitor is at the patient's bedside. It gives pleasure to the patient, especially if the visitor is a fellow "towny".

Wiltshire committee members again reported on their experience, and:

One man stated all he required was "a piece of decent soap", another wanted a safety razor so he might shave himself as he lay in bed, a third "just a few fags." In each case their wants were supplied.

By 1918, the committee was informed that there were now 128 hospitals in the capital for wounded soldiers.

On July 6, 1918, a report about the Association in the *Wiltshire Times* said 'an energetic hospital visitor' called

Percy Lapper Morse had been killed in action, aged 31.

In fact, he had died of wounds, the previous November, while serving as a 2nd Lieutentant with the Gloucestershire Regiment, and is buried at St Sever Cemetery, Rouen.

Morse, a solicitor, was the son of Levi Lapper Morse, the second Mayor of Swindon, who had also been an MP and had attended two annual dinners of the Association.

The dead soldier's childhood home was The Croft, Swindon.

The same report also made reference to Harold Nicholls, a committee member who had died in action the previous December (see page 158).

Although newspaper reports give the impression that the hospital visiting scheme was carried out by committee members only, in fact it was a much wider effort. When the Association were finally able to enjoy an annual dinner again, in January 1920, its chaplain, Rev Mills Robbins, pointed out that it involved 250 men and women.

This was immediately followed by a toast and a speech by Mr SE Walters that suggested that the efforts of the ladies during the war should lead to a change of attitude towards them in the Association:

The toast of "The Ladies" was submitted by Mr SE Walters. He said a great deal had been made about what the men had done during the past five years, but he thought he was not far wrong when he said it was the ladies who made it possible for the men to do what they had done.

They were surprised to find how

much the ladies had accomplished. He had taken a considerable interest in public work, particularly in his native town of Swindon, and he could speak with knowledge – considerable knowledge – of the work the ladies did in the great war which had just been brought to such a successful completion...

The Chairman had mentioned that... Wiltshire had produced some of the finest men the country had ever known, [but]... Wiltshire was proud of what its ladies had done.

When he remembered the great amount of Red Cross work Wiltshire ladies had done, the amount of money raised for charity and for the Wiltshire prisoners of war in Germany, he knew what the women had accomplished, and he was proud to be the civic head of the town which was the chief industrial centre of a county that had accomplished what Wiltshire had.

This was the signal for Mr CE Churchill, who was described as 'the ladies' champion', to have his say:

He was rather surprised that now the ladies had come into a measure of their right, one of them had not been asked to respond to the toast. They had obtained the vote, invaded the House of Commons and the magisterial bench, and were rapping at the ancient portals of the House of Lords and the Bar, and he thought one of them would be capable of replying on their own behalf. ■

915-1919

Hero Moonies' ultimate sacrifice

The First World War was just about to enter its final year when Royal Flying Corps corporal, Harold John Nicholls, was killed.

Nicholls, a bank clerk who was originally from Ashton Keynes, but had moved to Middlesex, was briefly a member of *The Association of Wiltshiremen in London*'s committee when he was lost, presumed drowned.

He was on board a former Royal Mail vessel that had been converted into the troopship, *HMT Aragon*, and was lying off the coast of Alexandria, Egypt, waiting for its escort.

According to some versions of the story, it was unable to enter the safe haven of Alexandria because of the suspected presence of mines.

Until then it had been an uneventful voyage from Marseilles for the *Aragon*, and had included a Christmas 1917 stopover at Malta for the 2,700 people on board, which included a contingent of 160 nurses. Then, at around 11am on December 30, and in very rough seas, the ship was hit by a torpedo fired by a German U-boat.

According to one of the nurses, who was writing to her parents:

I was down below, preparing for church service. Suddenly a fearful shock and our bonnie ship was hit under the aft-swell deck... Everybody was perfectly calm – not the slightest panic... We were marched into the boats and were lowered into the water, the Tommies who were left on deck cheering us when we reached the water safely.

Troops were lined up on deck and sang *Keep the Homes Fires Burning* while the boat listed, now obviously sinking.

One survivor later said: "I have heard the chorus 'Keep the home fires burning'

on many occasions, but I don't think I have ever heard it given with so much power."

Around 17 minutes after being hit, the boat sank, with the loss of 610 men, including Nicholls, who was days short of his 35th birthday. There was a second explosion as the ship's boilers touched the cold water.

His entry in the register of effects of dead servicemen shows Nicholl's body was never found.

The *Aragon*'s Captain, Francis Bateman, went down with his ship. According to witnesses, when he realised the sinking was imminent, he shouted: "Every man for himself, and God be with you."

Tragically, one of the ships that rushed to the aid of the *Aragon*, the destroyer *HMS Attack*, was also torpedoed, while alongside the stricken ship, and with up to 400 *Aragon* survivors on board.

It was literally blown in two, with both parts of the ship sinking within seven minutes. However, most of those on board the destroyer escaped, with only ten lost.

There is an irony to Nicholls being lost on the *Aragon* because there were a large number of railwaymen on board from the 96th Light Railway Operating Company, a unit formed by the Royal Engineers to lay narrow gauge track for the transportation of materials and men, to and from front lines.

And 76 of them perished.

Their ranks were made up from men with experience of working with at least ten difference railway companies, including the GWR.

Even worse was to follow for the Royal Engineers, the next day, when another troopship, SS Osmanieh, struck a mine, causing the loss of another 54 men from the 98th Light Railway Operating Company. ■

Above: Percy Lapper Morse's 'death penny', presented to his family after he died of wounds (see page 157). Opposite (top): a postcard of the *Aragon* when she was a mail ship. Opposite (bottom): the register of effects recording Harold Nicholl's death.

S.S. ARAGON OFF THE LIZARD.

THE ROYAL MAIL Cº.

Oilette

Neville-Cumming

W6126. R2060/8/17—100 Bks.—Wt. & Sons, Ltd 1284

Record No.	Registry No.	Soldier's Name	Regiment, Rank, No.	Date and Place of Death	Account and Date	CREDITS		
						£	s.	d.
671651	587489	Nicholls. Harold. John.	R. F. C. Cpl. 106748.	30.12.17. Woking (Officially accepted) believed drowned.	Woking 6/18. 1/19	√ 11 √ 4	17 —	1.

How we won the war

The Association of Wiltshiremen in London were finally able to put the First World War behind them and return to holding their annual dinners on January 24, 1920.

The attendance was down on pre-war dinners, but possibly only because they were unable to book the King's Hall in the Holborn Restaurant, and had to settle for the smaller Royal Venetian Chamber.

That meant some applications for tickets had to be refused, and even those lucky enough to get one couldn't necessarily be squeezed in to dine, only being admitted to the main gathering for the concert and speechmaking'.

Because of the death of Sir Richard Burbidge in 1917, there was a new President (who was also Chairman): Lord Roundway, who 'for a great many years had cheerfully borne the responsibilities of a very great landowner in the county, and chiefly in Devizes'.

The first speech was given to firebrand

MP, Jimmy Thomas (see page 162), who had the difficult job of summarising the war, and what lessons might be learned.

Despite the later controversy over the role of Field Marshal Douglas Haig, 1st Earl Haig, the commander of the British Expeditionary Force, Thomas gave him a warm tribute:

He would like to pay a word of tribute to the leader of the Army – the present Lord Haig – for the calm and deliberate manner in which he dealt with everything, no matter what the circumstances were. On one occasion he (the speaker) was talking to Lord Haig and told him that people in England were dismayed and alarmed with the outlook. His lordship's reply was that he had proved the men who were serving under him, and if they trusted them all would come right. Then, when the war was over and the victory was won, Sir Douglas'... first consideration was not for himself. He (the speaker) could say now that it was a fact that Sir Douglas abso-lutely refused all honours for himself, for he said his first duty was to those who had won the battles and enabled him to be so successful (applause). He hoped others would also think of the soldiers and sailors and not forget them now that the war was over.

For the first time, the Royal Air Force were toasted:

No-one five years ago, when it was in its infancy, thought there would be the wonderful development which the Air Force had made, and he thought every credit was due to the those men and boys for that great development.

Another MP, Sir Frederick Young, was next to stand up, and – given the spectacle of trench warfare and other horrors produced by the war, paid a bizarre tribute to the 'gallant and chivalrous conduct of the troops in France and elsewhere'.

One curious topic to come out of the annual dinner was the prospect of 'pilot-less planes'. Although not mentioned in the *North Wilts Herald*'s account, the *Birmingham Gazette* reported:

Speaking at a dinner of the Wiltshire-men in London, at the Holborn Restaurant... Mr JH Thomas, MP, referred to aviation work in the war, and said that the development in fighting aircraft was so great that, had the war continued, we could have sent aeroplanes up without pilots.

They were, indeed, developed in Britain and the United States during the First World War (pictured, left, courtesy of the Imperial War Museum). Britain's was called Aerial Target, and became the world's first 'drone' to fly under radio control, although it was not used operationally. Appropriately, it first flew at Upavon, Wiltshire, in 1917.

At the 1921 dinner, there was some disappointment at the failure to reach pre-war attendance figures, but one reason was the inability of many people from the county to get up to London and home the same day, apparently because of a lack of late trains. Although they were back in the roomy King's Hall, the attendance was around 300.

The aristocracy were still in the driving seats; the President was still Lord Round-way, and the Chairman was the 6th Earl of Radnor. There was no sign of Jimmy Thomas this year – but he would be back.

Earl Radnor waxed lyrical about the beauty of Wiltshire and its 'old-world towns', even giving Swindon a mention, and referring to 'our people, perhaps not very quick in the up-take, but shrewd, solid and always cheerful.'

George Terrell, MP for Chippenham (although not for very much longer) told the diners: 'The people he met in London… were really, as a whole, a most gloomy and dismal lot, but when he went down to Wiltshire they seemed quite smiling, merry and bright.'

But it seemed he hadn't received the note about the Association avoiding politics as he offered his opinion on the current 'black and gloomy outlook':

Every day produced a change of some kind or another, and he was full of hope that everything would turn out well… In spite of our grievances, Wiltshiremen as a whole were doing their bit. We had none of that industrial unrest and threats of revolution. We did not hear in Wiltshire of Lenin and Trotsky, and no one wanted to follow the example these men had set. We were all trying to do our best, and Wiltshire to-day was a fair example of what the great mass of feeling was in the country. Of course it was very easy to find fault. Labour was finding fault, the employers were finding fault, the consumer was finding fault, and the Government was perhaps not in quite as happy a condition as that in which it might be. Yet he firmly believed that considering what our country had gone through… that we were doing as well, if not better, than any other country in the world, and it was the sound common sense of our people that was pulling us through.

The *Wiltshire Times*' report offered no information on the musical (or any other) entertainment, and it was left to Alderman Jones, the Mayor of Swindon, to submit the toast of 'the ladies'.

But they were still not allowed to answer for themselves. ∎

Fireman, firebrand and friend

He was neither born in Swindon, nor did he die there. In fact, he only lived in the town for a paltry six years.

So why is it that the man dubbed 'The Artful Dodger' and whose remains repose in Radnor Street Cemetery, is regarded by many as one of the most prominent Swindonians of the early 20th century?

His rise from a disadvantaged background all the way to the Cabinet and the Privy Council would be noteworthy if it happened today – let alone 90 years ago.

His is a remarkable rags-to-riches story; of heroic working class struggle, unswerving ambition and awe-inspiring political nous. But it is also a story of commendable and enduring public service – even if it did all end in disgrace and censure.

James Henry 'Jimmy' Thomas was born in Newport, Monmouthshire, on October 3, 1874, the son of an unmarried mother. He left school at the age of 12 and, after a few menial jobs, joined the GWR, aged 15, in his hometown – initially as an engine cleaner, although subsequently rising to fireman.

Jimmy joined the Amalgamated Society of Railway Servants (ASRS) not long after he started work on the railway, eventually becoming chairman of his local union branch, aged just 23, in 1897.

This was a sign of things to come.

In 1899, Jimmy was moved to Swindon, and it was thought to be more about allowing the GWR greater visibility of this emerging union firebrand than career advancement. In other words:

they wanted to keep an eye on him. Indeed, he certainly didn't transfer for promotion because he stayed as a fireman for some while, only later securing the lowest rank of driver, known as pilotman, in 1902.

He was never assigned to the main line and remained for the most part on shunting duties. Later that year he became president of the Swindon Trades Council.

The 1901 Census records him as residing at 6 Salisbury Street, with his wife Agnes and one-year-old son, Anthony.

His growing family spent all their time in the Broadgreen area, also living for a while at 16 Manchester Road and 32 Broad Street.

And it was in Swindon that he made his initial forays into politics, winning Queens ward for the Labour Party in the 1901 council elections, and going on to serve as Chairman of the Finance and Law Committee during 1904/5, and Chairman of the Electricity and Tramways Committee in 1905/6.

In addition to his day job, family responsibilities and roles in local government, Jimmy continued to pursue his union activities. In 1903, aged 28, he joined the National Executive Committee of the ASRS, eventually becoming their youngest ever President in 1905.

But Jimmy was burning the candle at both ends, and there is a story that he was even once found asleep on the footplate. Perhaps it was the grudging respect shown by his departmental chief WH Stanier that meant he wasn't sacked on the spot.

Tragedy was to strike in 1905, though, when his 18-month-old daughter, Lilian May, passed away.

Such was Jimmy's growing reputation, that even the great Keir Hardie (soon to be the first leader of the Labour Party) interrupted a journey to alight at Swindon station and personally extend his condolences to the family.

A year later Jimmy took up the full-time role of organising secretary, and it was this that led him to take the difficult decision to leave the GWR and Swindon for good.

Fast-forward now to 1910, when Jimmy Thomas was elected as MP for that other famous railway town, Derby (ironically replacing incumbent Labour MP Richard Bell, also a former GWR employee).

During the First World War he was made a Privy Councillor, which was highly unusual given that he wasn't even a member of the government at the time.

Jimmy went on to lead national rail strikes in 1911 and 1919, and took a leading role in negotiations that resulted in the amalgamation of three railway

unions (The ASRS, the Pointsmen &
Signalman's Society and the General
Railway Workers' Union) to form the
National Union of Railwaymen (NUR)
in 1913.

Until then, railwaymen found it
impossible to speak with the force that
their overall numbers deserved. He
became only their second General
Secretary in 1917, and remained in post
until 1931.

Yet there was far more to come.

When the first Labour (albeit minority)
administration came to power in January
1924, under Ramsay MacDonald, Jimmy
was appointed Secretary of State for the
Colonies.

Following the 1929 General Election,
Labour emerged as the single largest
party, but again had to rely on Liberal
Party support to get its King's Speech
through Parliament. This time, Jimmy
was made Minister of Employment,
and also took the title of Lord Privy
Seal.

He was handed the urgent task (more
like a poisoned chalice) to seek a remedy
to rising unemployment, which was
affecting most industrialised
    nations at the time. ▶

MR. SIDNEY WEBB, M.P.　MR. JOHN WHEATLEY, M.P.　MR. F. W. JOWETT, M.P.

MR. CHARLES PHILIPS TREVELYAN, M.P.　LORD THOMSON.　LORD OLIVIER.　COL. JOSIAH WEDGWOOD, M.P.　MR. THOMAS SHAW, M.P.

MR. STEPHEN WALSH, M.P.　VISCOUNT CHELMSFORD.　MR. NOEL BUXTON, M.P.　MR. VERNON HARTSHORN, M.P.

THE RT. HON. WILLIAM ADAMSON, M.P.　MR. PHILIP SNOWDEN, M.P.　THE RT. HON. JAMES RAMSAY MACDONALD.　THE RT. HON. JAMES HENRY THOMAS, M.P.

LORD PARMOOR, K.C.V.O.　VISCOUNT HALDANE, Kt., O.M.　MR. JOHN R. CLYNES, M.P.　THE RT. HON. ARTHUR HENDERSON.

The first ever Labour Cabinet, in the gardens of 10/11 Downing Street after forming a minority government after the 1924 General Election. Former Swindon fireman and engine driver (and long-time supporter of *The Association of Wiltshiremen in London*), Jimmy Thomas, who had just been made Secretary of State for the Colonies, is seated in the front row, second from the right (appearing to put something in his waistcoat pocket). New Prime Minister Ramsay MacDonald is seated in the front row, fifth from the left.

Despite his best efforts, however, the unemployment figures continued to rise and in 1930 he was appointed to the newly formed Office of Dominion Affairs.

In 1931 Labour was seriously divided on the measures required to meet the economic crisis (proposals which included deep cuts to unemployment benefit) and a section of the government under Ramsay MacDonald formed a National Government of all the main political parties.

Most of the Labour Cabinet rejected this idea and resigned, but Jimmy Thomas was one of only three (along with MacDonald and Chancellor Philip Snowdon) who agreed to join the new coalition, continuing to serve as MP for Derby, and Secretary for the Colonies.

When the new government eventually introduced the deep cuts in public spending that had triggered all the unrest in the first place, Labour MPs were furious, and Thomas and the other two were expelled from the Labour Party. Thomas was then obliged to resign from his beloved NUR – losing his union pension in the process.

In the book *Political Diaries of CP Scott 1911-1928*, it is said of Thomas:

He was very shrewd and very quick, and knew how to handle men. He knew a great deal about foreign affairs and what he did not know he was not above learning. He could get up a subject with extreme rapidity and was an excellent speaker.

Jimmy Thomas held his government post until May 1936, when a Judicial Tribunal found that he had made an 'unauthorized disclosure' of budget secrets to his friends Sir Alfred Butt (the Conservative MP for Balham and Tooting) and Alfred 'Cosher' Bates, a

wealthy businessman. At the tribunal, Bates admitted giving Thomas £15,000, but claimed it was an advance for a proposed autobiography.

Despite a previously unblemished political career, Thomas resigned from the government and left Parliament in shame. In an emotional statement made to the House of Commons on June 11, 1936, he said he had never "consciously given a Budget secret away".

Despite the verdict, made without any direct evidence and with no right of appeal, he continued to protest his innocence.

After leaving Parliament, Thomas served as Chairman of British Amalgamated Transport Ltd, eventually retiring to Sussex. Surprisingly, and despite all his experience, he was never called upon to assist in any capacity during the Second World War, and passed away on January 21, 1949, aged 74, at his Dulwich home.

A memorial service was subsequently held at St Martin-in-the-Fields in London, which was attended by many political greats of the day, from across the party divide.

Jimmy was known to be able to mix well at all levels of society (in part because of his love of horse racing), was regarded as a natty dresser and a great teller of jokes, and became a close friend of King George V.

But, above and beyond everything, Jimmy Thomas remained at heart a railwayman.

When he started out, the power of the private railway companies was such that they could summarily dismiss an employee for union membership alone. He helped turn an exploited and oppressed group of workers into a powerful national political force, and gained a reputation as a shrewd

negotiator who preferred conciliation rather than confrontation – thus gaining the respect of his opponents.

Always a democrat and a champion of the underdog, Jimmy supported the restriction of the powers of the House of Lords, votes for women, and Dominion Home Rule for a united Ireland. His efforts helped demonstrate that Labour was a party 'fit to govern'.

And Jimmy Thomas received a touching tribute from Swindon railwaymen in the days following his death.

After cremation at Dulwich, his ashes were transported to Swindon by train and his remains were interred at Radnor Street Cemetery.

In the biography, *A Life For Unity*, Gregory Blaxland wrote:

Only the family stood by the graveside, while a biting wind blew beneath an iron grey sky. But further away, at a respectful distance from the chief mourners, stood a black human wall. It was composed of railwaymen from far and wide, 300 in all.

When the casket had been lowered and the last rites performed, Agnes approached these men, a coura-geous, upright figure, as steadfast to her husband at his death as she had been throughout their married life. Without a word being spoken, she shook hands with every one. There was a look of perfect serenity on her face as she reached the end of the line.

He had been taken back by the men to whom he belonged, and they had come, unasked, to show their true feelings towards the greatest champion they would ever have. ∎

A familiar face at the annual dinners of *The Association of Wiltshiremen in London* in the 1920s and 30s was one of the most respected physicians of his age.

Sir Thomas Jeeves Horder, (later 1st Baron Horder, pictured, below) was born just over the county border in Shaftesbury, Dorset, but was still a baby when his parents came to Swindon.

His eldest brother, EJ Horder, was head of the drapery business, Horder and Son, and for much of his youth, Thomas lived above the shop at 9 High Street, Old Town, Swindon, then boasting a substantial frontage that extended south from Lloyds Bank to the Goddard estate.

After matriculating at London University, he studied at St Bartholomew's Hospital. His progress was rapid and he came to be recognised as one of the greatest diagnosticians of the age.

He went on to become a physician to King Edward VII, King George V, King George VI, the newly-crowned Queen Elizabeth II and two prime ministers.

During the Second World War, he was a member of various committees advising the Ministry of Food on medical matters.

In two areas, Horder was a controversial figure.

He opposed many of Aneurin Bevan's plans for the National Health Service, and was a key advocate for eugenics, a belief that the human population can be improved by promoting or eliminating supposedly superior or inferior groups of people. ∎

Political footballs

If you are a student of international history, British politics and perhaps even human nature, then the 1922 meeting of *The Association of Wiltshiremen in London* offers a priceless view of where people thought they stood and how they should tackle the world's problems in the aftermath of the First World War.

A feature of many of the gatherings before the war – and the 1922 dinner showed the war had changed nothing in this respect – was the prevalence of political speeches, often with the insistence that the Association was strictly apolitical.

In 1922 there is evidence that some people thought a speech only counted as 'political' if someone else was making it.

There was a classic moment when the Chairman, the Earl of Pembroke, stood up and said – seemingly with a straight face – that 'the great pleasure to him in a gathering like that was that it was not political (hear, hear)', before offering this:

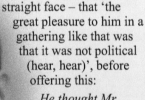

He thought Mr Thomas would agree with him that whatever political creed they held at the present moment they were determined on two things – firstly that those burdens which General Calley so aptly described, the burdens of taxation, should be lightened; secondly, that the safety of the British Empire must be guarded and the country not left in the position [that it was now in].

The reference to Mr (Jimmy) Thomas seems to anticipate that when his turn to speak came, this union man-cum-politician would get all political!

Major-General Calley had already spoken to demonstrate his unshakable faith in the British Empire – again seemingly in no doubt that this was not a 'political' stance:

The safety of the country had depended in the past and must depend in the future, in spite of any League of Nations – a splendid ideal, but human nature being what it is, and nations being simply individuals in the bulk, we could not trust entirely to specific intentions and treaties, and with an Empire like ours, with its frontiers in every quarter of the globe… we must have an efficient force of soldiers and sailors to act as the police of civilisation. He saw the other day that one of the means by which we were going to save money would be a very considerable reduction in the number of officers of both Navy and Army. He trusted sincerely that though it might be necessary to cut down the numbers to a certain extent, we would not have economy running wild in that direction.

1922

Offering a more thoughtful view was Charles Darbishire, an experienced international trader who, in recent years, had been involved in public and military service in Singapore, but who had recently become the Liberal candidate in Westbury (and would be elected, later that year).

His thoughts provide us with genuine insights, including an intriguing one about Britain's role in the war:

He had always felt… that if it were necessary for us to vindicate ourselves against the charge that we were responsible for the war, its originators and instigators, we need only point out that although in 1914 our Navy was undoubtedly supreme, it existed only for defence, because we were without an Army or an Air Force of sufficient magnitude to be of any use in international operations on a large scale. It was beyond question that we were inferior in those two branches of the services to both Germany and France, and it was a remarkable tribute to the characteristics of our race that at the signing of the Armistice we were in those respects better equipped and more efficient in every way than were any of our allies or of our enemies. I believe… these great characteristics of our race are born from the spirit of liberty and justice which have always been the guiding principles of British rule.

And what would happen next?:

We stand to-day, as I hope, at the thresh-hold of a new era initiated by the League of Nations and the Washington Conference. Let us not think that these great and noble qualities of heroic courage, self-sacrifice, great-heartedness to which

we are on the point of paying a tribute in this toast – let us not think that these qualities are not needful for the future. I pray and trust that they may be directed into other channels… leading us to international peace and lasting goodwill, and to freer, fuller, healthier, purer society (applause).

It was left to the President, Lord Roundway, to lighten the mood and remind those present of how pleasant their home county was – which he did with some skill:

Sometimes, he knew, we Wilt-shire people were told we were unde-monstrative. Whether we were so or not, he did not want to alter the Wiltshire man or the Wiltshire woman by one jot or one tittle. And if the stranger thought that their hearts were never moved, that they were incapable of enthusiasm or of giving expression to their feeling, he would say to that man – step into the King's Hall in the Holborn Restaurant and see Wiltshire men and Wiltshire women when they were at one of their (he might term them) family gatherings like the present.

It was then time for Brigadier-General George Palmer MP to toast 'the ladies' and, he said:

Without their presence much of the charm of that gathering would be ▶

George Llewellen Palmer had less than a year left of his short political career when he exchanged banter with Jimmy Thomas at the annual dinner of *The Association of Wiltshire-men in London*'s annual dinner in 1922.

Palmer (pictured below, from the pages of the *Wiltshire Times*) was a well-known figure in public life, especially in the Trowbridge area, who also had a distinguished military career.

Born at Berryfield Hall, near Melksham, in 1857, he was educated at Harrow.

In 1903/04 he was made High Sheriff of Wiltshire, but it was as an officer in the Royal Wiltshire Yeomanry that he made his name, commanding the regiment from 1910 to 1915.

In the First World War he commanded the 10th Mounted Brigade from 1915 to 1916, and retired at the rank of honorary Brigadier-General.

At the 1918 General Election, he won the Westbury seat as a Coalition Conservative, but lost it in November 1922, and never stood for parliament again.

When he died in 1932 his obituary in the *Wiltshire Times* said he was 'the donor of almshouses to Trowbridge and a generous benefactor of every charity in the town'. ∎

entirely lost. Up to the present, he proceeded, the women of the country, who were attaining as great power as the men, had never quite realised their power, but in a short time they would do so... Their word was of as much value as the men's.

Not that any ladies present would be asked to speak tonight, or even respond to the toast. That was down to Jimmy Thomas, who:

made a witty response to the toast, which kept the company in almost continuous laughter. Alluding to the fact that he was supposed, for the nuance, to be one of the other sex, he said that whilst certain people, noble lords for instance, could immediately change their positions, it was a difficult matter for a robust male like himself to suddenly do so.

Then he responded to Palmer, who had said that although he and Thomas sat on opposite sides of the House of Commons, they had often found themselves in the same lobby. 'It is true, of course,' he told Palmer, 'that you have been in the same lobby with Mr Thomas on a very few occasions, but may I remind you that those are the few occasions when you have been right (loud laughter); otherwise you have been wrong.'

Thomas was in fine form, and even his political opponents seemed to appreciate his wit, and they ended the night united by the fact that although they had their differences, they were all, in one way or another, Wiltshiremen – and the attendance was a healthy 350.

No attendance figure was given for the following dinner, in 1923, but the *North Wilts Herald*'s long list of prominent people who attended that night suggested it was another good turnout.

Field-Marshal Lord Methuen was in the chair, Lord Roundway was still President (although unable to attend because of illness) and they were still not political – as long as militarism and old-fashioned patriotism still didn't count.

The Chairman said he was 'looking to the future' by taking up two subjects:

One was with the British Legion, a great, new movement which brought ex-soldiers together and made them, to his mind, a great asset for the welfare of the country. But he felt still more earnestly on the second subject, which was the youth of this country. For the leaders there was no duty more important than to see to it that England's youth should be brought up in a proper way. He was frequently reported in the newspapers as speaking as a soldier. He was not, he was speaking as a citizen. Every girl and every boy was the better for knowing what to do for the defence (as apart from offence) of the country. Every girl who joined the Girl Guides and learnt hospital work would be useful in times of peace as well as war. Members of the various boys' organisations, too, were not only learning the use of arms, but were learning love of their country... They, in turn, must inculcate into the minds of the younger generation that love for country which every Englishman should possess.

The Mayor of Swindon (AE Harding) stood up in praise of Wiltshire, but:

The hub of Wiltshire, continued Mr Harding, was the town of which he happened to be head, and, while they had their warriors, their poets and their philosophers, it was engines that had really brought fame to the town and the county. The GWR had the finest rolling stock in the world.

This was a reference to the Railways Act 1921 (sometimes known as the Grouping Act) which consolidated Britain's railway companies into the 'big four': LNER, SR, LMS and GWR.

As usual, there was a toast to 'the ladies', which came from Reginald Mitchell Banks MP, with compliments on 'their undoubted political insight' and how 'in the sphere of science the fair sex had had substantial success'. However:

He was old-fashioned enough to think there was one sphere – the home – in which he preferred to see her. In her home, woman was a sovereign and every woman in that room was therefore necessarily a queen.

Would this finally be the year when a lady would be allowed to speak or at least respond to the toast?

No. But the irony was not lost on AJ Bonwick, MP, who was asked to respond on their behalf:

He thought it his duty to... ask some ladies what they would like him to say. He went to Wiltshire's most important town, which as they all knew, was the town of Chippenham. The result of his inquiries was that he was instructed to tell the Wiltshire association that if the committee had the audacity to couple the toast of "The Ladies" with the name of a man, then in future the ladies should insist upon proposing "The Gentlemen" coupled with the name of a lady.

The *North Wilts Herald*'s report gave no details of the entertainment provided during the evening, except: 'An excellent musical programme was contributed between the speeches, and during the dinner the Metropolitan Police Band played selections.'

If 1923 all seemed a little low key, the

following year's annual dinner would see the *Moonies* come back strongly.

The 1924 dinner, which was attended by around 400 people, was given a big billing by the *Wiltshire Times*:

On Saturday evening the King's Hall of the Holborn Restaurant was the scene of a great gathering of men and women of Wiltshire. It was the thirty-second of its kind and was presided over by the Marquess of Ailesbury, among his supporters being one Cabinet Minister, five other Members of Parliament, one ex-Member, now a Parliamentary candidate for Wiltshire, another ex-Member of Parilament, three ex-Parliamentary candidates for Wiltshire, three Wiltshire Mayors.

The Cabinet Minister was none other than that veteran of *Moonies* dinners, Jimmy Thomas, fresh from being appointed Secertary of State to the Colonies by Prime Minister Ramsay MacDonald in the first ever Labour government, albeit in a hung parliament that would be defeated before the end of the year.

If those present were expecting another witty speech from Thomas, they found him quite sombre:

The world they had to deal with was a stricken, distracted, sorrowful one, and they had to endeavour to restore confidence. Whatever lessons they had to learn from the war period, that was the most important, and they would all wish that they would never again go through the hell and horror of war (applause). This was something worth aiming at. He believed that in aiming at this the Government would have the good will of all parties (cheers), because there was no man and no woman who

could be other than convinced that if there were to be a great war in the future the real test would be, not what nation would survive, but whether civilisation itself would survive (cheers).

He had clearly made the decision not to be too political, or at least not party-political, but this unwritten (albeit often ignored) rule, did not seem to apply to Reginald Mitchell Banks MP:

Mr Mitchell Banks, MP, proposed "The Imperial Forces," saying that with Mr Thomas on the Parliamentary footplate that they need have no fear that they would be derailed or that we would fail to see the signal. But there were others in the Government of whom he could not say the same.

Another MP, AJ Bonwick, was more interested in Wiltshire's current status:

He had... read recently that "Wiltshire had decreased in importance, until at the present time she slept in peace, untroubled by the turmoils at large." When he read those words he thought of Swindon, where were built the best engines in the world.

The toast of "the Ladies" was proposed by Mr CW Darbishire 'in a pleasing and entertaining speech', and Sir James Currie responded.

And everyone had an optimistic note to take home:

The Chairman announced that the King had promised to visit Swindon, inspect the works there, and open the new wing of the hospital.

Scheduled for the following month, (April), it would be the first official visit in Swindon by a reigning British monarch. ∎

A regular attendee at the annual dinners and a sparring partner of JH Thomas (see page 162), Reginald Mitchell Banks was Conservative Member of Parliament for Swindon from 1922 to 1929, and again from 1931 to 1934.

Born in Liverpool in 1880, he was educated at Rugby and Christ Church, Oxford, where he was senior classical scholar, becoming one of the country's most prominent lawyers.

He was knighted in 1928.

The *North Wilts Herald* printed a glowing obituary following his death in 1940, which included:

No politician enjoyed greater popularity in Swindon than Sir Reginald, and his ability in politics and in law was acknowledged by opponents and friends alike. At one time it was expected he would have secured the post of Solicitor-General.

He... was regarded as one of the most brilliant of Tory back-benchers. No mere party hack, he was a man of independent thought and fearless expression, and it was generally thought that it was because of his outspokenness he did not get Cabinet rank, a recognition to which his ability and knowledge entitled him... A young barrister seeking his laurels at the Bar, he was first returned for Swindon in 1922 on the retirement of Sir Frederick Young.

Sir Reginald won the next two elections, [then, in 1929] he lost to Dr Addison...But in the 1931 election Sir Reginald won the seat back with a 5,000 majority. He left politics on being appointed County Court judge at Hull.

Enlisting as a private in the East Surrey Regiment in 1914, he was commissioned in the Indian Army Reserve and attached to the 1/5 Gurkha Rifles in 1915. He served in India and Mesopotamia. ∎

Wiltshiremen going west

In 1924, the success of *The Association of Wiltshiremen in London* inspired a group of men to go west – and set up another society, this time in Bristol.

A meeting to consider the idea was held on January 17, 1924, at the Artistes and Press Club, in Park Row, Bristol.

The first general meeting was to follow at the Grand Hotel in Broad Street, on February 15, where the rules of the new society were passed, and where the election of officers and the council, as well as enrolment of members, followed.

It was hoped that the new group, *The Society of Wiltshiremen (Moonrakers) in Bristol*, would 'bring old friends together' and 'hold out a helping hand to those who were not able to help themselves'.

Solicitor Henry Reginald Wansbrough was to become its first President.

Writer, playwright and council member Thomas Jay was to represent the new society at the dinner of the *Association of Wiltshiremen in London* on March 15, 1924, although it appears to be the case that the reciprocal representation happened, the London group were not officially represented at a Bristol dinner until two years later, in the shape of Mr George Lansdown JP, of Trowbridge.

The first annual dinner was held at the Grand Hotel in Broad Street, Bristol, on February 20, 1925, for around 100 members and friends, including the Lord Mayor and the High Sheriff (Mr FO Wills). A social event took place at the same venue the following December, which was attended by 120 members and friends.

It represented a nostalgic return to Bristol for a fellowship organisation of Wiltshire men – perhaps seeking to occupy a place in the civic and social life of the city once occupied by the Wiltshire Society #2, just over 140 years previously (see page 15).

Honorary Vice-presidents included Field Marshall Lord Methuen, the Earl of Radnor and the Marquess of Bath, and later on, the Earl of Pembroke and Lord Long of Wraxall. However, there is no evidence that any of them ever attended a meeting or social function of the society in Bristol.

Nevertheless, there were some relatively high-profile attendees at the annual dinners, such as Alderman Frank Moore, then-Lord Mayor of Bristol, who became President for 1926/27, and, the following year, Sir Felix Pole, General Manager of the GWR, was a guest.

At the dinner on February 10, 1928, Major the Hon Eric Long MP not only joined the assembled company as a prominent member of *The Wiltshire Society*, but even sang *The Vly Be on the Turmuts* (see page 174).

And at the 6th annual dinner in 1930, the Presiding Chairman was Mr WH Eyles, a former Lord Mayor of Bristol, and he was supported by Col RW Awdry (President of *The Wiltshire Society*).

However, although the dinner was deemed 'socially speaking, a great success', it was regretted that 'there were not more of our members present'.

From this point onwards, the organisation was starting to lose members through disinterest; worse still: it was failing to attract new ones. Subscription revenues were falling, and a general air of despondency creeping into its affairs – all made worse by the death in office of President, Councillor WH Eyles, and some other key members.

The Annual General

The Society of
WILTSHIREMEN ("Moonrakers") IN BRISTOL.

—

ANNUAL DINNER

HELD AT THE

GRAND HOTEL,
.. BRISTOL, ..

WEDNESDAY, 6th FEBRUARY, 1929.

—

President—JOHN E. PRITCHARD, ESQ., F.S.A.

Meeting arranged for April 1930 was cancelled 'due to unforeseen circumstances', as was the annual dinner scheduled for February 1931.

Nevertheless, Henry Frederick Thynne, the Right Hon Viscount Weymouth (in his year of office as President of *The Wiltshire Society* and soon-to-be MP for Frome), would also assume the office of President of *The Society of Wiltshiremen (Moonrakers) in Bristol* for 1931/32.

It was a valiant attempt to revive the ailing society, and it was stated in the press that 'Viscount Weymouth's acceptance of the office of president should however, produce many new members'.

Further warning signs were apparent when a report appeared in the *Western Daily Press* in May 1931, following the society's Annual General Meeting, in which it was

1931 — 1932

The Society of Wiltshiremen ("Moonrakers") in Bristol

President :
RT. HON. VISCOUNT WEYMOUTH.

Vice-Presidents :
H. REGINALD WANSBROUGH.
EDWARD LOWTHER.
Ald. FRANK MOORE, J.P.

Chairman of Council :
J. E. PRITCHARD, F.S.A.,
22 St. John's Road, Clifton.

Hon. Treasurer :
W. THICK,
3 Windsor Road, St. Andrew's Park,
Bristol.

Secretary :
CHAS. T. DAVIS,
43 Broad Street, Bristol.
(Tel. 1503).

unanimously resolved that 'the society continue the benevolent work which was started principally through the efforts of Mr HR Wansbrough, more than eight years ago'.

Despite apathy elsewhere, the one event that always seemed to be well supported was the Society's annual outing.

The Marquess of Bath hosted a visit to Longleat on June 18, 1924, when members travelled 'in three of the luxurious pneumatic-tyred motor coaches belonging to Bristol Tramways & Carriage Co Ltd'.

There followed excursions to Stonehenge, Grittleton House and Stourhead House, with Lord Methuen hosting a visit to Corsham Court and Edington in June 1929 – something that was particularly well-received.

Sadly, even this run of success came to an end when it was reported that the 1930 trip to Fonthill Abbey was poorly attended.

Notice of the forthcoming AGM in the Windsor Room of the Grand Hotel on April 26, 1932, appeared in the *Western Daily Press* and all members were requested to attend, particularly since the response to previous announcements had been 'so lacking in enthusiasm that the time has arrived when it must be decided... whether the Society can be continued'.

It took an unusually long time before this vexed question could be satisfactorily resolved (doubtless exacerbated by the resignation of the treasurer), with the Society set to enter a period of stasis in the interim.

At a Special Meeting held on January 30, 1935, it was unanimously decided that the Society be wound up, and the funds remaining in the organisation's coffers split between *The Wiltshire Society* and the *Bristol Lord Mayor's Hospital Fund*.

Its demise was a personal blow to Henry Wansbrough, who had vested so much of his time and expertise in an organisation which was always much more about promoting fraternity and goodwill among members, rather than the pressure of achieving specific charitable aims.

Indeed, little is to be found in print about the scope of its benevolent activities, and what evidence there is appears to be limited to donations to the Lord Mayor's Christmas Dinner Fund in 1925 and 1926, as well as moderate relief given to 'distressed Moonrakers' in 1926 and 1932.

It was only in 1930 that a proposal to establish a benevolent fund in the city ('to help their fellow Wiltshiremen when they fell on evil days and to give them a little relief in cases of real distress') was formally adopted, but by then concern was already creeping in that insufficient revenue was being generated to match even its limited ambitions.

Most commentators and historians would accept that *The Society of Wiltshiremen (Moonrakers) in Bristol* never really thrived at any point during its brief existence, and hence was particularly vulnerable to financial headwinds following the onset of the Great Depression in late 1929.

As a final mark of gratitude and respect for his efforts, Wansbrough was presented with the President's Badge in perpetuity, which was only fair, given that he was 'the founder of the Society, and had also subscribed liberally to its funds'. ∎

Opposite and left: a menu card for the 1929 annual dinner, and the Society's rule book

Moonies on the move

In 1925, *The Association of Wiltshire-men in London* held their annual dinner in a new venue. Reports offered no explanation why the Holborn Restaurant, which had been the venue for every dinner since 1897, was not chosen, and they convened in the Connaught Rooms, Great Queen Street (pictured, in 2024), instead.

There was a new President, the Marquess of Ailesbury (replacing Lord Roundway), and he would remain President until the Second World War. For the moment he was also Presiding Chairman.

The *North Wilts Herald* gave comparatively sparse details of proceedings and made no mention of how many attended, but the company included at least four MPs, and two key guests.

One was Sir Felix Pole (pictured), who was born in Little Bedwyn in 1877, joined the GWR as a telegraph lad at Swindon in 1891, and had been General Manager of the company since 1921.

He said:

Wiltshiremen sometimes forgot one great claim to fame that their county possessed, that it was the home of the finest engines in the world, engines which unquestionably held the record for power and speed. He yielded to no one in his admiration for the old county, and he imagined they all had but one desire, that they might live long to enjoy its beauties

and the hospitalities and everything associated with it, and that when their time did come they might be laid to rest in its friendly soil.

Also present was Mr W Brown, of New Scotland Yard (see page 202), who told the diners that he 'went to London from Chitterne [near Warminster], 38 years ago'.

The job of toasting 'the ladies' fell to Percy Hurd MP, who pointed out:

Men had had the good sense to put women into positions of responsibility... Indeed women were taking such a big place in the affairs of the country and in the affairs of the Wiltshire Society that it might be that the committee of that society would soon consider altering its title to that of the "Society of Wiltshiremen and Wiltshirewomen in London."

Not that they should be allowed to respond to the toast, of course, so Capt WW Shaw MP was asked to do the honours.

Reginald Mitchell Banks MP was given the job of toasting the Chairman, and took the opportu-nity to share his views on the House of Lords, which he said, was 'quite unreformed, quite incapable of reformation (according to some), yet it... contained more experts upon more subjects than any other gathering ...in the world.' ∎

Warning: mind your turmuts

Almost as traditional as the story of the Moonrakers is the Wiltshire dialect folk song, *The Vly Be on the Turmut* (or, as one internet source translates it, for the benefit of the unenlighted: 'The Fly is on the Turnip').

The song is the unofficial anthem of Wiltshire, and was a slightly more official marching song of the Wiltshire Regiment.

According to the Rifles Berkshire and Wiltshire Museum, the 1st Battalion of the regiment used to have *The Lincolnshire Poacher* as its anthem (a bizarre and clearly inappropriate choice), but switched to *The Vly Be on the Turmut* in 1932.

However, there is a much longer history to it than that, as the annual dinner of *The Association of Wiltshiremen in London* revealed in 1922.

Speaker George Lansdown JP recalled:

> In the 70s or 80s, when Lord Pembroke was a Major in the Wiltshire Volunteers, and the night before the end of the annual training on Homington Down, or some other part of the Plain; they finished with a great pow-wow and sing-song round the blazing faggot pile. The star turn of the evening was always "The vly be on the turnips" by Lord Pembroke.

Lansdown urged the current Lord Pembroke, who was then Chairman of the Association, to give the assembled a rendition of the song.

Pembroke waited his turn to speak before addressing the request, saying:

> Thanks for the success of the evening were also due to the very excellent artistes who had given such a charming musical performance – and on that topic might he tell Mr Lansdown that if he thought the Chairman was going to sing "The vly be on the turmut," after the wonderful music they had had that evening, he was mistaken (laughter).

Precisely when the regiment first adopted the song is lost in the mists of time, along with the song's origins; like many traditional folk songs, it is an unknown number of centuries old, and was probably sung in various forms over the years, with alternative lyrics.

Versions are said to have existed in Oxfordshire and Gloucestershire, and the song is often confused with another, *The Turmut-Hoer's* (or *Turmot-Hoer's*) *Song*, with which it shares the line 'The vly, the vly, the vly be on the turmut,' which forms half of the chorus.

The song's persistence in the 21st century is partly due to successive MPs for Salisbury – first Robert Key, then John Glen – maintaining the tradition (that the BBC claims is more than 300 years old) of successful candidates from that constituency being obliged to sing the song from the balcony of the city's White Hart Hotel after winning an election.

Four years after it was requested to be sung at the Association's dinner, it was finally sung in 1926, becoming a regular feature of every dinner from then on, and a firm favourite.

Ironically, one of the guests at the 1926 dinner was Alfred Williams (see page 176), who, a few years earlier, had embarked on a major project to transcribe the lyrics of local folk songs in the area, and although he collected more than a thousand, *The Vly Be on the Turmut* wasn't one of them.

The report of the 1926 dinner states:

After the toast of "Wilts our County," the orchestra rendered, with fine effect, the old County song "The Vly be on the Turmuts," and all the diners sang in true Wiltshire style one verse and the chorus of the old "classic," as someone was heard to describe it.

In 1927:

During dinner, selections of music were rendered by the orchestra by the "P" Division of the Metropolitan Police under the conductorship of Constable Boardman. Especially well received was the playing of the march of the Wiltshire Regiment, "The Vly be on the Turmut."

In 1928 and 1933, the verses were sung by Major the Hon Eric Long, the MP for West Wilts.

It seemed to prove particularly rousing when it was sung in 1930, albeit imperfectly:

It was when the Wiltshire classic, "The Vly be on the Turmuts," was sung, following the toast of the evening, "Wiltshire, our county and Wiltshiremen in London," that the county atmosphere became more pronounced, although it must be admitted that there is room for considerable improvement in the rendering of the song at this annual gathering.

Then, in 1935:

Mr TC Newman of Swindon, mounted the platform and, dressed in billy-cock hat and red neckerchief, sang that Wiltshire classic which is always a feature of this gathering – "The Vly be on the Turmuts." Though it had obviously not been rehearsed by the general company, it was received with enthusiasm – "turmuts' being produced on the stage somewhat after the manner in which a conjurer produces his rabbit from the hat.

Four years later, Newman was back, but had to share the limelight:

Following the toast, Mr TC Newman (Swindon) and Mr Fred Chivers (Devizes), both of whom were dressed as country landsmen, sang what is termed the Wiltshire hymn, "The Vly be on the Turmuts" which was enthusiastically received.

The tradition continued after the Second World War, and when the annual dinner of 1949 clashed with the FA Cup final, it was reported:

London… was not entirely given over to the men of Leicester and Wolverhampton… One small corner of the great city – the Holborn Restaurant, to be exact – rang during the evening with the hearty strains of "The Vly," indicating that exiles from Wiltshire were meeting and creating a little piece of West Country in London itself.

In 1951 and 1952, the singing was led by celebrated baritone Alfred Salter (see page 213), who was dressed in 'gaiters and breeches, smock and round felt hat'.

The singing of the song would even prove to be the penultimate action of the Association when, at the 1954 (and last)

annual dinner, 'The proceedings concluded with the singing of "The Vly be on the turmits" and "Auld Lang Syne."'

The Wiltshire Regiment ceased to exist, five years later, when it was amalgamated with The Royal Berkshire Regiment (Princess Charlotte of Wales's) to form The Duke Of Edinburgh's Royal Regiment (Berkshire and Wiltshire) in 1959.

Unlike the Association and the Regiment, however, folk songs can go on forever, and although their lyrics are never fixed, the current accepted version of *The Vly Be on the Turmut* seems to be:

Chorus:
The vly, the vly,
The vly be on the turmut,
'Tis all me eye,
For Oi to try,
To keep vlies off them turmuts.

The vust place as Oi went to wurk;
It were wi' Varmer Gower,
Who vowed and swore as 'ow Oi Were
*   a vust class turmut 'oer;*
The second place Oi went to wurk,
They paid Oi by the job,
If Oi'd a-knowed a little more, Oi'd
*   sooner bin in quod.*

– Chorus –

The last place as Oi went to wurk,
They zent ver Oi a-mowin',
Oi zent wurd back,
Oi'd zunner get the zack,
Than gi'e up turmut 'oein'.
Now all you jolly varmer chaps,
What boides at 'ome zo warm,
Oi'll now conclude my ditty wi'e
*   a-wishin' you no 'arm.*

– Chorus – ∎

You could say Alfred Williams and *The Association of Wiltshiremen in London* were made for each other.

Usually remembered as *The Hammerman Poet*, Williams, who was born in South Marston in 1877, was so much more: a writer of sublime prose; a social observer whose 1915 book, *Life in a Railway Factory* is arguably the most important book in the history of Swindon and its GWR Works; a nationally important collector of folk song lyrics – and he served in the First World War, returning home from India on November 11, 1919, exactly a year after the fighting had stopped.

But he is also the archetypal Wiltshire villager, who was far smarter than some would give a South Marston lad credit for – a latterday moonraker who became a self-taught polymath.

So when they talked about the special qualities inherent in some Wiltshiremen, his fellow *Moonies* needed to look no further. He was mentioned several times at the annual dinners before he finally got to actually attend one.

In 1913, when Alfred was still a working railwayman, Colonel Calley told the assembled Association:

> *Wiltshire had produced two men of recent years who had been gifted with the ability and power of expressing in proper language those feelings which they all felt, but were unable to express – he referred to Richard Jefferies, and, at the present*

Left: Alfred Williams and his wife Mary, probably on their wedding day in 1903 (Courtesy of Swindon Libraries/Local Studies). Opposite: South Marston, photographed in 2017. Alfred's birthplace, Cambria Cottage, is at the bottom right, facing the junction. Dryden Cottage, where most of his works were written, is to the left, on the opposite side of the road. (Courtesy of Noel Beauchamp)

Alfred, the self-taught polymath

time, the Boiler Shop of the Swindon Works had produced a worthy successor to him in Mr Alfred Williams, whose poetry, he hoped, they had all read (cheers).

Calley was wrong on two counts: Williams actually worked in Number 18 Stamping Shop; more importantly: most of those present probably hadn't read his poetry (or his books).

In fact, Alfred struggled to make a living from writing, and when ill health forced him to give up his day job in the Works, what he was able to scratch together from market gardening was barely enough, and he was almost literally starving when he died.

He and his devoted wife Mary had only survived until then because of ad-hoc 'pensions' won for him by his friends, on the rare times when he swallowed his pride and accepted charity.

His friends and admirers straddled the whole political spectrum, from Lord Fitzmaurice, a Liberal peer, to Reuben George, who is considered the father of the Labour Party in Swindon.

Despite the obvious admiration of members of the Association, Alfred's appearance at the 1926 dinner is surprising. For one thing, it would have been very difficult for him to afford the train fare to London at that time, let alone the cost of a meal in a posh venue like the Connaught Rooms; either he somehow scraped it together or they somehow persuaded him to let them pay his expenses, but both seem unlikely.

He is also something of a controversial figure because *Life in a Railway Factory* was critical of the GWR in general and middle management in particular, which didn't go down well with the company; they probably would have sacked him if

he hadn't already left. So the fact the Association greeted him warmly tells us they saw him as *one of them*.

In stark contrast to his 'factory book', his 1912 work, *A Wiltshire Village*, was – in more ways than one – right up the *Moonies*' street.

A more vivid and affectionate celebration of the beauty of the county and its people, history and traditions has never been written, and as such it embodies everything *Moonies* said at their dinners, every year, about Wiltshire. And so did Alfred.

He died in 1930; distraught because of Mary's terminal cancer, he collapsed in the house the couple had recently built – literally, with their own hands – and was found the next day.

The death certificate said it was a heart attack that killed him, but a broken heart is probably more accurate. ∎

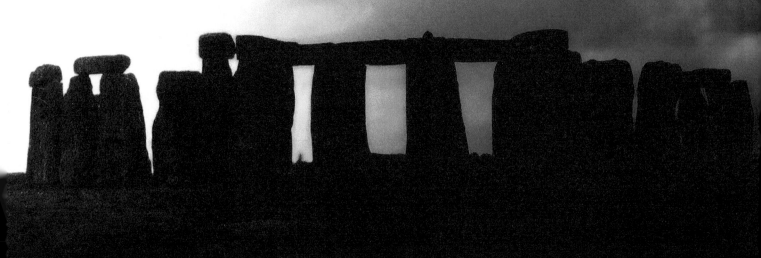

'The paradise of antiquary'

If there were any fears that a change of venue would bring about a change of fortunes, the annual dinner of 1926, which was again at the Connaught Rooms, would have set everyone straight.

The BBC were even there to broadcast part of it on the radio (see page 180). There were 350 present, the Marquess of Ailesbury was still President, but there was a new Chairman, WJ Hopkins.

The nature of the gatherings changed in the middle of the 1920s, with the previous preoccupation with politics, patriotism and militarism swept away by a quite romantic appreciation of literature, the genuine beauty of Wiltshire and inspirational people.

This year was a case in point.

'Pride in the county was voiced in no uncertain terms by the speakers,' said the *North Wilts Herald*'s report.

The first major speech was by Henry Wickham Steed, a former editor of *The Times*, who was East Anglian by birth, but claimed Wiltshire ancestry. He said:

To him Wiltshire was a place of sheer delight. Even the railway engines were green and golden, very different from the dull blue or oily black of the East Anglican loco- motives. Then the soft speech of the Wiltshire people, lighter than that of Zummerzet, less hard than that of Darzet, fell upon his ear like music.

In the early 1930s, Steed – a complex character whom some consider to be an anti-semite – would be one of the first commentators to raise alarm bells over the rise of Adolf Hitler. This makes his speech to the Association all the more surprising because of its optimism, as he predicted:

A part of the great transformation which was about to begin, the turning of our black coal into the blue electric current that kills pace and defies distance might change for the better the whole life of town and country, reviving rural crafts, teaching city dwellers the delights of pure air and clean sunlight and changing grimy, congested England into Merry England again.

The Association was optimistic too, and confident of the annual dinner's status – because when the apologies for absence were read, it revealed that invitations had gone out to the Prime Minister, the Lord Mayor of London and various other VIPs (who all politely declined).

Another speaker said there was 'a large number of the gentler and fairer sex' present, although they appear to have given up the idea of raising a toast to them, at least for now.

A main speaker was Alderman WG Adams, the Mayor of Swindon (one of three mayors present), who said he was 'a native born Mayor of the largest town in Wiltshire and he was therefore "a proper Moonie"'.

He also hinted at a big following of *Moonies* back home when he read a telegram that had been received that evening, saying: 'Fraternal greetings to Wiltshiremen assembled in London, from six hundred clubmen at dinner in the Drill Hall, Swindon.'

And, he added:

The town possessed the finest railway works belonging to the GWR Company which had the finest service in the world. He regretted that the General Manager, Sir Felix Pole, who was in Swindon the previous evening, was unable to be present with his brother Wiltshiremen that evening. The 14,000 workmen employed in the railway works at Swindon were proud of their handi- work, and it was gratifying to note that the greatest goodwill prevailed between employers and employees.

This final comment is significant because the dinner was being held less than six weeks before the General Strike, which tested relations between employers and employees in all industries, not least among railway workers, whose support (for miners) was crucial.

Meanwhile, Jimmy Thomas (see page 162), despite now being on the Opposition benches, played a key role in the build-up to the strike (which eventually lasted nine days), coming close to brokering a deal between the TUC and Stanley Baldwin, the Prime Minister.

Then it was time for a speech from Alfred Williams, the so-called 'Hammerman Poet', who had, in fact, long since retired (through ill health) from his job as a hammerman with the GWR in Swindon (see page 176).

The theme of his talk was poets, particularly how they were often misconstrued, and he insisted:

Really, poets were very much like other people, being plain and practical – they had to be, or they would soon starve. They could take it from him that poets and authors were about the worst paid of all in the social order to-day, and yet their numbers increased – there was no lack of recruits.

In hindsight it is a poignant comment, since Williams's final years were marked by poverty, and hunger contributed to his early death, four years later, at the age of 53. But he ended his speech on a positive note:

He considered that Wiltshire had ▶

Radio Times, March 19th, 1926.

BROADCASTING A GREAT OPERA.

BBC

THE RADIO TIMES

THE OFFICIAL ORGAN OF THE B.B.C.

EVERY FRIDAY.   Two Pence.

Vol. 10. No. 133.   Registered at the G.P.O. as a Newspaper.

OFFICIAL PROGRAMMES
for the week beginning
SUNDAY,   March 21st.

IMPORTANT TO READERS.

The editorial address of "The Radio Times" and of the British Broadcasting Company, Ltd., is 2, Savoy Hill, Strand, London, W.C.2. RATES OF SUBSCRIPTION to "The Radio Times" (including postage): Twelve Months (Foreign), 13s. 6d.; Twelve Months (British), 11s. 6d.

The Glory of Russian Opera.

By ALBERT COATES, the Famous Conductor.

COMPARATIVELY little Russian opera has been heard in England. Generally speaking, it is less familiar to English audiences than are the operas of Italy, France, and Germany. It is difficult to understand why this should be, since Russian operas are so full of colour, life and movement. They are mostly built up of simple folk tunes, for the Russians know, just as Wagner did, that the finest melodies are always the simple ones.

    * * *

When I was Director of the Imperial Opera House at Petrograd, the operas performed were, of course, mostly Russian, though Wagner was a great favourite there, and my musical apprenticeship in Germany made me equally at home in either school. It was shortly after I arrived in Petrograd that the first performance of the sacred opera *Kitesh* was given. The composer, Rimsky-Korsakov, had an indefatigable temperament, and not only composed works himself, but used also to orchestrate and help his friends with their work.

The opera *Kitesh* is typically Russian. It is based on a monastic legend, and interspersed with the sacred character of the work are some of the most moving and characteristic episodes in Russian life, folk lore and descriptive battle scenes.

The work had an immense success in Russia, and wherever it was performed the houses were always crowded to overflowing. It takes a place in Russian literature equal to that of *Parsifal* in the German.

At Barcelona two years ago—my first visit there—I persuaded the Director of the Opera to let me produce *Kitesh*. He agreed,

Mr. ALBERT COATES.

and the result was the same overwhelming success in Spain as that which had been experienced in Russia. The opera will now form part of the regular Russian repertoire and will be given in Barcelona again next year.

On my return to England, I had the pleasure of co-operating with the B.B.C., and they suggested that I should conduct an opera for them in the spring. I proposed a concert performance of *Kitesh*, and the suggestion was accepted with alacrity. This performance will take place on March 30th.

    * * *

The opera is actually some four hours in length, and much of it would be difficult to convey in a concert version; we have, therefore, arranged to shorten it without losing in any way the continuity of the musical narrative.

The third act is particularly fine. The battle song of the young prince, the solemn chant of old King Jury, and the great choral prayer of the people to the Virgin, culminating in the miracle of the city's invisibility and the appearance of the great Cross of light —the inspiration is so lofty that words cannot describe it.

We English are inclined to be somewhat conservative in our tastes, whether musical or otherwise; but having lived most of my

(Continued overleaf in column 3.)

[March 19th, 1926.   RADIO TIMES   591

2LO
365 M.

LONDON PROGRAMMES.
(Continued from the previous page.)

Week Beginning March 21st.

10.0.—Time Signal from Greenwich. [Con...] Weather, New...

...no Duets.

...6 10.30 p.m. will be ...nce, given by Mr. ...and Miss Isobel Gray, ...ard from this station ...ers will remember ...Gray played the ...recitals of music ...ael Pollard was ...f the Royal Academy ...of twenty-two, and ...low. He is a fine ...and has appeared ...le and other con...me is of the way,

...Hallé Pensions ...come pension for ...Hallé Orchestra ...compelled to ...ce. The orchestra ...ans of securing ...ng of an annual ...orchestra at full ...some of the most ...their repertoire. ...e is one which ...ut to musicians. ...has offered his ...and Mr. Arthur ...violin parts. ...from Holden... ...s laid out on ... necessitate

the employment of a large modern orchestra, including tubas, and falls into several sections, the most important of these being the Love Scene, the Battle Scene, and the Finale.

From the musical point of view, the work may be regarded more in the nature of an autobiography dealing with the life and artistic struggles of Strauss himself, since a number of melodies taken from his instrumental and vocal works are drawn into the general musical texture. At the outset, an introductory section of great nobility based upon an ascending arpeggio theme for horns is heard; afterwards we come to an ugly little phrase for woodwind, representing the adversaries (critics). This is used both alone and in combination with a three-note theme for two tubas in fifths; said to be a musical setting of the name of a German critic who was well known as one of Strauss's most bitter opponents.

Some exhaustive treatment in this material now ensues, and we then arrive at the Love Scene, an episode of great beauty, followed very shortly by the Battle Scene, illustrating the composer's fight with his adversaries, ex, perhaps, the critics to whom his works were not palatable. The concluding pages of the work now concerned with a leading theme of great tranquillity, and deal with a later period of the composer's life, following upon which, numerous quotations from his works are drawn into the general scheme, not only singly, but also in combination.

...MES.   **Week Beginning March 21st.**

...IC.   **FRIDAY, March 26th.**
...CAFE DE   10.30 a.m.—Time Signal and Weather
...AND, and   Forecast.
...DANCE   11.0-1.0.—THE RADIO QUARTET
...é de Paris.   and GEORGINA TANNER
    (Soprano), FREDERICK
...25th.   GREGORY (Baritone), ANITA
    HARRISON (Piano).
...Weather   1.0-3.0. } Programme S.B. from
   3.45-10.25. } London.
...UARTET
...AMPLIN   10.25 (approx.)—Shipping Forecast.
...NNEDY
...ROBERT   10.30-12.0.—Programme S.B. from
    London.

    SATURDAY, March 27th.

...Maibrook.   10.30 a.m.—Time Signal and Weather
    Forecast.
...R.C.O.   1.0.—Time Signal from Greenwich.
...perston
...Coates   4.0-9.5.—Programme S.B. from Lon-
...40th`   don.
...Percy
...Elgar   9.5.   Annual Dinner of
...anford   THE WILTSHIRE MEN
    in London.
...from   Speeches:
   THE MARQUIS OF AILSBURY.
    Mr. WICKHAM STEED.
...from   During the Evening will be sung
    Some Songs of Wiltshire.
   Relayed from The Connaught
...from   Rooms, London.
   9.30.—Programme S.B. from London.
   10.25 (approx.)—Shipping Forecast.
   10.30-12.0.—Programme S.B. from
    London.

The listing showing the BBC's broadcast of the annual dinner in 1926 (courtesy of *The Radio Times*).

the strongest character and the finest dialect in the South of England.

A positive point was also made by the next speaker, JH Willis, who reminded diners of the Association's wider aims:

He said [it] did not exist simply to promote whist drives and dances, or even annual dinners. They had something else to devote their activities to. He instanced a case of recent occurrence where an old Wiltshireman, over 80 years of age, fell ill, and was in straitened circumstances. The Association came to his aid, and helped him to the end of his days.

This was a good point at which to pay a compliment 'to the splendid work that was being done by the hon secretary (Mr Coward), and he also paid a tribute to the previous secretary (Mr GB Moore), who worked so hard and successfully for many years, and whom they were glad to see present in the gathering that evening'.

The Association seemed to be in fine fettle, with every reason to be optimistic for the future.

Attendance was slightly down, at 300, when they reconvened in 1927, at the same venue for the third year in succession (although now referred to as 'Connaught Chambers').

Also completing a hat-trick was the President, the Marquess of Ailesbury, while Sir Thomas Horder (see page 166) was Chairman. In what is believed to be an unprecedented move, he and Lady Horder hosted a pre-dinner reception.

The meeting started with a telegram from Buckingham Palace, no less, which read:

The King sincerely thanks Wilt-shiremen in London assembled at their annual dinner for their message of loyal greeting and wishes them a ▶

Alderman Thomas Charles Newman (1878-1941) attended eleven *Association of Wiltshiremen in London* dinners between 1926 and 1939, singing the Wiltshire anthem on several occasions.

His rendition of *The Vly Be on the Turmut* (see page 174) must have been renowned in Swindon, because it was mentioned in his obituary in the *North Wilts Herald* as 'always a popular feature of the musical proceedings'.

Newman (pictured below, courtesy of Swindon Libraries/Local Studies) went down in history as the first Mayor of Swindon to accompany a reigning British monarch on a tour of the town: the visit of George V and Queen Mary in 1924. The same year saw the buildling of a new sewage works at Rodbourne, at a cost of £50,000, and the opening of tennis courts at the Town Gardens.

Born and bred in Swindon, he was educated at Sanford Street School under John Williams (see page 30), and began his career as a printer's 'devil', eventually going on to own his own prints works, The Borough Press.

A tireless councillor, after a record 12 years on the Corporation, Newman became an Alderman in 1921,

eventually sitting on the Council for 32 years, for many as Chairman of the Finance Committee. For a short time he was also a member of Wiltshire County Council.

He was Chairman of the committee in charge of the creation of the new Civic Offices, which were opened in 1938.

But his council duties were only part of his public service. He was President and Chairman of the Nursing Association for 15 years, founder of the Borough Football League, Table Tennis, Shooting and Billiards Leagues, and the Wheelers Cycling Club.

He was also President of the North Wilts Motor-Cycle Club, the Victoria Cricket Club and the Swindon Glee Singers; Vice-president of Swindon Cricket Club, Swindon Amateur Musical and Dramatic Society, the Conservative Club, and the Junior Imperial League; and Treasurer of the Unionist Association, the Swindon Swimming Club and the Choral Society.

He became the President of the Swindon Rotary Club, and was also a prominent Freemason.

And somehow he found some spare time to devote to his two favourite hobbies, gardening and angling. He died in October 1941, aged 63. ∎

successful re-union. *His Majesty gratefully appreciates their kind reference to the safe return of the Duke and Duchess of York.'*

This last remark was about the future King George VI and the future Queen Elizabeth the Queen Mother, who embarked on an extensive tour of Australia and New Zealand on January 6, 1927, and would not return until June 27. They took with them Princess (later Queen) Elizabeth, who would reach her first birthday a month after the Association's dinner that year.

Sir Thomas Horder made a speech that was typical of many over the years, extolling the virtues and especially the natural beauty of Wiltshire, but with an eloquence that makes it worth quoting at length, especially as he made sure not to forget the special case that was (and is) Swindon when describing the landscape:

Wiltshire men and women did not even require imagination to feel stirred with enthusiasm when their county was being discussed. Here all could be abundantly satisfied. Did they not love the rolling downland, and delight to let their eyes rest upon the peaceful distant vales? Let them
stand *on the edge of Barbury or Liddington Camp, walk over the hills from Ogbourne to Lambourn, or drive from Marlborough by way of Oare or Huish to Pewsey, and the most insatiable soul would be filled. Did they love to wander in the forest avenue and glade of Savernake, where ancient oaks and beeches were to be seen? Did they admire ancient monuments? It was common knowledge that Wiltshire was the Paradise of the antiquary, providing at Stonehenge, Amesbury, Silbury, and at a dozen other spots a feast of interest and conjecture that could not be found anywhere else in the world.*

Was it the glories of the Cathedral that they sought? Though Wiltshire possessed but one, that one was a pile so magnificent and so unique, both in its site and its structure, that it drew from the American poet Emerson, the expression, "Surely it is the apple of the eye of England."

Then if we were modern in our tastes and found pleasure, even beauty, in machinery, and in the contemplation of the conquests of the engineer, we could look to Swindon. Here were to be found the premier locomotive works of the world, where the whole
history and development of the railway and its tremendous issues could be seen and studied.

Details of the following year's dinner (1928) are scarcer than in earlier years, but the Assocation still seem to have been on a high, and there were 'several hundred' in attendance:

The great entrance hall and lobbies of the Connaught Rooms, Great Queen Street, London, were on Saturday evening pervaded with something of the breeziness of the rolling Wiltshire Downs, when several hundred people, members of the Society of Wiltshiremen in London and their friends, fore-gathered on the occasion of the 36th annual dinner of that very useful organisation.

This year the Chairman was the Marquess of Lansdowne, who, as the Earl of Kerry, had presided in 1914. The guest list included three MPs, the Duke of Somerset, and the Mayors of Devizes, Marlborough and Malmesbury.

Lansdowne used his position to make an appeal on a subject that is still an issue, a century later:

As President of the Wiltshire Archaeological Society, his lordship made an appeal for support for the fund being raised to secure the ground surrounding Stonehenge. Stonehenge, he said, was like a beautiful picture, but it wanted a

Harry Preater only attended five annual dinners of *The Association of Wiltshiremen in London*, but was a leading local businessman and

Freemason. His name still lives on in some circles, as the Harry C Preater Masonic Lodge No 8204 still holds its meetings at The Planks in Old Town.

Preater (pictured, left, in Masonic regalia) was the eldest of the nine children of Charles Preater and his wife, Mary Jane. Born in Swindon in 1880, he spent part of his childhood at the New Inn in Cromwell Street, where his father was landlord.

In 1894, not long after the Town Flour

frame; that frame had been in danger of being entirely destroyed by the erection of unsightly buildings in the immediate vicinity of the ancient monument. That danger had been averted by the purchase of the ground bounding the monument, a portion of the purchase price of which had still to be raised, and he would commend the appeal being made for assistance in this direction to their sympathetic consideration.

Major the Hon Eric Long also made an appeal:

for the support of the Wiltshire Society which, he said, did great work in apprenticing Wiltshire boys; this was a society which was deserving of the wholehearted support of every Wiltshire man.

Back on the agenda again, this year, were the ladies, who were toasted by Reginald Mitchell Banks MP, but the day when they would be allowed to respond themselves had not yet come.

The event ended on a happy note, however, with a telegram from Windsor Castle, which read:

The King has received with much pleasure the loyal message which you have sent on behalf of the Wiltshiremen in London assembled at their annual reunion. His Majesty warmly thanks them for their greeting, and trusts they are spending an enjoyable evening.

You can bet they did!

They were on the move again in 1929, after four years at the Connaught Rooms, their annual dinner switching to the Grand Room of the Hotel Cecil.

The Presiding Chairman was Sir Felix Pole, the President was still the Marquess of Ailesbury, and there was an attendance of more than 300.

The toast of the evening was of 'Wiltshire, OUR county and Wiltshiremen in London,' but the Chairman suggested 'there also ought to have been added to the toast, "Wiltshire-men in London on a night out"'.

These were good times for the Association, even though the country was in the depths of an economic depression, as Lord Bledisloe reminded them:

A cloud at present rested upon the greatest and most vital of their industries; there was indeed a "vly of depression on the Wiltshire turmut". Individually and collectively, to whatever part of the State they belonged, they must do all in their power to set that industry on a permanently firm and prosperous basis. At any rate, Wiltshire farmers, of whom for his sins he was not one, were facing their struggles with a stout heart and, relatively speaking, with no small confidence in the future.

And he added:

Wilts was a county of fair women

and quite incorrupt men. It was a land that produced width of outlook, cheerfulness of disposition, simplicity of faith and honesty of purpose.

Next was the star turn, Jimmy Thomas MP:

The telegraph office, he said, had been exceedingly busy that night. Mr Lloyd George [the former Prime Minister, now leader of the Liberal Party again] *had wired him: "Delighted to know you are attending the Wilts dinner. Please assure them that I am the one man that can give them the moon."*

Knowing that Sir Felix [Pole] *was in the chair and knowing that Sir Felix and he jointly ran the Great Western Railway, Mr Stanley Baldwin* [the Prime Minister] *had wired: "Dear Jim (as from one Prime Minister to a prospective Prime Minister), delighted to know you are attending dinner. Please convey to those present that they are our only hope."*

He also 'poked much fun' at the bachelorhood of Captain Victor Cazalet, the MP for Chippenham (who was present), probably in the knowledge that Cazalet was homosexual.

A dashing veteran of the First World War, he had a colourful life; he strongly supported General Franco's fascists in the Spanish Civil War, was the godfather of actress Elizabeth Taylor, and died in a plane crash in 1943. ■

Mills (see page 138) were built, he joined F Skurray & Son as a miller's clerk, eventually rising to become the manager of Skurray's Motor Engineers Ltd, operating from the same location in Princes Street.

By early 1922, he had founded HC Preater Ltd, and taken over the Ford dealership previously owned by Ernest Skurray, who in turn moved to The Square, Old Town, and set up Skurray's new business on the site of the former VWH Repository.

For 11 years Preater was a magistrate, and he was also President of the Swindon Rotary Club. During the Second World War, along with his wife Lilian, he played an active role in the work of the Red Cross; he was Secretary of its *Penny-a-week Fund*, while Lilian was the Honorary Commandant of the 68th Wilts Detachment.

When he died in 1968, Preater left an estate to the value of £47,121. ■

Lighting up the gloomy thirties

The Association returned to Hotel Cecil for the first annual dinner of the 1930s, chaired by Sir Kynaston Studd (see page 148), and with the Marquess of Ailesbury still President.

Despite the ongoing Depression, the annual dinners continued to attract large attendances, this year's reckoned to be over 400.

Such was the expectation of people of high office attending that the *North Wilts Herald*'s report of the occasion said that 'only one' MP was present (Captain Cazalet) and 'only two' Mayors (of Marlborough and Wilton).

The menu included *Hors d'oeuvre Netheravon, Creme Wiltonia, Supreme de Sole Kynaston, Boeuf Marlborough* and *Poulet Savernake*.

This was clearly part of a concerted effort to lighten the mood and continue to change the character of the occasion, as the *North Wilts Herald* explained and welcomed:

Those responsible for the arrangement are to be commended on their courage in curtailing the number of speeches and on their decision that these should be as short as possible. The heavy orations of a few years ago had given place to shorter and brighter speeches and more time for music, while the closure of the dinner proceedings at half-past nine provided the opportunity of devoting two hours and a half to dancing and general fraternisation – a departure inaugurated last year, which seemed to be very much appreciated.

And as if to confirm that times definitely were changing: when 'the ladies' were toasted by Sir Lawrence Chubb, a lady was actually allowed to respond for the first time.

She was a Mrs Lovett, but the report gave no information about her or why she was chosen for the overdue honour. All we know about her is she attended the dinner in 1923, and otherwise 1930 was her only other recorded appearance.

The main speech was by Sir Kynaston Studd, who:

related how the first cricket match in which he took part was between the schoolboys of Wiltshire and Hampshire when, thanks to the courtesy and kindness of the captain of the opposite side, he got 123 runs. Wiltshire was famous for its Downs, and as a small boy he and his brother had to turn out early in the morning to ride his father's steeplechasers.

The Marquess of Ailesbury replied by saying he 'quite envied Sir Kynaston in having been able to ride over the Downs before there was any wire there'.

The changing formula of the dinners appears to have been successful, because when they reconvened in 1931, the *North Wilts Herald* said:

The toast list was short, the speeches brief, and an excellent musical pro-gramme had been arranged, the idea of finishing the dinner early and devoting a couple of hours to dancing being evidently a popular departure.

This produced an 'unusually large number who went up from the old county to re-unite with men and women whose lot is now cast in the metropolis',

although no attendance figure was reported.

It all took place in another new venue: the 'large banqueting hall and the surrounding suite of rooms at the Hotel Victoria, London' (on Northumberland Avenue, pictured opposite, in 2024) and the honours were a family affair, with the Marquess of Ailesbury as President, as usual, and his son, the Earl of Cardigan, the Presiding Chairman.

The chief speaker was Jimmy Thomas, now Secretary of State for the Dominions. After some political banter and more joking ('amid considerable laughter'), Thomas's mood turned much more serious:

It would be idle to deny, said Mr Thomas, that in responding to this toast one was fully conscious of the difficult times through which we were passing. The Government was not unmindful of its responsibility. From 1914-18 this nation passed through a crisis which was unprecedented in the world's history. During those four years, our people were faced with a burden that no people had ever faced before, but no greater mistake was made than to assume that when the armistice was declared and peace was proclaimed, our difficulties were over.

Far from it; before the year was over, there would be a split in the Labour Party that would lead to the formation of a coalition under Ramsay MacDonald, and when Thomas supported it, he was expelled from the party and the NUR.

Despite everything, the annual dinners continued to go from strength to strength.

But how much longer could it last? ∎

CHELTENHAM FLYER

A NEW RAILWAY BOOK FOR BOYS OF ALL AGES

FULLY ILLUSTRATED
PRICE ONE SHILLING

CHELTENHAM FLYER
GWR
WORLD'S FASTEST TRAIN

At the annual dinner of the Association in 1932, it was noted that the 'Swindon contingent' had arrived in London on the *Cheltenham Flyer*.

It was a nickname given to the *Cheltenham Spa Express*, which ran from Paddington to Cheltenham Spa, via Swindon, and vice versa.

The Mayor of Swindon, Alderman Calderwood, also made reference to it when he spoke at the dinner:

Swindon's chief claim was that it produced the best of everything for the best of railways. The town's little band of 51 pilgrims travelled to London that day on the world famous Cheltenham Flyer – 75½ miles in just over one hour, and usually there were a few minutes to spare on scheduled time. Such an excellent service brought the Wiltshiremen of London very near to home.

Six months later, in September 1932, the Swindon to London service was timed at 65 minutes, giving an average speed of 71.3 mph (114.7 km/h).

It was the first time any train in the world had been scheduled at over 70 mph (110 km/h).

Cheltenham Flyers were all pulled by Swindon-built locomotives, such as *Caerphilly Castle*, which is on display at the Steam Museum in Swindon with a *Cheltenham Flyer* plaque on the front of its boiler. ■

Now we're flying

If *The Association of Wiltshiremen in London* could be said to have had a home, it was the Holborn Restaurant, where they met from 1897 to 1924.

It is not known why they didn't book the venue for 1925 and used other venues in the intervening years – nor why they decided to return there in 1932.

And they returned in style on February 27, with around 400 filling the epic King's Hall.

The Marquess of Ailesbury's long run as President was still continuing, but ill health meant that he sent a deputy, his son, the Earl of Cardigan. The Presiding Chairman was Lord Roundway: not the same man who had been President in the 1920s – that was the 1st Baron, who died in 1925 – but his son, the 2nd Baron, Edward Murray Colston.

He pointed out that he fulfilled both requirements of the Association – because he was born in Wiltshire, but was living in London.

The *North Wilts Herald* gave details of the party that had travelled up from Swindon:

Wiltshire exiles were greeted by their own kith and kin from all parts of the county, but the greatest pilgrimage of all was that sent out from Swindon. Organised by Mr WJ King and Councillor TC Newman, the Swindon contingent, led by the Mayor (Ald JL Calderwood) numbered more than 50 strong and travelled by Special Saloon on the Cheltenham Flyer.

When he spoke, Alderman Calderwood pointed to Swindon as a success story, something that is all the more remarkable in hindsight, against the backdrop of the global Depression of the 1930s:

Although a young borough, they were rapidly growing up and consolidating their position as a great industrial centre. He referred to the various industries in the town, including the new chiming clock factory [Garrard's] which had an attractive "stand" at the British Industries Fair. Swindon was also preparing in the matter of electricity, and its new water supply scheme, for all those new industries they hoped to tempt to the town.

Jimmy Thomas again made the keynote speech, but before he got up, Sir Felix Pole paid tribute to him for joining the coalition National Government, even though it led to his exclusion from the Labour Party and the NUR.

"In that great political upheaval," he said, "Mr Thomas played his part manfully. He did the right thing and I was delighted when I heard that he had retained the seat for Derby."

Despite its usual humour, in hindsight, Thomas's speech seems unsuited to the changed nature of the dinners at this time. However, amid his talk of tariffs and fiscal reform, and references to the grave problems facing the world, there was some personal poignancy: ▶

John Lindow Calderwood (pictured, below) attended the annual dinner of *The Association of Wiltshiremen in London* as the Mayor of Swindon in 1932, but his best years were still ahead of him.

Born in 1888, in Cumberland, he was the son of a surgeon, but became an articled clerk to London solicitors, Messrs Cree & Son.

After receiving his law degree in 1910, he qualified as a solicitor two years later, eventually joining the Swindon firm of Townsend, Jones & Wood (later Townsend, Wood & Calderwood) in Cricklade Street.

He was commissioned as a Second Lieutenant during the First World War, and rose to the rank of Captain.

After returning to Swindon in 1919, he became one of the most prominent local politicians in the next four decades.

His home from the 1930s until his death in 1960 was The Hermitage in Old Town.

He played a prominent role in establishing the Arts Centre (at its original location in the former Methodist Hall in Regent Street), and the formation of the borough library service, and in 1932 formed the Swindon Council of Social Services, becoming President until 1949.

He was elected to Wiltshire County Council in 1947, became Chairman in 1949, and remained in post until his death. Calderwood was given the Freedom of Swindon in 1950, and awarded the CBE in 1957, for services to local government. ∎

I never believed that it would have been possible for me to attend any gathering and say that I have now ceased to be connected with the railway. I was an errand boy at 7s [35p] a week on the GWR; I was a fireman and I was an engine-driver. I can never be other than a railwayman, no matter what I may pretend; my ties with Swindon are too deep-rooted and sacred. I shall never forget my life and my associations with Wiltshire.

Although I have been amongst you as an engine-driver, as a labour leader, and as a member of four different Governments, I have never felt my responsibilities so great as at the present moment. My one object and my one aim must be to see that those who gave us their confidence, who pinned their faith and their hope in a National Government, shall not be let down by time and circumstance.

The organisers took further steps to lighten proceedings when they returned to the Holborn Restaurant for the 1933 dinner, perhaps because of Thomas's long speech the year before (although he did not attend this time):

An effort was made to limit speeches to three minutes, and to assist the chairman, a warning device similar to traffic lights was erected in the hall. At the beginning of a speech the blue light shone, the amber light shone as a warning that time was almost up, and when the red light was switched on, speakers came to a hurried finish.

Around 400 were in attendance, including the President, the Marquess of Ailesbury. One of his duties was to make a presentation to the Honorary Secretary of more than ten years, Mr GM Coward; he was given a gold cigarette case, while Mrs Coward was presented with a diamond ring.

In the chair, and completing his first public engagement, having recently come of age, was Walter Long, 2nd Viscount, of Wrax-all, the son of Walter Long, the 1st Viscount, who had been the Presiding Chairman in 1912. The young Viscount does not appear to have been subject to the 'traffic light' control, thankfully – because he gave a rare insight into the Association's activities and charitable work, which is lacking from almost all other annual dinners:

Enjoyable, too, were the games and competitions organised by the Association, which afforded such excellent opportunities of maintaining the "county spirit". Perhaps the most important of all the activities of the Association was helping Wiltshire-men in trouble. The hon secretary told him that assistance had been given to every deserving case that came before the Council during the past year – and to some undeserving ones as well.

This reference to 'deserving' and 'undeserving' is connected with the Poor Law, established 99 years earlier. It created a distinc-tion between those who were by nature hardworking and were in poverty through no fault of their own, and were therefore deserving of charity, as opposed to the rest. The fact that the Asso-ciation was giving support to the 'undeserving' poor is interesting and perhaps surprising.

The theme of highlighting the Association's other activities was carried over into a speech by John Willis, but he also emphasised the need for it to attract younger members:

We are very anxious that all young people from the dear old county should join the association. They will meet old friends and make new ones if they attend the whist and bridge drives and if they attend our dances I feel certain that in the arms of the opposite sex dancing to the tune of "Wheezy Anna" is bound to end in matrimony.

Dealing with another side of the Association's activities, Mr Willis urged, "Do not forget the sports", adding:

They had a true array of cups presented by their President and Sir Felix Pole for which they could compete. On the charitable side, any cases that came to their notice they did their utmost to assist.

There was a toast to 'the Ladies', but the precedent of allowing one of them to respond was not followed this time, and it was left to Lord Horder, who 'thought perhaps he had been asked to reply for them because at the end of the week, women would have no words left'.

Then, 'amid laughter', he added: "We ladies do thank you very sincerely."

Once the last 'traffic light' had flashed, it was time for the entertainment, which seems to have taken an exotic (and even erotic) turn – something that would have been unthinkable, a few years earlier:

After dinner, there was dancing until midnight, and an excellent cabaret performance with Edna Squire-Brown [pictured, opposite], a clever contortionist dancer, was included. Mr HH Perkins, hon musical director of the association, arranged the concert items during the evening. ∎

Right: Wiltshiremen (and women) photographed by *The Tatler* in 1934 (courtesy of Illustrated London News Group)

WILTSHIRE MEN IN LONDON

THE MARQUESS OF AILESBURY (President) AND LADY HILTON YOUNG

THE MARCHIONESS OF AILESBURY AND LORD HORDER (Chairman)

LADY HORDER AND THE RIGHT HON. J. H. THOMAS

MR. AND MRS. HARRIS

MR. H. H. PERKINS (Hon. Musical Director), MR. F. CHIVERS, AND MR. G. M. COWARD (Hon. Sec.)

MR. AND THE HON. MRS. A. F. DOGGETT

THE MAYOR AND MAYORESS OF SWINDON (Mr. and Mrs. W. H. Bickham)

Over 400 Wiltshiremen and women gathered together for the annual dinner at the Holborn Restaurant and to drink a toast to Christopher Wren, Thomas Lawrence, Richard Jefferies, and other great Wiltshiremen, and in the chair was another very distinguished Wiltshireman, Lord Horder, Physician-in-Ordinary to the Prince of Wales, whilst the Marquess of Ailesbury, the President of the Wiltshire Society, was also present and undertook the responsible task of proposing "The Ladies" to which Lady Hilton Young responded. Lord Horder's daughter, the Hon. Mrs. Cullinan, is in another picture, and the Right Hon. Jim Thomas' daughter is Mrs. Harris, seen in another picture. Mr. Fred Chivers, the late Mayor of Devizes, added the right touch of atmosphere by singing "The Vly Be On the Turmuts." A most successful evening!

Photographs by Arthur Owen

DR. AND THE HON. MRS. E. K. CULLINAN (Lord Horder's daughter)

Jimmy Thomas's last stand

There was another 'large gathering' at 1934's annual dinner, which had Lord Horder in the chair, and the Marquess of Ailesbury was President for the tenth time.

It was also the last time that Jimmy Thomas would attend, and when he rose to speak, he was greeted by 'continued applause'.

This, the many compliments he received from other speakers, and some of the contents of his own speech make it seem that they somehow realised it was his swansong, although they could not have known. He started by saying:

> I am going to say quite seriously that there is no gathering and no society and no body of men and women to whom I could more truthfully say, 'Thank you for what you did for me' than to a gathering of Wiltshiremen and Wiltshire women.
>
> My early association with Wiltshire was as a young man with an ambitious feeling that I could contribute something to my country's good, not unmindful of the fact that the past tradition meant vast privileges. I entered a new era which did not mean wealth, or name or position, but service to my country.
>
> Could there be anything of which I am more proud, of which I am grateful and of which I express my appreciation than of the fact that it was in Wiltshire, in Swindon, that I was given my first opportunity to serve my country?

Then he turned to the problems facing the world:

> The real problem of unemployment is the fact that between the ages of 17 and 20 the brain is like a sponge, ready to sop up evil as well as good. And the evil is that we have too many of your young folk walking the streets sopping up evil at a time when their character ought to be formed in the other direction.
>
> How happy we ought to be to-night that we are the only country in the world which can say that we have not only arrested, but that we have turned the tide. It is as certain as I am speaking here that we have at last mastered our unemployment problem.
>
> I should be deceiving you if I did not frankly admit that every day and every hour is fraught with difficult and new problems...
>
> They talk of revolutions that are sometimes reflected in bloodshed which we saw a few weeks ago in Austria... The world can never be the same as it was. God knows what the future may be.
>
> Friends, you hear of Blackshirts, Whiteshirts and Greenshirts, of dictatorships of the right, and dictatorships of the left. I beg of you to maintain that old British tradition that preserves untrammelled this magnificent constitution – a constitution which enables me to-night to respond as Secretary of State to a toast presented at a Wiltshire gathering, just as I came as a humble railway fireman in this same room and under the same auspices.
>
> The first time I was invited to this gathering was when as a young fireman I came from Swindon earning 24 shillings a week. To-night I respond as a responsible Secretary of State. What greater tribute could there be to the democratic character of our constitution?
>
> You men and women of Wiltshire, yours is a great county, a beautiful county, a county that gives hope and inspiration to all who visit it. In literature, arts, science and politics Wiltshire has given great men and women who have left their mark in the history of this country.

Lord Horder also talked about great Wiltshiremen, and he named three in particular: the painter, Sir Thomas Lawrence, Sir Christopher Wren and Richard Jefferies.

Lawrence (1769-1830) was actually born in Bristol, but began painting when he was living in Devizes, where his father was an innkeeper at the Bear Hotel; the family moved to Bath when he was ten.

His greatest tribute was to Jefferies:

> Richard Jefferies, was not only Wiltshire born but also Wiltshire bred. He was a Wiltshireman through and through. He was the most modern of the three... Lawrence's portraits would fade away, and St Paul's would crumble to dust, but Jefferies' word pictures in which he described the soil and the pasture, the sunrise and the sunset, and the wind and the rain as they made their appeal to him in the native county, could never die because they lived on and on in the minds of those who had eyes to read and minds to understand.

The Chairman also dwelled on the aims of the Association:

The activities of their... society were various, embracing whist, bridge and dancing. The sports members met for tennis, golf, and bowls, and there were beautiful cups, one presented by their president and the golfing cup by Sir Felix Pole.

The traditional toast to 'the Ladies' was not only responded to by a lady this year, but by a *Lady*: Lady Hilton Young.

Meanwhile, JH Willis said he wanted to make particular mention of his home town, Swindon:

He thought they were entitled to it. Swindon men formed the Association many years ago, and Swindon people formed at least a section of that gathering, and they were deeply indebted to Swindon people for what they had done to support the Association.

Every year that passed in the 1930s brought an increased feeling of doom, but the annual dinners of *The Association of Wiltshiremen in London* continued to enjoy what was probably their heyday.

No attendance figure was given for the 1935 dinner, which was held at the Holborn Restaurant again, but it had the same enthusiastic crowd – apparently as determined as ever to at least temporarily put the world's problems to one side.

Although Jimmy Thomas could not be there, he telephoned the venue to dictate an encouraging message:

Give my kind regards and best wishes to the Wiltshiremen and women now assembled in London.

Tell them that in spite of the pessimists, the old country is still on top and will remain so. Wiltshire people do not understand the meaning of defeat and they reflect the determination of their race in difficult times. It is the duty of all to pull together, and that is the motto for to-day.

As if to underline the grandeur of the annual dinners compared with the charitable objectives of the Association,

Pictures from *The Tatler* in March 1935, taken at the annual dinner that took place the previous month. Above: the Marquess of Ailesbury and Mrs AG Street. Right: Lady Wright and WW Wakefield MP.

the *North Wilts Herald* report said:

Lord Wright, who presided, read many other messages of good wishes, including one from Buckingham Palace in reply to the loyal message customarily sent to the King and Queen on this occasion.

Another came from a little orphan boy whom Wiltshiremen in London have befriended and agreed to maintain at the Alexandra Orphanage. "I hope you will all have a good time," said the boy, who enclosed his photograph, which was passed round the tables.

The evening had a theme of literature, with AG Street, author of *Farmer's Glory*, one of the speakers (see page 196).

(see page 196).

Another speaker was FT Hobbs, Mayor of Swindon:

He recalled the melancholy fact that for the past five years the employees in that great undertaking [Swindon Railway Works] had been working short-time and suggested that, this being the railway centenary year, it would be appropriate to ▶

1935

WEST COUNTRYMEN IN CARICATURE

L.H. BENTALL J.P.

STONE HENGE

W. NICHOLSON

G.M. COWARD
Hon. Secretary

Chairman—
Rt. Hon. LORD KENNET OF THE DENE
P.C., G.B.E., D.S.O., D.S.C.

H.H. PERKINS
Hon. Treasurer.

Z. STILES ALLEN J.P.
Mayor of St Marylebone.

B.G. WORT
Member of the Council.

W.W.
WAKEFIELD, M.P.
*The famous
England Rugby
Captain,
who proposed
"The Chairman"*

LT. COL. HUGHES
*Mayor
of
Marlboro'.*

FRED CHIVERS
*Ex Mayor
of
"VIZES".*

THE SOCIETY OF WILTSHIREMEN—BY "MEL"

The forty-fourth Annual Dinner of the Society was held in London on Leap Year Day. The Rt. Hon. Lord Kennet of the Dene, as chairman, proposed the toast of "Wiltshire, Our County, The County." As Sir Edward Hilton Young he was in *Vindictive* during the raid on Zeebrugge. During the dinner Lady Kennet presented the County Golf Trophies to Mr. B. G. Wort and Mr. H. H. Perkins. The Mayor of St. Marylebone, also a Wiltshireman, responded to the principal toast, and the famous and popular "Wakers" proposed the health of the Chairman

---

mark the occasion by paying the workpeople for their holidays, and that the Company should say to the men: "We will mark this epoch in the history of railways. We will pay you for the holidays you are bound to take."

That would be welcomed as a great relief to those responsible for some 40,000 dependants who were forced to take ten days' holiday during the summer every year.

It is a timely reminder to us that while the annual shutdown of the Works, known locally as 'Trip Week', is often remembered with nostalgia, many families spent all year recovering from the cost of unpaid leave and the holiday.

'There were 300 guests at the tables' at the annual dinner of 1936, and 'quite a good proportion of them were ladies, who have grown in numbers in recent years'.

And one lady in particular was making history, in two senses: Alderman Mrs May George (see page 194), who was not only the first female Mayor of Swindon, but the first woman to be present at an annual dinner as a civic head. Unlike many previous mayors attending the dinners, however, who seemed routinely invited to speak, she apparently wasn't.

The Chairman was Lord Kennet of the Dene PC, GBE, DSO, DSE 'better known generally, perhaps,

Pictures from *The Bystander* magazine in May 1936, showing *The Association of Wiltshiremen in London*'s golf day at Woodcote Park, near Purley, Surrey, where they played for The Liberty Cup. Above (from left): the Marquess of Ailesbury, Leonard Bentall, Capt Ivor Stuart Liberty, NJT Neilson. Right, top: GM Coward (Honorary Secretary) and C Jeater. Right, bottom: HH Perkins (Honorary Treasurer) and AG Pears. Opposite: a cartoon view of the 1936 dinner in *The Tatler* (courtesy of Illustrated London News Group).

as formerly Sir Hilton Young', and he started on an optimistic note:

We were fortunate, he went on, in our new Sovereign – King Edward VIII – who had the great advantage of youth at a time when we were looking to youth to establish peace and prosperity in times to come.

His optimism was severely misplaced as the King, who had succeeded George V, just over six weeks earlier, would abdicate, nine months later.

And there was no getting away from the pessimism surrounding world affairs, with WW Wakefield, MP for Swindon, telling the gathering: "We hope the necessity for the occasion of war may never arise, but notwithstanding that, there is a necessity of our being prepared for war."

This ended the formal part of the proceedings. The subsequent two hours or so were, in accordance with recent custom, devoted to dancing. ■

May the first

It took May George, Swindon's first lady mayor, a long time to reach office. She was elected as councillor for the South Ward as early as 1921, and was made an alderman ten years later, finally becoming Mayor in 1935-36.

Her appointment caused council officials a dilemma. No-one knew how to address her; it was reported that speakers at public meetings didn't know whether to introduce her as *Mr* or *Mrs* Mayor.

It seems the *The Association of Wiltshiremen in London* didn't quite know how to deal with her, either. When she attended the 1936 dinner, the North Wilts Herald noted:

For the first time in the long history of the gathering, a woman was present as a civil head – Alderman Mrs May George, Mayor of Swindon.

Despite the tradition apparently being that mayors attending the dinner would be invited to make a speech, or at least propose and/or respond to toasts, in this case she remained silent.

Born in 1883 as May Williams, she was the daughter of a railway guard, but not – as some people believed – related to a former Mayor of Swindon, Reuben George.

In the Borough's official year book, where the councillors and aldermen are listed with their profession or occupation, May George is recorded simply as a married woman, but she was a former teacher, and believed women should play a prominent role in public life – and led by example.

Throughout her political career she worked tirelessly for the needs of women and children, and was instrumental in establishing a standard of care at Swindon's Kingshill Maternity Home that made it an example for the whole country.

She served on numerous committees, including Health, Market and Cemetery; Watch and Pleasure; Finance and Law; and Education. She was also a member of the Guardians, Local Employment, and Pensions Committees.

And she was still working, only hours before she died. She collapsed at her home at 17 Croft Road, on the evening of April 20, 1943, after attending a Finance Committee meeting at the council offices, and died the following day; the Mayor, AJB Selwood, said her premature death could have been due to overwork.

"When I saw her... I was not altogether happy about her appearance," he said. "I had occasion to telephone her later that evening – we had a conversation, and she wished me good-night – for the last time."

May's funeral was in Carmarthen, and there was a memorial service at Christ Church, Swindon. Floral tributes were sent by the many organisations she had campaigned for in Swindon, including the matron and staff at the Isolation Hospital, the Swindon Youth Organisation Council and the staff and children at Olive House and The Limes children's homes.

Her obituary in the *Advertiser* said: "Mrs George died as she would have wished – working. No woman – or man – put so much into public work as she did." ■

The authoress Edith Maud Olivier MBE has the distinction of being the first woman allowed to give a proper speech to *The Association of Wiltshiremen in London* (in 1939), when she was Mayor of Wilton.

Born in Wilton in 1872, she was one of ten siblings, and was related to the actor Sir Laurence Olivier through her paternal grandfather.

Schooled at home, she went to St Hugh's College, Oxford, but completed only four terms, before leaving because of asthma.

Edith formed a deep but platonic friendship with the artist Rex Whistler, who painted her in 1939 (pictured, left), and her other friends included Cecil Beaton and Siegfried Sassoon.

All of her many books had a strong country flavour, and she said Wiltshire was the epitome of rural England.

Her first novel, *The Love Child*, was published in 1927, while her autobiographical writings included *Without Knowing Mr Walkley* (1938) and *Edith: From Her Journals 1924-48*.

Moonrakings: A Little Book of Wiltshire Stories (co-curated with Margaret KS Edwards) was reprinted in 1979 to celebrate the Diamond Jubilee of the Wiltshire Federation of Women's Institutes.

Her non-fiction titles include *The Eccentric Life of Alexander Cruden* (1934) and *Four Victorian Ladies of Wiltshire* (1945).

She died in May 1948. Her final book, *Wiltshire* (part of the *County Books* series), was published posthumously in 1951. ■

MOONRAKING
BY
A.G. STREET

Strawberry
Roan

A. G. Street

COUNTRY
CALENDAR
by
A. G. STREET

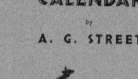

Illustrated by
LIONEL EDWARDS, R.I.

A.G.
STREET
Farmer's
Glory

Decorations by Gwendolen Raverat

FABER

FABER paper covered EDITIONS

FROM

The Sedgebury
Platoon prepared
A. G. ST

PENGUIN
BOOKS

FARMER'S
GLORY

A.G. STREET

IN HIS OWN
COUNTRY

A Selection
from the Writings
of
A.G. STREET

FARMER'S GLORY
A. G. STREET

Introduced by
JAMES REBANKS

TO BE A
FARMER'S
BOY

Faber and Faber

A.G.
STREET

FARM

A

COMPLETE   UNABRIDGED

2/-

A.G. STREET

MOONRAKING

ILLUSTRATED BY

STRAWBERRY
ROAN
A NOVEL BY
A.G. STREET

A.G.
STREET

Bobby
Bocker

A.G. STREET

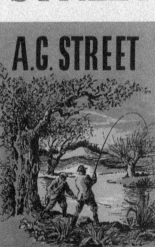

Fish and Chips

BY A
AUTHOR

EN
FU

Farmer's Glory

Arthur Street (AG Street to his readers) attended several annual dinners of *The Association of Wiltshire-men in London*, and appears to have been inspired by it to write about about the moonrakers legend.

A year after attending the 1935 dinner he published *Moonraking*, one of more than 30 books he wrote in a career spanning four decades.

He was born at Ditchampton Farm, Wilton, near Salisbury, on April 7, 1892, and was educated at Dauntsey's School, where agriculture was part of the curriculum.

He left in 1907, at the age of 16, and spent some years learning farming from his father, before emigrating to Winnipeg, Canada, in around 1911.

There he worked as a farm labourer, returning to Wilton in 1914, and later taking over the tenancy following his father's death.

Following the onset of the great agricultural depression in the 1920s and 1930s, he decided to try writing as a means of supplementing his farm income.

His best-known book was *Farmer's Glory*, first published in 1932, which described his time in Canada, and his return to Wiltshire.

It was an immediate bestseller, not only saving his farm, but bringing his name to a wider public.

He wrote a weekly column for *Farmers Weekly* for 30 years, and was also a prolific radio broadcaster, appearing on *The Brains Trust* and many other BBC radio programmes.

He continued to farm after he became a popular author, his writing becoming particularly well known for portraying agriculture in all its pragmatic and stark reality. His use of West Country dialect strengthened his imagery of rural life.

His books were mainly light fiction, often based on the Wiltshire farming community and therefore, to some degree, autobiographical.

His book *Strawberry Roan* was later turned into a film starring the future *Dr Who* actor, William Hartnell.

He left Ditchampton Farm in 1951 because of encroaching residential development, and moved to Mill Farm at South Newton.

His obituary in the *Western Daily Press* said:

A book written in the little spare time a working farmer has at his disposal proved to be the turning point in the career of AG Street, farmer, author, broadcaster.

Before he wrote his book, "Farmer's Glory," he was struggling to keep things going at Ditchampton Farm, Wiltshire...

It was the start of a career which made him one of the best-known names in broadcasting for his talks of the countryside and as a star of the programme "Any Questions".

His turnover of books was quite prolific, considering that he was, and remained, a farmer.

Nearly all his books had a flavour of the countryside. Some critics complained that his books were too brutal in their realism, but Street would say that it was his intention to show the countryside as it is and not as anybody might think it ought to be. ∎

Different perspectives

Below: the only menu card thought to survive from the pre-war annual dinners of *The Association of Wiltshiremen in London*. Note the instruction that everyone *without exception* must join in with *The Vly Be on the Turmuts*.

The success of *The Association of Wiltshiremen in London*'s annual dinners showed no sign of abating in 1937, when 'a large company' attended the gathering at the Holborn Restaurant.

There were five mayors present: from Swindon (Alderman LJ Newman), Devizes, Calne, Marlborough and Chippenham. Owing to the absence of the President, the Marquess of Ailesbury,

· FUIMUS ·

President:
THE MOST HONOURABLE
THE MARQUESS OF AILESBURY, D.S.O., D.L., J.P.

"Know this thy Countie Wiltshire, look up and thank God."

The
Forty-Fifth Annual Dinner

King's Hall, Holborn Restaurant,
Saturday 27th February, 1937.

Chairman.
THE MOST HONOURABLE
THE MARQUESS OF AILESBURY,
D.S.O., D.L., J.P.

WILTSHIREMEN IN LONDON.

MENU.

" 'Tis now upon the point of Dinner-time"

Huîtres Natives
ou
Hors-d'œuvre Variés
" My soul tasted that heavenly food, which gives new
appetite."

Queue de Bœuf Claire
Crème Germaine
" Famish'd people must be slowly nurst,
And fed by spoonfuls, else they always burst."

Saumon bouilli sauce Hollandaise
"From the rude sea's enraged and foaming mouth."

Vol-au-Vent Toulouse
Choufleur Polonaise

Poulet rôti au Bacon
Salade de Saison
Croustilles
" Can one desire too much of a good thing?"

Bombe glacée Plombière
Gaufrettes
" The daintiest last to make the end most sweet."

Croûte au Fromage

Dessert   **Café**
" Coffee, which makes the politician wise,
And see through all things with his half-shut eyes."

"Who rises from a feast with that keen appetite that
he sits down?"

who was suffering from influenza, his son, the Earl of Cardigan (along with his wife, the Countess) presided, and they received guests in the Throne Room, before they dined in the King's Hall.

The Earl proposed the toast ("Wilt-shire our county, the County") and, as was customary, spent some time talking about the beauty of the Wiltshire countryside, but offering a different perspective. His first remark, that 'most people went about in motor-cars' is certainly inaccurate, because car ownership was beyond the reach of 'most people' until years after the end of the Second World War, although the 1930s saw motoring come within the reach of the middle classes.

Not that the vast majority of the population would have been able to associate themselves with the privileged lifestyle evident in his following comments, as reported by the *North Wilts Herald*:

He made his "living" by writing about cars, and in his spare time he was bored to death with the wretched ▶

WILTSHIREMEN IN LONDON.

TOAST LIST.
TEMPUS FUGIT.

His Most Gracious Majesty The King.
THE CHAIRMAN.

Her Majesty The Queen,
and other Members of the Royal Family.
THE CHAIRMAN.

" Wiltshire our County, THE County."

Proposer	THE CHAIRMAN
Responder	H. G. MAURICE, ESQ., C.B.

The County Mayors.

Proposer	A. G. STREET, ESQ.
Responder ...	HIS WORSHIP THE MAYOR OF MARLBOROUGH
	(ALDERMAN THOMAS FREE, J.P.)

GOLF TROPHIES.

PRESIDENT'S BOWL.	*Holder:* H. H. PERKINS
FELIX POLE CUP.	*Holder:* B. G. WORT
FRY CUP for Bowls	*Holder:* F. T. PIKE

All Golfers must compete for the "Liberty" Cup at the WOODCOTE PARK GOLF CLUB, COULSDON on MONDAY, APRIL 19th NEXT.

Our President, The Most Hon. The Marquess of Ailesbury, D.S.O., will preside at the luncheon supported by the Right Hon. The Lord Mayor of London who will take the first card.

This is an "open" meeting and non Golfers may come to the Luncheon.

The " 9 o'clock " Toast—All Absent Friends.
" Memory is the treasury and guardian of all things."
THE CHAIRMAN.

The Chairman.

Proposer ...	CAPTAIN IVOR STEWART-LIBERTY, M.C., J.P.

Toastmaster: COLIN SYMON.

WILTSHIREMEN IN LONDON.

MUSIC.
" Let the sounds of music creep into our ears."

" THE " CLASSIC."
After the Toast " Wiltshire, our County "
MR. JAMES WORT will sing in dialect
" THE VLY BE ON THE TURMUTS "
and all diners, *without exception*, must join in the
MOONRAKER'S HYMN.

RAYMOND NEWELL ... ... Baritone

CABARET.

LILYAN DANIA AND MALO
A charming Dancing team from the leading Cabarets.

OTTO AND HUGO WITH ANN
Ann is delightful—Otto and Hugo, quite mad!!

EDDIE BANCROFT
Eccentric Dancing Comedian.

SYDNEY JEROME AND HIS BROADCASTING BAND
will play during Dinner and for Dancing, 9.30 till 11.59

At 11.59—

" Happy did we meet and we'll be happy until we meet again."

Hon. Treasurer:	Honorary Secretary:
H. H. PERKINS, ESQ.,	G. M. COWARD,
Studley,	The Chase, Coulsdon.
Upper Teddington Rd.,	
Hampton Wick.	

things, and if he wanted to enjoy himself he flew.

Nevertheless, he provided a new insight into the county, which most of those present would never have experienced – the view from the air:

The aeroplane has this great advantage over the motor-car," said Earl Cardigan. "Once you have got it in the air – unless you are a complete fool – you can just let the machine take you along and you can sit back and enjoy the view. It is a wonderful view as one passes over Wiltshire – the wide sweeping downs rolling in the broad valleys; the dark line of the woodland; the silver threads of the streams tracing winding paths through the hamlets, and here and there the groups of the market towns with their broad main streets... I don't know where in any country, you can have a happier prospect.

The next item on the agenda brought them down to earth nicely: everybody joining in with *The Vly Be on the Turmuts.*

The Association sent its now traditional telegram to the King – George VI, who had succeeded less than three months previously, and had not yet been crowned, so it wished him 'a long and peaceful reign', perhaps realising, by now, that it would probably be anything but peaceful.

A reply from his Private Secretary was duly received during the evening, which they had clearly decided to make the most of, this year:

When the uniformed Post Office telegraph messenger arrived at the entrance to the dining hall, his presence, with a message from his Majesty, was announced by the toast

master. A signal for his admittance was given, and, to the accompaniment of the roll of the drums of the orchestra, the messenger marched smartly to Lord Cardigan, delivered the telegram, saluted and marched out of the hall.

With the entertainments no longer restricted to performances by noted Wiltshiremen or women, Sydney Jerome and his broadcasting band played selections during dinner and also for the dance later, and songs by the well-known baritone, Raymond Newell, interspersed the speeches.

Most of the company danced until midnight, and enjoyed thoroughly the excellent cabaret.

'The 46th Annual Dinner of the Society of Wiltshiremen in London was held in the King's Hall at the Holborn Restaurant on Saturday evening,' said the *North Wilts Herald* in March 1938. 'It was a brilliant function attended by some 350 guests.'

And it got an ecclesiastical seal of approval for the first time, thanks to the attendance of the Bishop of Salisbury, who also became the Association's chaplain, while Lord Horder was once again Chairman.

But it was left to a policeman to make the first key speech. He was Superintendent William 'Farmer' Brown MBE (see page 202), who had been arguably the most famous real-life policeman of the day, and who told the assembled:

When he retired from the Force to which he had the honour to belong for nearly forty years, his old colleagues asked him what he proposed to do and he replied that his intention was to obey the natural call to his native county, which he did. Proceeding to extol the virtues of

Wiltshire, Mr Brown recalled what they had heard on former occasions from their President (the Marquess of Ailesbury) as to prominent Wiltshiremen and the beauties of the wonderful Downs and Plains and of Stonehenge. He himself personally admired those Downs... where one used to see hundreds of acres of lovely corn waving in the breeze. Now, however, one saw nothing but miles of military tanks and aerodromes instead of the waving corn.

He also referred to another 'blot on the fair county': foot-and-mouth disease, of which there had been a European-wide outbreak in 1937 and 1938, and which, Brown noted, 'denuded the hill-sides of cattle and sheep'.

The Chairman also made reference to this pandemic:

The County Associations in London have, most of them... dwindled somewhat. I am informed that the Wiltshire people share with Dorsetshire and the Yorkshire Tykes the distinction of not having dwindled. Despite that serious state of affairs to which Mr Brown has referred, what I understand is a disease which has baffled the most astute veterinary doctors, through which our county has suffered cruelly – a burden which has fallen very heavily upon Wiltshire, paralysing the markets and taking a great toll of the cattle – despite all that we have to-night some 350 Wiltshire people sitting round these tables.

So, you see, they have courage and enterprise, and a desire to mix with their fellows. If these things are to be taken as a measure of the men's and the women's relations to the body politic and the body social, then we can take heart, because it is quite clear that Wiltshire people at all events never say die.

But, as he quickly moved on to explain, there was worse news looming:

To-night we have several regrets. Mr Wakefield (the Member for Swindon) who was to have proposed the toast that Mr Brown so ably undertook, is not with us. There seems to have been some political excitement within the last few days – something to do with dictators [laughter] – but I would have thought that any matters having to do with dictators would have been of less consequence than the Wiltshiremen's dinner. After all, dictators are transient things, whereas Wiltshire is bound up with the more permanent factors in life. I am rather surprised at Mr Wakefield. I think he should have been here [laughter].

It is difficult to know what incident, particularly, Horder was referring to. What is clear, however, is how events in Europe were now affecting everyday life in Britain, and one response to the potential catastrophe that was looming was to laugh at it.

When it was time for the Mayor of Swindon, Major HE Niblett, to speak, he mounted something of a defence of the town after 'Priestley… told them that Swindon should be wiped off the face of the earth.'

Swindon's beautiful art deco Civic Offices, built in 1937-39, which the Mayor referred to, in his speech at the 1938 annual dinner, as a new 'Town Hall' (courtesy of Swindon Libraries/Local Studies)

This was a reference to the author, JB Priestley, whose 1934 book, *English Journey*, was critical of Swindon's 'Victorian tenements'.

After pointing out that 'They had at Swindon the finest railway works in the Kingdom, where they turned out not only good men from Wiltshire, but the finest engines and carriages that could be possibly put on the lines to run,' Niblett added:

We are only a young town so far as that goes. We have been in existence for only about 40 years, as you may say. Where our town offices stand there was formerly a farm near which was a pond with ducks swimming upon it. Now we have a Town Hall which is, however, too small and we are compelled to shift our offices from there and put them in a new place. Presently we hope to have a Town Hall in the centre of the borough which will be a credit, not only to Swindon but to the county in general, and to North Wilts in particular.

It's a reference to the partly built Civic Offices, not a 'Town Hall' as such.

The speeches concluded for another year, 'the remainder of the evening, until midnight, was devoted to a cabaret and dancing'.

Just one more year of dancing remained before events would take a darker but not completely unexpected turn. ∎

'Farmer' Brown's casebook

His colleagues called him 'Farmer Brown', the newspapers said he was 'the terror of bank note forgers and coiners', and the villains – they knew him as 'The Guv'nor'.

Born on August 25, 1872, at Chitterne, halfway between Warminster and Stonehenge, William Frederick Brown was the son of a schoolmaster, but left Wiltshire in 1894 to become a policeman, and went on to be arguably the most famous and celebrated real-life detective of the first half of the 20th century.

Like a true moon-raker, 'Farmer Brown' was much smarter than he at first appeared. Beneath 'his robust appearance' and the broad Wiltshire accent that gave him his nickname was a shrewd man and 'one of the cleverest detectives in the country' according to one of his obituaries.

'His uncanny way of detecting crime,' said *The People*, 'and following the smallest clues, led to his rapid promotion.'

As a Constable he worked in Lambeth, and quickly began climbing the ranks.

In 1911 he became Divisional Detective Inspector in the Wapping East area, and during the First World War was said to have done invaluable work for the Intelligence Department, tracking down German spies.

By 1921 he had become Chief Inspector at Scotland Yard, and after another three years had moved up to be Superintendent in charge of the Central Office. This made him part of what national newspapers and their readers knew as 'the Big Five' – the senior leadership team at Scotland Yard that was sometimes referred to as the 'Police Cabinet'.

Throughout his career he was genial and highly respected – even by the criminals.

THE DAILY MIRROR, Tuesday, March 28, 1922.

The 'Joys' of Spring-cleaning : See Page 13

The Daily Mirror

NET SALE NEARLY TWICE THAT OF ANY OTHER DAILY PICTURE NEWSPAPER

TICS   RONALD TRUE AT FLAT MURDER INQUEST

Ronald True taking notes at the resumed inquest yesterday on Gertrude Yates, found dead in her flat. The coroner's jury returned a verdict of wilful murder against him.

The People said of him:

> *One feature of his personality is that his closest friends do not consider that he has an enemy. On many occasions he has been praised by even the most hardened criminals in the dock for his courteous treatment of them, and his fairness in giving evidence against them.*

And according to the *Bath Chronicle*:

> *Wrong-doers fear him because of his dogged determination. He never admits failure. A powerfully built man, the Superintendent in private life is a delightful companion.*

From 1926 he was Area Superintendent, putting him in charge of all London policing operations south of the River Thames.

Brown's speciality was bringing forgers to justice, but he also led a string of high-profile murder enquiries, including the 'Lonely Villa Crime' in 1921, when Brown apprehended a strangler, Fred Wood.

And it was a murder that first brought him to the attention of the public, the brutal killing of a prostitute by Ronald True in 1922 – what became known as the *Kensington Flat Murder*.

Ironically, of all of Brown's cases, it was probably the easiest to solve and prove, although it did involve a tricky arrest that could have gone horribly wrong.

True was tried and convicted for the murder of a prostitute, Gertrude Yates (aka Olive Young), on the morning of March 5, 1922. He bludgeoned her five times with a rolling pin, before thrusting a towel in her mouth and strangling her with a dressing gown cord.

Although born illegitimate, True's mother married a rich aristocrat, and he was a former RFC/RAF airman, which added extra spice to the case, and would become significant later.

In committing the murder, True left a trail of evidence to link him to the crime, including witnesses putting him at the scene.

'Short of putting a notice in the paper that he had committed the murder,' the Daily Mirror reported, 'the way he behaved after he left the flat showed that he must have been mad.'

At his trial, Brown revealed that a private investigator, former Chief Inspector Stockley, gave ▶

HEIR TO WED

MARCH 19, 1932

SCOTLAND YARD'S GREATEST

Superintendent   *Superintendent*   *Superintendent*   *Superintendent J.A. Ashley*

Opposite: young PC Brown, shortly after leaving Chitterne for Lambeth. Left: part of the *Daily Mirror*'s coverage of the *Kensington Flat Murder*, and part of an article in *The People* about Scotland Yard. Above: 'Farmer' Brown's calling card while one of the *Big Five*. (Courtesy of Sue Robinson/ www.chitternenowandthen.uk)

Chief Inspector W. F. Brown,
CRIMINAL INVESTIGATION DEPARTMENT,
NEW SCOTLAND YARD.

TELEPHONE: VICTORIA 7000.

information about where True might be found. He had been hired by True's wife and other relatives who 'were very anxious about his conduct' and wanted to find him. They confirmed that he was a drug taker with a morphine habit.

Brown tracked him to the Hammersmith Palace of Varieties, where he had paid for a private box using some of the money he had stolen from his victim, and at 9.45pm – about 14 hours after the murder – Brown moved in, assisted by three other officers.

The murderer, who was carrying a loaded revolver, was persuaded to calmly leave the box, and they arrested him.

Brown told him he was going to arrange an identity parade, but True saved him the trouble, saying: "I admit I am that man your witnesses say they saw."

It was one of the most sensational and infamous murder cases of the inter-war period, partly because True's death sentence was later commuted, on grounds of insanity.

Many argued the reprieve was because of his privileged background, and his victim's low status, and it was compared with the case of an 18-year-old pantry boy named Henry Jacoby, presided over by the same judge.

Jacoby had murdered 65-year-old Lady Alice White and was sentenced to death, just days before True's trial began, and he received no reprieve. For this reason, True's case was later brought up in debates on capital punishment in Parliament.

One of the former "Big Five" at Scotland Yard, and the man who arrested Ronald True for the murder of a woman in a London flat, Superintendent William, Brown, is spending his retirement in the house where he was born at Chitterne, near Warminster.

A 1937 cutting, showing 'Farmer' Brown in his retirement (courtesy of Sue Robinson/www.chitternenowandthen.uk)

The True case was never forgotten, generating sensational stories of his lifestyle in what the press liked to call 'Broadmoor Criminal Lunatic Asylum', along with ill-informed predictions of his imminent release.

Brown was awarded the MBE in 1931 for his services to policing, and retired the following year, returning to Chitterne, where villagers called him 'Tec Brown'. He became a member of Warminster and Westbury Rural District Council, the leader of the local Home Guard in the Second World War and a Justice of the Peace.

His appearance at *The Association of Wiltshire-men in London*'s annual dinner of 1938 – effectively as the guest of honour – was another fitting tribute.

'Farmer' Brown died in his sleep in 1941, at the age of 68, most national newspapers printing affectionate obituaries – and all of them referring to his famous arrest of Ronald True, nearly two decades earlier.

He was survived by his wife, Mary Ann, whom he had married in 1904; their only daughter, Lilian, who was born in 1911, died just before her second birthday, but the couple later adopted their nephew, Maurice. ∎

Mayors ready for war

They had been there before, of course: all dressed up for a glitzy night at the Holborn Restaurant, all but certain that a catastrophic war was just around the corner.

The date was February 25, 1939, just over six months before Britain would once again declare war on Germany.

If the war was barely mentioned, it was clearly on everybody's minds.

The Marquess of Ailesbury was President – for what would turn out to be the last time – and for one night, also Chairman. Among the 'between 300 and 400 guests' were no fewer than five mayors, including one lady: Edith Olivier, the authoress who was also Mayor of Wilton (see page 195).

She made what was arguably (based on the newspaper reports over the years) the first proper speech by a woman to *The Association of Wiltshiremen in London*. During it, she made reference to a current world champion who was living in Wiltshire: a cow called Cherry (see page 206).

The next speaker, Mr HG Maurice, had an obvious eye on the forthcoming war, and felt mayors might inspire victory:

The Mayors of England stand for a great tradition, and one to which we cling, perhaps more tenaciously today than ever before when our peace and quiet is disturbed by Dictators, bellowing like excited stags, their challenges from end to end of Europe.

Our Mayors stand for a system of government which carries with it the liberty of the people, a system which does not aim at the glorification of individuals, nor at the spoliation of individuals, but at the advancement of the public good.

And it is because the Mayors stand for this tradition that we honour them. We honour them because they stand for the spirit which is bred in us, which knows no unwholesome spoliation or racial enmities.

Mr FW Eden, the Mayor of Devizes, pointed out that Wiltshire was about to have a key role in hostilities:

The Wiltshire Mayors were true leaders of the municipalities... in the county finding room and training grounds for the largest combination of His Majesty's land and air forces in the country... The year 1939, with the world in a state of war, bloodless or otherwise, filled them with feelings of pride and determination.

It all sounded rather like they were trying to convince themselves that it would all be OK in the end – and soon all the talking was over.

The hall was then vacated and transformed into a ballroom, where a cabaret entertainment was given, and dancing provided for to music by Sydney Jerome and his orchestra, who had enlivened the proceedings during the dinner, as also had Miss Ellen Hill, who delightfully sang songs from her repertoire.

What had, in many ways, been a glorious decade for the Association was over. ■

Right: an advertisement published in the *North Wilts Herald* in February 1939, including details of the train to the annual dinner, costing six shillings and threepence (31½p).

GWR CHEAP TRIPS

– FROM –

Swindon Junction
WITH MANY BOOKINGS FROM SURROUNDING STATIONS.

Depart—

Annual Dinner of Wiltshiremen in London.

SATURDAY, February 25.
2.20 p.m. To LONDON 6/3. (Return 9.25, 9.50 p.m., or 12.30 night).

SUNDAY, February 26.
11.13 a.m. To BATH, BRISTOL, 3/2, WESTON-SUPER-MARE 4/9.
11.20 a.m. To STROUD 2/8, GLOUCESTER, CHELTENHAM SPA 3/8.
12.15 p.m. To READING 4/2, EALING (Broadway) and LONDON 6/3. Restaurant-Car Train.

SATURDAY, March 4.
1.13 p.m. To LONDON 6/3. Restaurant-Car Train. (Return 9.25, 9.50 p.m., or 12.30 night).

SUNDAY, March 5.
11.13 a.m. To BATH, BRISTOL 3/2, WESTON-SUPER-MARE 4/9.
11.20 a.m. To STROUD 2/8, GLOUCESTER, CHELTENHAM SPA 3/8.

SATURDAYS.
6.20 p.m. Evening Trip to OXFORD 2/1. (Return 11.15 p.m.).

VISIT THE BRITISH INDUSTRIES FAIR,
London & Birmingham.
(TO MARCH 3).

Full details, conditions of issue of tickets, etc., obtainable at G.W.R. Stations, Offices and Agencies.

JAMES MILNE, General Manager.

Cherry the Wonder Cow

It is probably saying a lot about the lacklustre nature of the *Moonies'* last annual dinner before the war that the star of the show – and she wasn't even there (because nobody had sent her an invitation) – was a dairy cow from Amesbury.

But 'Cherry the Short-horned cow' or (as some newspapers quickly dubbed her) 'Cherry the Wonder Cow' was a national sensation in the spring of 1939.

An eight-year-old, all-red, non-pedigree cow of the Shorthorn variety, she was originally bought as a heifer at auction in Salisbury, and immediately joined Messrs Wort & Way's herd at Redhouse Farm, Amesbury.

She didn't look champion material to most. Even after she hit the headlines, a newspaper reporter wrote that she had 'a shape at which experts scoff'.

But beauty is in the eye of the beholder, and it was all about the eye of farm manager Alex McKie, who had only joined the business the previous year. He said: "She "looked the 'milky' type."

And he was right. In May 1938, following the birth of her fifth calf, Cherry broke the world record with a yield of 14 gallons (63.6 litres)) in 24 hours, beating the previous best by nearly a gallon.

Her average yield was 11 gallons (50 litres) a day – enough to supply 69 families with their average milk intake, and more than six times the volume produced by an average cow at the time.

But her work was only just beginning.

Shortly after noon on Good Friday, April 7, 1939, in front of a crowd of spectators and 'a large party of

newspaper men', it was declared that Cherry had produced 4,164 gallons (18,929 litres)) over a 12-month period, beating the previous world record holder, Ormsby Butter King, from the USA, by over 300 gallons.

The record secured, Cherry was led back to her shed for a rest, while her owners laid on a luncheon for a hundred guests. Sometime later they signed a deal with the suppliers of her dairy cake that saw Cherry appear in newspaper advertisements for their products (pictured, below).

Each day she would eat 28lbs (12.7kg) of dairy cake, 40lbs (18.1kg) of additives, 7lbs (3.2kg) of meadow hay, 5lbs (2.3kg) of bran and flaked maize – and two mangelwurzels.

One of the secrets of Cherry's success was the vast amount of water she drank during her

record-breaking year: at least 35 gallons (159 litres) a day, and often more, with a handful of salt thrown in to make her thirsty.

But it also required a lot of hard work and dedication on the part of McKie, who milked her by hand. He often devoted 16-

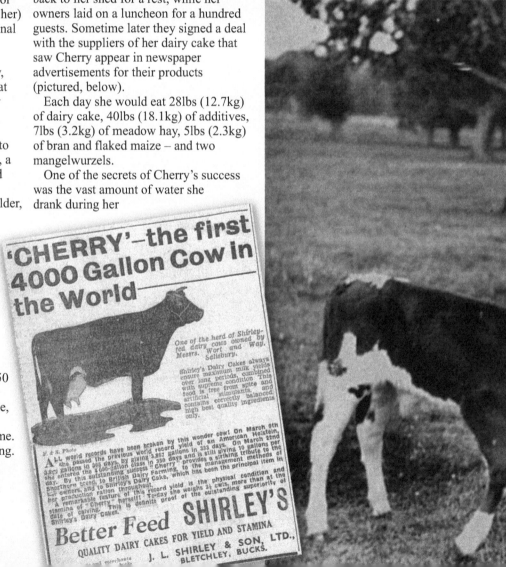

'CHERRY' – the first 4000 Gallon Cow in the World

One of the herd of Shirley-fed dairy cows owned by Messrs. Wort and Way, Salisbury.

Shirley's Dairy Cakes always ensure maximum milk yields over long periods, combined with supreme condition. This food is free from spice and artificial stimulants, and contains correctly balanced high best quality ingredients only.

Y. & S. Photo

ALL world records have been broken by this wonder cow! On March 6th she passed the previous world record yield of an American Holstein, 3,861 gallons in 365 days, by giving 3,867 gallons in 333 days. On March 22nd she entered the 4,000-gallon class in 350 days and is still giving 10 gallons per day. By this outstanding success of Cherry provides a striking tribute to the Shorthorn breed to British Dairy Farming, to the management methods of her owners, and to Shirley's Dairy Cake, which has been the principal item in her production ration throughout.

A remarkable feature of this record yield is the physical condition and stamina of 'Cherry' herself. Today she weighs 31 cwts, more than at the date of calving. This is definite proof of the outstanding superiority of Shirley's Dairy Cakes.

Better Feed SHIRLEY'S

QUALITY DAIRY CAKES FOR YIELD AND STAMINA

J. L. SHIRLEY & SON, LTD.
BLETCHLEY, BUCKS.

18 hours a day to keeping her fed and nourished, assisted by his son, Robert.

"You can imagine what a tie it is," he said. "Four milkings a day from half-past five in the morning to 11 o-clock at night for eleven months, Sundays included – it wants a bit of sticking."

And Cherry (pictured, below, with one of her calves) was not the friendliest of cows, being described as 'a somewhat bad-tempered matron'.

With rationing imminent because of the approaching war, there was a serious side to all the hype, however, as Prof R Boutflour, Principal of the Royal Agricultural College at Cirencester, told reporters.

"There was never a prouder day in my life than the present one," he said. "I have spent most of my life trying to show what cows could do... we have come to a real red letter day in cow performance." ∎

CHERRY'S FINAL EFFORT
Wilts Cow's New World Record Stands at 4,164 Gallons in 365 Days

HONOUR FOR 14-YEARS-OLD MILKER

BY PETER GURN...

CHERRY, THE NEW WORLD ALL-BREEDS RECORD-HOLDER. COMPARE HER MODEST DIMENSIONS WITH THOSE OF THE PREVIOUS HOLDER OF THE RECORD, SHOWN BELOW

The Wiltshiremen return

Although they were unable to continue the annual dinners during the Second World War, there is some evidence that *The Association of Wiltshiremen in London* were still active.

The Honorary Secretary, GM Coward, was busy instigating and running a *Comforts Fund*, which it seems was originally (at least) in the name of the Association.

It primarily supplied gifts to members of the Wiltshire Regiment who were prisoners of war, and seems to have been inspired by those taken prisoner after Dunkirk in 1940.

Some kind of organisation was still in place in November 1943 – or they were at least in contact with one another – because a short article in the *Bath Weekly Chronicle and Herald* explained:

Princess Elizabeth will attain her 18th birthday and her majority in April next, a coming-of-age which will be of great significance for all those lands and peoples who own allegiance to the Crown. His Majesty the King is now choosing a title for the Princess. The Society of Wiltshiremen in London have in humble duty put forward the suggestion that this should be the "Duchess of Wessex."

Then, in September 1944, an edition of the *Wiltshire Times* made reference to a telegram sent to wish Miss Louise Alley a happy 101st birthday from 'the Council of Wiltshiremen in London'.

But it was the sad duty of the *Wiltshire Times*, on September 8, 1945, to report the death of Mr GM Coward, aged 66. He had been Honorary Secretary since 1918, and sounds like the kind of stalwart that every social organisation needs, and depends on, year in, year out. But it would be wrong to call him a completely 'unsung hero'.

He had been the subject of the very last toast of the last dinner before the war, proposed by the Chairman, who said 'they were almost entirely indebted to Mr Coward for the splendid evening they had enjoyed'.

The son of an engine driver, his obituary stated that although he had been born in Mere, Wiltshire, he had left at the age of 17, and had worked for Messrs Liberty and Co for 45 years. He had also served in the last war, in the RFC/RAF.

The *Wiltshire Times* said of him:

He particularly delighted in the organisation of the annual dinner, and he had a flair for selecting brilliant young artists for the entertainment. No one knew and understood Wiltshiremen better than GM Coward, and we mourn his loss and send our heartfelt sympathy to his widow.

The Association always referred to him by his initials, and only additional research has revealed that they stood for George Mayo.

At least we have a photograph of him; he was a keen golfer, so appears with fellow Moonie golfers on page 193.

It appears that much of the success of the Association between the wars was because of the work he did, and probably the main reason it would take time to restart the annual dinners after the war was his absence.

Another reason was rationing. The end of the war didn't mean the end of rationing, which continued in some form until 1954, and it would have been extremely difficult to organise the kind of lavish event enjoyed over so many years before the war.

At least the Holborn Restaurant had survived The Blitz, although the image, opposite, which was taken about a quarter of a mile away in 1940, demonstrates how fortuitous that was.

It was the spring of 1948 before the Association was finally revived, following a luncheon at the Holborn Restaurant on March 24 – where else? – when a meeting of the 'Council Committee' was held. In the chair was Mr HH (Henry Hubert) 'Herbert' Perkins (see page 211). He had been Chairman of the Association's Council since 1937, and he set out the challenge facing them:

The Chairman stated that during and since the War, in common with many other Associations, their activities had been considerably curtailed, and on the death, two years ago, of their zealous Hon Secretary, Mr Coward, to whom he paid a glowing tribute for his untiring efforts on behalf of Wiltshiremen in London, both on the Social and Benevolent side, they were faced with the difficulty of obtaining a suitable and preferably younger man to take his place.

That man would be Arthur W Miles Webb.

Originally from Calne, Miles Webb had been Secretary of Bath Junior Conservatives, the founder of a dramatic society in Bath, and a member of Calne Town Council during the war, when he was also the local Ministry of Information officer. He also did 'a great deal of other war work'.

They also discussed who the new President might be. The Marquess of Ailesbury had moved away to Jersey and 'intimated that he would like to relinquish' the post, so they unanimously agreed to 'invite a prominent Wiltshireman to honour the Association by accepting the position'.

A report in the *Wiltshire Times* in the following August revealed that this was the Duke of Somerset, who had been the Lord Lieutenant of Wiltshire since ▶

1942, and he had agreed to be President.

A short article in the *Wiltshire Times* in February 1949 revealed another problem with restarting the Association: a lack of records:

Mr Miles Webb announced that during the war-time bombing the Society lost the most recent register of members and they were unable to contact the majority of old members. With a few names they had been able to form the nucleus of a new membership.

At last, a meeting for members of the reborn Association was fixed, as reported in the *Wiltshire Times* in January 1949 – even if the paper wasn't quite sure what to call them:

The first function of the newly-formed Wiltshiremen in London Society will be an informal cocktail party on Feb 15th at Oddennio's Hotel, Regent Street, London, 7-9pm, at which members will be able to meet the new President, the Duke of Somerset, DSO, OBE, and members of the Council. A general meeting will follow.

Membership is growing slowly and anyone who is interested should get in touch with the Hon Secretary, Mr A W Miles Webb... The annual dinner will take place on April 30th.

So everything was finally set for the revival, and the *Wiltshire Times* reminded its readers of its origins in March 1949, concluding:

The association has many years of useful work behind it and has brought pleasure to countless Moonrakers caught up in the impersonal activities of the seething millions. ∎

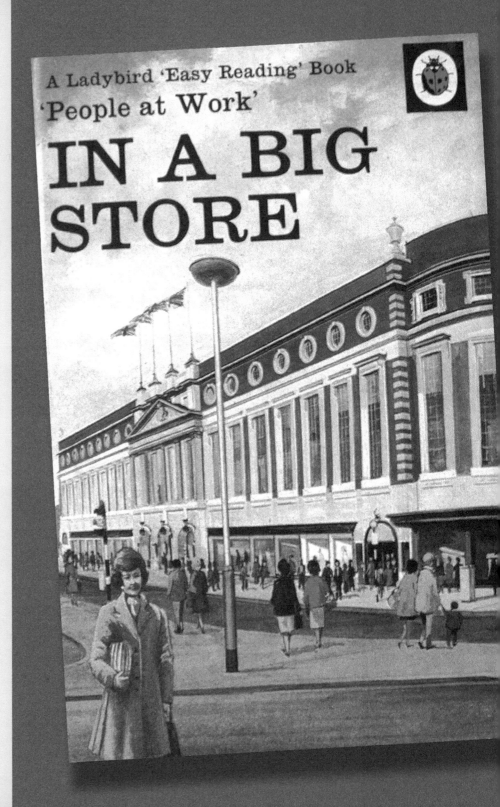

Mr Perkins at your service

The man who hoped to restore the Association to its pre-war eminence, and the Chairman of its council for the whole of the post-war period was (as he was always referred to by the Association) Mr HH Perkins.

Baptised Henry Hubert but usually known as Herbert, Perkins was another brilliant businessman with a connection to prestigious department stores.

While Harrods genius Sir Richard Burbidge (see page 134) was from South Wraxall, near Bradford on Avon, Perkins was born in the town itself (on September 15, 1879), and this was clearly one of the reasons he found himself working for Burbidge at Harrods.

Lord Horder was later to tell diners at an annual dinner that he was glad to see Perkins present as he had been one of the original members when the Association was founded in 1901, so he had probably moved to London from Wiltshire by then – although it wasn't until 1913 that his name is recorded in the press as having attended an annual dinner.

Perkins (who is pictured on pages 192 and 193) worked for Harrods from March 1904, but left in September 1909 to become mail order and publicity manager at Bentall's in Kingston upon Thames. Then, in 1917, he was jointly (with one other) put in charge of the company when Leonard Bentall (who is another of the golfers pictured on pages 192 and 193) relinquished full control.

By the outbreak of the Second World War, he was listed as 'Director and Secretary' of a department store, and living in Twickenham.

In the meantime he had become heavily involved in the annual dinners of the Association. He was Honorary Musical Director in 1933/4, and then Honorary Treasurer until 1948.

It can be no coincidence that the fortunes of Bentalls, who would eventually open a chain of nine stores, underwent a huge upturn after Perkins joined them.

They became a famous and highly respected brand, to the extent that when toy car manufacturers Dinky produced a model of a delivery van in 1939, it was painted in Bentalls livery (pictured, below).

The store thrived under Perkins's management, and even after his death (in 1968, aged 89), continued to be highly respected; when *Ladybird* produced one of its famous books for children in 1973, called *In The Big Store*, it was the real-life Bentalls that they based it on.

Bentalls was purchased by the Fenwick group in 2001, and the Kingston store kept its original name until 2023.

After reviving the Association, not even Perkins's skills and efforts could ultimately turn its fortunes around, although when it finally floundered, in 1954, he was roundly praised:

The thanks of all were now due to Mr Perkins (Chairman) and Mr Miles Webb and the members of the Council for the valiant way in which they had carried on in the face of insurmountable difficulties. ∎

Back in business at the 'banquet'

Ten years and 64 days after their previous gathering, members of *The Association of Wiltshiremen in London* finally sat down to an annual dinner again on Saturday, April 30, 1949.

Only it wasn't billed as a dinner anymore, but rather a 'banquet', although the venue was the same: the Holborn Restaurant.

The Presiding Chairman was Viscount Long of Wraxall, who was also acting as President in the absence of the indisposed Duke of Somerset. The guests included four mayors – of Swindon, Devizes, Calne and Wilton – plus Robert Grimston, the MP for West Wilts, and 'over 150' others.

Swindon singer Alfred Salter 'clad in rustic smock and hat, led the singing of "The Vly," and sang other appropriate songs'. And there was music from Sydney Jerome, just as there had been, before the war.

The Mayor of Swindon, WJ Davis, had some toasting duties, then moved on to pay Swindon an awkward compliment:

Wiltshire... was a lovely, ancient and rural county. Swindon, by comparison, might be described as a "poor relation of the pushing kind." (Laughter). This poor relation, a young upstart of barely a century,

though claiming in some respects to have come of age, and to be old and large enough to be freed from the county's paternal control, had shown

that it, as readily as any other town, could recognise, respect and rejoice in the ancient traditions and rural beauty of the county of which it formed so contrasting a part.

This was a cue for Lord Long to use the platform to give the company 'a few "home truths" about what was going on in Wiltshire' so 'they might realise the desecration of their wonderful county which had been going on slowly but surely, year after year, in his lifetime':

It may be, he said, that none of us will deny that it is for the benefit of the country as a whole, but it is worth remembering that one-seventh of the acreage of our county no longer belongs to the people of the county, but is owned by one or other Ministries. When are we going to stop it?

It probably wasn't what people wanted to hear, and other speeches followed with a similarly pessimistic note, mostly about local government, before a 'humorous speech' by Reginald Arkell lightened the mood.

Arkell was a scriptwriter, comic novelist and poet, but he also founded, edited and published magazines, including *Men Only*. He was reportedly a Wiltshiremen, but was actually born in Lechlade, Gloucestershire, in 1881. However, he did live in Wiltshire – and died there, at his home in Marston Meysey, in 1959.

The last speaker was Instr Rear-Admiral Sir Arthur Hall, Director of Studies and Dean of the Royal Naval College, Greenwich. He thanked the Chairman of the Society's Council (Herbert Perkins) and the Hon Secretary (Arthur Miles Webb) for the enterprise they had shown in organising the first post-war 'banquet'.

It had certainly been a success, but perhaps a qualified one.

A follow-up report in the *Wiltshire Times* in May 1949 revealed that the membership had grown – from just 16 a year earlier, to 133, but there was some concern over the average age of those attending the dinner.

Under the headline 'Younger members wanted', the paper's correspondent said: 'The Wiltshiremen in London are… I am told, finding it difficult to obtain enough new, younger members to keep a healthy balance between the young and the not-so-young,' adding:

Members I talked with at the dinner said they want younger people going from Wiltshire to live in London to feel that by joining the Society they will be able to meet friends who know their home districts and can help them to feel at home in their new surroundings.

Membership was still a concern in December 1949, because the President, Council Chairman and Secretary all signed a letter to the *Wiltshire Times*, setting out the aims of the Association and urging potential new members to get in touch. Near the end of the letter, it was

pointed out that they were open to women members, as well as men, perhaps revealing fears that it was being seen as a predominantly male society again.

They were clearly trying to come up with new ways of promoting the Association, as a short article in the *Bath Weekly Chronicle and Herald* demonstrates, again in December 1949:

Mr AW Miles Webb… tells me that the members of the Wiltshiremen in London… want, as an association, to pay a yearly visit to a Wiltshire town. Which one, I wonder, will be the first to send them an invitation?

In other words: *The Association of Wiltshiremen in London* – in Wiltshire. There is no record of any such visits taking place.

There was a change of venue in 1950, Restaurant Frascati getting the nod over the Holborn Restaurant for some reason, although it would be a one-off.

The attendance was slightly up on the previous year, at 160, but still half that of pre-war levels, even though the guest list was impressive, including Viscount and Viscountess Long of ▶

When *The Association of Wiltshiremen in London* needed someone to lead the traditional singing of *The Vly Be on the Turmuts* after the Second World War, there was probably only one candidate: Alfred Salter.

By then Salter had made his name locally as a singing star, and nationally as a fine baritone who was often heard on the radio, but he turned down the chance of a professional career in 1945.

However, he was cheered as he sang the 'Wiltshire anthem' at dinners in 1949, 1951 and 1952.

Born in 1907 and raised in Rodbourne, Alfred attended Even Swindon School under headmaster, Henry Day, but was slow in coming to the attention of audiences.

As a soloist he won minor honours in the Swindon Eisteddfod Awards in 1930 and 1933, but became a stalwart of the *GWR (Swindon) Amateur Theatrical Society*, both as an actor and member of the chorus.

During the war he would often be seen performing at a plethora of fundraising and benefit concerts throughout Swindon, often with Bert Fluck (father of Diana Fluck, aka Diana Dors) as his accompanist.

He also travelled to army camps, military hospitals and factories, giving concerts, and he made more than 20 radio appearances.

A piece headed 'Town's star singer dies' appeared in the *Swindon Advertiser* on April 26, 1971, announcing his death at the age of 64.

By then he had moved to Southampton Street.

When asked why he never went professional, Alfred said: "I don't like the cut-throat life of a professional artiste." ∎

ON THE AIR.

Mr. Alfred Salter, of Jennings-street, Swindon, whose portrait is printed here, broadcast on Saturday for the third time in eight months.

Mr. Salter, a pleasing baritone, has had successes at all the principal musical festivals in the West and South of England, and is well known on the concert platform.

Left: a cutting from the *North Wilts Herald* in 1935

Wraxall; Lord Goddard of Aldbourne, the Lord Chief Justice of England; Christopher Hollis, MP for Devizes; the Mayors of Swindon, Salisbury and Devizes; and Lord Oaksey, who, as Lord Justice Lawrence, presided over the Nuremberg Trials (see page 216).

This time the new President, the Duke of Somerset, also attended, and he started off with an appeal on behalf of a newly established fund in aid of Salisbury Cathedral, which was 'in a very dangerous condition, and a portion of it will have to be pulled down and rebuilt', at an estimated cost of £40,000.

But the President was not in a positive mood:

> *He went on to speak of the desecration of the Wiltshire countryside by various government departments. The military authorities were still occupying the lovely old village of Imber in the centre of the downs; there was the camp at Crabtree,*

> *near Longleat, where young boys of the county went to earn £6 or £7 a week for doing nothing; wireless masts had been established on the Downs for the benefit of the Police – the Police deserved all the help they could get, but he felt it was a pity the Downs had to be used for that purpose; all over the county there were dumps of dud ammunition and army stores decayed beyond all use, lying about, which nobody took the least interest in; and there was the "awful cement works" going up at Westbury ... God help us when it gets going. I have seen the effects of it in other places, and although they say they can get rid of the refuse, it is not so.*

On Imber, he had a point; its population was evicted so the village could provide practice for urban warfare training during the war, and it is still 'a ghost town' even now, out of bounds to the public, except for certain weekends of the year. 'The camp at Crabtree' was actually RAF

Crabtree, a large storage depot opened in 1943, and staffed by around 200.

Lord Oaksey focused a little more on the glories of the county and admitted:

> *he could scarcely describe himself as a Wiltshireman in London, he was rather a Londoner in Wiltshire, having been in Wiltshire only for the past 40 years. Comparisons were odious, even among counties, but he believed people from other counties would willingly admit that there was no county that surpassed the glorious beauties of Wiltshire, with its antiquities, its glorious countryside and downs, its sporting facilities, its beautiful churches, towns and villages, and great houses.*

Christopher Hollis MP brought things back down to earth. His complaint was over the erosion of local government, and he said he 'hoped no reforming zeal would reduce [the county's town's] to nullity and rob them of their ancient privileges'.

Next up was the Mayor of Salisbury, complaining about boundary changes that meant Wiltshire had shrunken, but the Mayor of Swindon (Francis Akers) tilted the mood of the gathering back to upbeat:

> *He was proud to say, as Mayor of Swindon and an alderman for the county, that his town was taking its share in the county's responsibilities and administration. A large proportion of its citizens had been drawn from the surrounding countryside at a time when there was little real encouragement to toil on the land, and now*

"Balcony", Restaurant Frascati, London.

Left: a postcard from the venue for the 1950 'banquet': Restaurant Frascati, which was at 26-32 Oxford Street

Swindon was able to repay the county and nation by the skill and ability of its artisans. Rural and urban Wiltshire were fast coming to know one another better and to appreciate their mutual dependence. The old idea that townsmen were clever, and countrymen dull-witted was quite out of date.

If it was all a little too serious, at least there was the entertainment to look forward to:

Music was played during dinner by Sydney Jerome's light orchestra, with an interlude while Billy Williams sang the Wiltshire "classic" "The Vly" in traditional smock, breeches and leggings, and the gathering ended with dancing.

There was a postscript to the 1950 dinner, following a meeting of the Council on July 18, at Restaurant Frascati, showing that the Association's charitable work was ongoing.

A report of the meeting in the *Wiltshire Times* revealed:

a letter was received from a Warminster man living in Australia, who, with his wife and son, are returning to England... The hon secretary has arranged accommodation for the party, transport from Tilbury, and other assistance... Such services are always available in London for Wiltshire people. ■

Right: pages from *The Tatler* after the magazine sent its photographer to snap the VIPs at the 1950 'banquet'. (courtesy of Illustrated London News Group).

Viscount Long of Wraxall, one of the Vice-Presidents of the Wiltshiremen In London, who proposed the health of the chairman, chatting with Lord Oaksey, who proposed the toast "Our County." The dinner was at Frascati's

WILTSHIREMEN SANG THE "MOONRAKERS' ANTHEM"

As Part of the Very Pleasant Entertainment at Their 49th Annual Banquet in London

The Duke and Duchess of Somerset. The Duke, who took the chair, is Lord Lieutenant of Wiltshire and president of the society

Col. W. S. Shepherd, chairman of the London Branch, Old Comrades' Association, Wilts Regt., with Capt. G. M. Warren

Mr. and Mrs. H. Cassey, with Council members Mr. R. Cassey and Mr. E. W. Palmer

Mrs. George Gibbons, her son-in-law, Instr. Rear-Admiral Sir Arthur Hall, and her daughter, Lady Hall

Mr. and Mrs. H. C. Preater and the Mayor and Mayoress of Salisbury, Councillor and Mrs. S. N. Bigwood

Oaksey brought Nazis to justice

Members of *The Association of Wiltshiremen in London* often got to rub shoulders with some important names in history over the years – and those attending the annual dinners in 1950 and 1953 were in the presence of a man who had just made history.

He was Lord Oaksey, who had presided over the Nuremberg Trials that brought some of Nazi Germany's war criminals to justice, sending some of them to their deaths in 1946.

As he told diners in 1950, he wasn't a Wiltshireman, but had lived in the county for the last 40 years.

Oaksey – or to give him his full title: Geoffrey Lawrence, 1st Baron Oaksey, DSO PC DL TD – was born in London in 1880, the youngest son of Lord Trevethin.

A second lieutenant in the Royal Field Artillery Territorial Force, he served with the Royal Artillery in France during the First World War, and received the DSO in 1918.

However, his trade was the law, and after serving as Attorney for the Jockey Club, became a King's Counsel in 1927, eventually being made Lord Justice of Appeal in 1944.

But it was as the lead judge in the Nuremberg Trials (pictured, opposite), which began in November 1945 and lasted just over a year, that Oaksey is best remembered.

They eventually saw 24 people indicted on three broad counts: conspiracy, crimes against peace, war crimes and crimes against humanity. It led to 12 defendants receiving the death penalty, while seven were given life sentences and three were acquitted. One other committed suicide before the trials began, and one was too ill to stand trial.

Oaksey was praised for his part in what was a complex, difficult and, in some respects, thankless job; although the *New York Times* said 'he won tributes from all parts of the world for his impartiality and fairness'.

He retired in 1957, and devoted the rest of his life to his 160-acre Hill Farm, at Oaksey, where he had a passion for rearing cows. A former President of the British Dairy Farmers' Association, he kept pedigree Guernseys.

He died at Oaksey in August 1978, aged 90. His son, John, was a well-known jockey and racing journalist and broadcaster. ∎

The President: up to his old tricks

The Duke of Somerset – Evelyn Francis Edward Seymour, 17th Duke of Somerset, to be precise – was President of the Association from 1948 until 1951, and as the Lord Lieutenant of Wiltshire was a fairly obvious choice.

But the Duke was not your archetypal aristocrat.

Born in Ceylon (Sri Lanka) in 1882, he was educated at Blundell's School, Tiverton, and then Sandhurst, before serving in the Boer War, Aden (in 1903), and then the First World War, when he took command of the 10th Battalion, The Royal Dublin Fusiliers. In 1918 he was awarded the DSO, followed by the OBE in 1919.

He returned to the army in the Second World War, at first commanding a battalion of The Devonshire Regiment, later becoming a Colonel on the General Staff.

At the Coronation of King George VI in 1937, he bore the King's Sceptre with the Cross.

He had succeeded his father as 17th Duke in 1931, and lived at Maiden Bradley, near Warminster.

There he took an active interest in the preservation of historic churches, the *British Legion* and a range of other causes, including the *National Playing Fields Association*.

His leisure pursuits were what you would expect of a country gentleman –

hunting, shooting, fishing, golf, cricket – but for many years he was a member of the Magic Circle, which he joined in 1907.

His interest in magic was aroused when he saw a performance at the Electric Theatre, Crystal Palace, and he became a pupil of professional magician Ernest Noakes, gradually building up a repertoire of nearly a hundred tricks, which he would perform for friends.

In 1935 he became President of the Magic Circle.

He died in 1954, after a period of ill health that was probably the reason for stepping down as President of *The Association of Wiltshiremen in London*. ∎

*leaf
year*

Wiltshiremen  in London

President:

His Grace the Duke of Somerset, D.S.O., O.B.E.
Lord Lieutenant of Wiltshire

— o —

" Know this thy Countie Wiltshire, look up and thank God "

Golden Jubilee
BANQUET

held at the

Holborn Restaurant, London, W.C.1

on

Wednesday, May 2nd, 1951

" When May with cowslip-braided locks
Walks through the land in green attire"
Bayard Taylor

Chairman:

His Grace the Duke of Somerset, D.S.O., O.B.E.

There was, according to the *Wiltshire Times*, 'a large number' of Wiltshiremen present when the Association gathered at the Holborn Restaurant on May 2, 1951, but their abridged version of events (compared with reports of previous years in the press) perhaps spoke volumes.

No actual attendance figure was given, and also missing were the lists of attendees, common in years gone by.

There wasn't even any confirmation of which county mayors or other VIPs were present, unless they made a speech.

And yet it was, as the programme declared (pictured, left) the golden jubilee, being half a century since *The Moonies in London* officially became *The Association of Wiltshiremen in London*. Not that this was mentioned in the *Wiltshire Times*'s report; there doesn't seem to have been anything special to mark the milestone – another sign, perhaps, that the whole thing was in decline.

Alfred Salter (see page 213) returned to lead the singing of *The Vly Be on the Turmuts*, and the author AG Street (see page 196) gave 'an attractive speech, much of it in humorous vein'.

He observed:

The last time he spoke at that function, in the early thirties, Wiltshire had little industrialism and what with having no sea coast, the modern crowd went straight through it. Since the war a lot of people were stopping. He knew it showed good taste, but there was a duty on Moonrakers to teach these people to become good Moonrakers and to love Wiltshire.

The end of the road

And there were plenty of reasons to love it:

Referring to the Society of Wiltshiremen in London, Mr Street said: "It is always good that country people, especially Wiltshire people, who are taken by circumstances to live in the horrid discomfort of a modern city like London, should find a way of meeting occasionally, and enjoying some conversation based on country common sense.

Without that regular dose of comforting medicine, life for them would indeed be a dreary business. I assure you, if I treated any of my livestock on my farms in Wiltshire the way human beings are treated in this city, I should be prosecuted. (Laughter).

The President, the Duke of Somerset, 'reviewed outstanding events in the county in the past year, including the visits of the Duchess of Kent to Salisbury and the Princess Elizabeth to Swindon'.

Mrs McCubbin Fraser responded to the toast of 'the ladies', and all that was left was for Alfred Salter to sing 'a number of West Country songs' and for Sydney Jerome and his quartet (scaled down from the orchestra of previous years) to provide the music for dancing.

More signs that the Association was flagging were apparent the following year, 1952, which would be the last time they met at the Holborn Restaurant.

The event still wasn't getting the press coverage of previous eras, although the *Wiltshire Times*'s upbeat report did suggest that the event was at least a partial success.

There was a new President, Lord Horder (who was also the Presiding Chairman), and there was a new monarch to toast and send a telegram to.

Queen Elizabeth II had ascended the throne less than three months earlier, and replied by telegram from Windsor Castle to say: 'Please convey to the Wiltshiremen in London dining together this evening my sincere thanks for their kind and loyal message of good wishes. – Elizabeth R'

In the meantime, 'Mr Alfred Salter, of Swindon, in gaiters and breeches, smock and round felt hat' got on with the serious business of leading the singing of *The Vly Be on the Turmuts*.

No attendance figure was given, but in terms of county mayors attending, the score was four: Salisbury, Devizes, Marlborough and Wilton.

Once again the imagined desecration of Wiltshire countryside was a theme, the Mayor of Salisbury (SE Chalk) stating:

"I trust there is no danger of losing some of the beauty spots which have made Wiltshire famous .... and that all local authorities and the appropriate government departments will always bear this important matter in mind and see that the beautiful countryside is not spoilt by the erection of unsightly buildings."

The Mayor of Marlborough said he had hoped to bring along Gordon Richards, the great jockey, as a guest, but he had a previous engagement. Richards, who would become the only jockey to be knighted, the following year, was born in Shropshire, but had a long association with Beckhampton, near Avebury.

'The evening ended with dancing to Sydney Jerome's Dance Orchestra' (not just a quartet, this time) and members went home, perhaps wondering whether the Association was bouncing back.

If they did, then they were to be disappointed.

The next annual dinner took place on March 24, 1953, at the venue with arguably the most attractive exterior, St Ermin's Hotel, in Westminster, but it would effectively be the Association's last.

Later reports on the winding down of the Association suggest that only 50 people attended in 1953, and the *Wiltshire Times* – the only newspaper to file any report – summed up the whole event in the following few words:

Tribute to Queen Mary was paid by Viscount Long in proposing the toast of "The County Mayors" at the 52nd annual dinner of the Society of Wiltshiremen in London held at the St. Ermin's Hotel, Westminster, on Tuesday evening. He said that her late Majesty had by her charm captured all their hearts and had set them all a wonderful example.

Lord Long appealed to the Mayors for greater effort in Civil Defence recruiting and organisation. Lord Horder presided over a large company and amongst the speakers were Lord Oaksey, who proposed "Wiltshire our county," and Lord Kennet.

They didn't even take the trouble to mention *The Vly Be on the Turmuts*.

There is no record of an annual dinner in the spring of 1954, but it was reported that at the AGM in July: ▶

They had come to the conclusion that there was little use in going on since few people were now interested in these County Associations when, in London, there were so many other distractions, besides the home interests of Radio and Television... alas, enthusiasm waned and it became more and more difficult to retain the interest of all the members; other calls on their time were proving too strong for us and it seemed useless to try to carry on with a mere fifty people. Thus, reluctantly, we decided to wind up our affairs.

There was, however (thanks to the generosity of Mr HH Perkins and his wife) to be a complimentary farewell dinner – on November 20, 1954.

For this they went back to St Ermin's Hotel (pictured, right, in 2024), and it was attended by around 40 people – 'mainly Council Members and their wives or husbands'.

Arthur Miles Webb 'was presented with two West Country pictures – signed artists' proofs – and a convex mirror, in token of the members' thanks for his work from 1948 to 1954, during which time a valiant effort had been made to revive the old Society which had been so strong in pre-war days'.

It was suggested that they should meet annually, 'and so keep a pilot light burning' – but if they ever did, there is no record of it.

There were only two things left to do: a final rendition of *The Vly Be on the Turmuts*, followed by the singing of *Auld Lang Syne*.

The Association of Wiltshiremen in London was over – and soon to be forgotten.

Until now. ∎

Appendices

Date and Location of Dinners

March 13 – Plumstead
March 12 – Prince Alfred Hotel, Plumstead
March 10 – Railway Tavern, Plumstead
March 9 – Railway Tavern, Plumstead
March 8 – Bridge House Hotel
March 14 – Bridge House Hotel
March 12 – Champion Hotel
March 18 – Bridge House Hotel
March 3 – Bridge House Hotel
March 16 – Bridge House Hotel
March 21 – Horse Shoe Hotel
March 13 – Holborn Restaurant
No dinner
March 11 – Holborn Restaurant
March 10 – Holborn Restaurant
March 9 – Holborn Restaurant
March 8 – Holborn Restaurant
February 21 – Holborn Restaurant
March 5 – Holborn Restaurant
April 15 – Holborn Restaurant
March 3 – Holborn Restaurant
March 2 – Holborn Restaurant
March 7 – Holborn Restaurant
March 13 – Holborn Restaurant
March 12 – Holborn Restaurant
March 11 – Holborn Restaurant
March 9 – Holborn Restaurant
March 8 – Holborn Restaurant
March 7 – Holborn Restaurant
No dinner
No dinner
No dinner
No dinner
No dinner

January 24 – Holborn Restaurant
January 22 – Holborn Restaurant
February 25 – Holborn Restaurant
February 17 – Holborn Restaurant
March 15 – Holborn Restaurant
February 14 – Connaught Rooms
March 27 – Connaught Rooms
April 2 – Connaught Rooms
April 21 – Connaught Rooms
March 2 – Hotel Cecil
March 1 – Hotel Cecil
March 21 – Hotel Victoria
February 27 – Holborn Restaurant
February 25 – Holborn Restaurant
February 24 – Holborn Restaurant
February 23 – Holborn Restaurant
February 29 – Holborn Restaurant
February 27 – Holborn Restaurant
February 26 – Holborn Restaurant
February 25 – Holborn Restaurant
No dinner
No dinner
No dinner
No dinner
No dinner
No dinner
No dinner
No dinner
No dinner
April 30 – Holborn Restaurant
April 18 – Restaurant Frascati
May 2 – Holborn Restaurant
April 19 – Holborn Restaurant
March 24 – St Ermin's Hotel
November 20 – St Ermin's Hotel
(farewell dinner)

Principal Officers & Presiding Chairmen – 1886-1919

	President	Chairman	Presiding Chairman	Council Chairman	Honorary Secretary
1886		John Templeman			John Templeman
1887		John Templeman			John Templeman
1888		John Templeman			John Templeman
1889		John Templeman			John Templeman
1890		John Templeman			JR Howcroft
1891		John Templeman			JR Howcroft
1892		John Templeman			J Innes
1893		John Templeman			FS Wallington
1894		John Templeman			FS Wallington
1895		John Templeman			FS Wallington
1896		John Templeman			FS Wallington
1897		WE Morris			FS Wallington
1898		(unknown)			FS Wallington
1899		T Hooper Deacon			FS Wallington
1900		T Hooper Deacon			FS Wallington
1901		GJ Churchward			FS Wallington
1902	Richard Burbidge		Sir John Goldney		GB Moore
1903	Richard Burbidge		Sir John Goldney		GB Moore
1904	Richard Burbidge		Marquess of Bath		GB Moore
1905	Richard Burbidge		General Lord Methuen	George Avenell	GB Moore
1906	Richard Burbidge		Earl of Radnor	George Avenell	GB Moore
1907	Richard Burbidge		Marquess of Ailesbury	George Avenell	GB Moore
1908	Richard Burbidge		Lord Fitzmaurice	George Avenell	GB Moore
1909	Richard Burbidge		Baron Roundway	George Avenell	GB Moore
1910	Richard Burbidge		Earl of Pembroke	George Avenell	GB Moore
1911	Richard Burbidge		Richard Burbidge	George Avenell	GB Moore
1912	Richard Burbidge		Viscount Long	EPY Hillier	GB Moore
1913	Richard Burbidge		Col TCP Calley	EPY Hillier	GB Moore
1914	Richard Burbidge		Earl of Kerry	EPY Hillier	GB Moore
1915	Richard Burbidge			EPY Hillier	GB Moore
1916	Sir Richard Burbidge			EPY Hillier	GB Moore
1917	Sir Richard Burbidge			EPY Hillier	GB Moore
1918	Baron Roundway			EPY Hillier	GB Moore
1919	Baron Roundway			EPY Hillier	GB Moore

Principal Officers & Presiding Chairmen – 1920-1954

President	Chairman	Presiding Chairman	Council Chairman	Honorary Secretary
Baron Roundway		Baron Roundway	EPY Hillier/WJ Hopkins	GB Moore
Baron Roundway		Earl of Radnor	WJ Hopkins	GB Moore
Baron Roundway		Earl of Pembroke	WJ Hopkins	GB Moore
Baron Roundway		Lord Methuen	WJ Hopkins	GB Moore
Baron Roundway		Marquess of Ailesbury	WJ Hopkins	GM Coward
Marquess of Ailesbury		Marquess of Ailesbury	WJ Hopkins	GM Coward
Marquess of Ailesbury		WJ Hopkins	WJ Hopkins	GM Coward
Marquess of Ailesbury		Sir Thomas Horder	WJ Hopkins	GM Coward
Marquess of Ailesbury		Marquess of Lansdowne	JH Willis	GM Coward
Marquess of Ailesbury		Sir Felix Pole	JH Willis	GM Coward
Marquess of Ailesbury		Sir Kynaston Studd	JH Willis	GM Coward
Marquess of Ailesbury		Earl of Cardigan	JH Willis	GM Coward
Marquess of Ailesbury		Baron Roundway	JH Willis	GM Coward
Marquess of Ailesbury		Viscount Long of Wraxall	JH Willis	GM Coward
Marquess of Ailesbury		Baron Horder	JH Willis	GM Coward
Marquess of Ailesbury		Baron Wright	JH Willis	GM Coward
Marquess of Ailesbury		Lord Kennet of the Dene	JH Willis	GM Coward
Marquess of Ailesbury		Earl of Cardigan	JH Willis/HH Perkins	GM Coward
Marquess of Ailesbury		Baron Horder	HH Perkins	GM Coward
Marquess of Ailesbury		Marquess of Ailesbury	HH Perkins	GM Coward
Marquess of Ailesbury			HH Perkins	GM Coward
Marquess of Ailesbury			HH Perkins	GM Coward
Marquess of Ailesbury			HH Perkins	GM Coward
Marquess of Ailesbury			HH Perkins	GM Coward
Marquess of Ailesbury			HH Perkins	GM Coward
Marquess of Ailesbury			HH Perkins	GM Coward
Marquess of Ailesbury			HH Perkins	
Marquess of Ailesbury			HH Perkins	
Marquess of Ailesbury/Duke of Somerset			HH Perkins	AW Miles Webb
Duke of Somerset		Viscount Long of Wraxall	HH Perkins	AW Miles Webb
Duke of Somerset		Duke of Somerset	HH Perkins	AW Miles Webb
Duke of Somerset		Duke of Somerset	HH Perkins	AW Miles Webb
Baron Horder		Baron Horder	HH Perkins	AW Miles Webb
Baron Horder		Baron Horder	HH Perkins	AW Miles Webb
Baron Horder			HH Perkins	AW Miles Webb

An Extract from the Association Rules (1951)

NAME

The name of the Association is "WILTSHIREMEN IN LONDON"

OBJECTS

2 a) To make grants in temporary relief of deserving Wiltshiremen in London who may be in need of assistance
   b) To assist generally Wiltshiremen in London and Wiltshire institutions
   c) Other kindred objects as the Council may think fit
   d) To afford Wiltshiremen, by periodical gatherings, the opportunity of meeting and of keeping in touch with one another and of Wiltshire happenings

DEFINITION

3 The term "Wiltshiremen" for the purposes of the Association, shall be deemed to mean and include the following:
   a) Persons of either sex born in Wiltshire
   b) Persons of either sex of Wiltshire parentage on either side
   c) Persons not coming under the above two definitions but who are associated with the county of Wilts, by marriage, residence or otherwise, to the satisfaction of the Council

FUNDS

4 The Association is supported by:
   a) Donations
   b) Annual subscriptions
   c) Legacies

MEMBERSHIP

5 a) The Association shall consist of a President, Vice-Presidents, Council of fifteen or more Members, Life and Annual Subscribers, an Hon Chaplain, an Hon Treasurer, Hon Auditors, an Hon Secretary, Assistant Secretary
   b) Every Subscriber to the funds of the Association shall thereby become a Member of the Association, and be deemed to acquiesce in and submit to the rules for the time being of the Association
   c) Subscriptions to the funds of the Association are not limited, and an Annual Subscription of 10/6 and upwards constitutes the Subscriber a Member of the Association, entitled to vote at the annual and other meetings of the Association. Subscriptions shall be deemed payable on January 1st each year
   d) A donation of Five Guineas and upwards to the funds of the Association constitutes the donor a Life Member of the Association

Menu for the Golden Jubilee Banquet (1951)

Les Hors d'oeuvres Variés

ou

La Crème de Tomate

***

Les Filets de Sole Margéury

***

Le Poulet Rôti Italienne

Les Petit Pois

et

Les Pommes Rissolées

***

Le Biscuit Glacé Hericart

Gaufrettes

***

Le Café

Moonraker (1926) (recited (in part) at the annual dinner in 1927)
By David Fincham

Dig me a grave on Wiltshire soil,
Lay me alone, and where
My ghost can take
Monnraker's air.

I would not wait for Judgment Day
In consecrated ground
With graveyard walls
To hedge me round.

I have no love to mingle dust
With clergy, oaf, or squire;
I'll take my chance
Of nether Fire.

I could not rest with Christian men,
Cramped in a narrow plot,
And watch and watch
Moonrakers rot.

I want no mumbled funeral,
But the wild trees over,
And the soft grass
For my cover.

Then will I walk, if ghosts can choose,
From White Sheet Hill to Knook,
And swim ghost dogs
Across the brook.

At dawn, before the world is up,
I'll see the otters play,
And drench my feet
In dew-wet hay.

Starve-all Bottom and Cricklade Ridge
Will greet my steps again,
And I will range
Over the Plain.

I would not share with God's Elect
One foot of Zion's Hill,
If I could be
Moonraker still.

Where Are My Schoolmates Gone? (as sung at the annual dinners in 1893-6 & 1899)
Music by Frederick Buckley, words by BE Woolf

Oh where are my school mates gone,
The shy, the dull and the gay?
They have left me all heart-sick and lone,
To drag out life's short'ning day.

The school yet remains where it stood,
When its moss cover'd roof I first saw,
The play-ground my eyes 'gin to flood,
When I think of the play-ground of yore.

The spire, too, that pointed to truth,
The fall in its bubbling rage,

So vast in the days of my youth,
So small in the night of my age.

Oh where are my schoolmates gone,
Do they yet toss on life's stormy waves,
Or sleep a sleep peaceful and lone,
'Neath the flow'rs that bloom o'er their
graves?

What day-dreams are mine to enjoy,
As I sit and gaze into the past,
Till again I am changed to a boy,

And, ah, me! Dreams too airy to last.

Farewell, scatter'd friends of my youth,
'Tis your mem'ry dims these old eyes,
May your thoughts, like yon spire, point
to truth,
And we'll talk o'er the past in the skies.

Oh where are my school mates gone,
The shy, the dull and the gay?
They have left me all heart-sick and lone,
To drag out life's short'ning day.

Presidents of The Society of Wiltshiremen ("Moonrakers") in Bristol

1924/5: H Reginald Wansbrough
1925/6: H Reginald Wansbrough
1926/7: Ald Frank Moore JP

1927/8: Ald Frank Moore JP
1928/9: John E Pritchard F.S.A
1929/30: Ald William Henry Eyles

1930/1: Ald William Henry Eyles
1931/2: Viscount Weymouth

227

King John and the Abbott of Canterbury (anon, sang to the tune of Derry Down)

These lyrics are from a report distributed by John E Pritchard of The Society of Wiltshiremen ("Moonrakers") in Bristol, following his research in 1926. He discovered a printed copy dated 1779, relating to The Wiltshire Society #2, and the lyrics were on the back.

I
I'll tell you a Story, a Story anon,
Of a noble Prince, and they call'd him King John,
And he was a Prince, and a Prince of great Might,
He held up great Wrong, and he put down great Right.

Derry down, down, down, derry down.

II
I'll tell you a Story, a Story so merry,
Concerning the Abbot of Canterbury;
And of his House-keeping, and high Renown,
Which made him repair to fair London Town.

III
Oh! Oh! Brother Abbot I've heard tell of thee,
That thou keepest a better house than me;
And of thy House-keeping and high Renown,
I fear thou hast Treason against my Crown.

IV
I hope my good Liege, you owe me no Grudge,
For spending of my own true gotten Goods:
Say the King, if thou answer me not Questions Three,
Thy Head shall be taken from Thy Body.

V
When I am so high upon my Steed,
With my Crown of Gold upon my Head,

Among all my Nobility with Joy and much Mirth,
Thou shalt tell me, to a Penny, what I am worth.

VI
And from the next Question thou shalt not flout,
But tell me how long I shall be riding the World about;
And from the last Question thou shalt not shrink,
But tell to me truly what 'tis I do think.

VII
O these are hard Questions for my shallow Wit,
And I cannot answer your Grace as yet;
Except you will give me about Three Days' Space,
Then I'll do my Endeavour to answer your Grace.

VIII
Well! Three Days' Space I will thee give,
And that is the longest that thou hast to live;
For if Thou dost not answer these Questions right,
Thy Head shall be taken from thy Body quite.

IX
Now as the Shepherd was folding his Flock,
He spy'd the old Abbot a riding along;
O Master Abbot, you're welcome home,
What News have you brought from our King John?

X
Bad News! Bad News! I will thee give,

For I have but Three Days' Space to live;
For if I don't answer him Questions three,
My Head's to be taken from my Body.

XI
When he is so high upon his Steed,
With his Crown of Gold upon his Head,
Among all his Nobility, with Joy and much Mirth,
I must tell him, to One Penny, what he is worth.

XII
And from the next Question I must not flout,
But tell him how long he shall be riding the World about;
And from the third Question I must not shrink,
But to tell to him truly what 'tis he does think.

XIII
O Master Abbot did you never hear it,
How a Fool may learn a Wife Man Wit;
Lend me but your Horse, and your Apparel,
I'll away to fair London, and answer the Quarrel.

XIV
Well, now I'm so high upon my Steed,
With my Crown of Gold upon my Head,
Among all my Nobility, with Joy and much Mirth,
Thou shalt tell me, to One Penny, what I am worth.

XV
Why, 'twas for Thirty Pence our SAVIOUR was sold
Unto the false Jews as I have been told,
And Nine and Twenty is the worth of thee,
For I think thou art One Penny worse than He.

XVI
Now from the next Question thou shalt not flout,
But tell me how long I shall be riding the World about;
You must rise with the Sun, and go on with the same,
Until the next Morning it riseth again.

XVII
As for Exactness, be sure that you see,
Keep right with its Center, as right as can be;
And then I am sure you need never to doubt,
But in Twenty-four Hours you'll ride it about.

XVIII
Now from the next Question thou shalt not shrink,
But tell to me truly, what 'tis I do think;
And that I can do, which will make your Heart merry,
You think I'm the Abbot of Canterbury;
But I am his Shepherd, and that you may see,
I am come to beg Pardon for him and for me.

Derry down, down, down, derry down.

Presidents of The Wiltshire Feast (Wiltshire Society #2)

1727: John Holton
1728: Anthony Whitehead
1729: James Still
1731: John Sainsbury
1732: Ralph Good
1733: Captain Parnall
1739: Edward Marsh
1741: William Atkinson
1742: Charles Willis
1745: John Clark
1746: William Arnold
1747: John Mereweather
1749: William Wansey
1750: Richard Smith
1751: Roger Rice
1752: John Lane

1753: John Waters
1754: James Getley
1755: George Pullin
1756: Henry Gardiner
1757: John Clark
1758: Anthony Barrett
1759: William Barrett
1760: Mr Neat (of Pill)
1761: James Edwards
1762: Mr White (Schoolmaster in Shirehampton)
1763: John Mullins/Thomas Manley
1764: James West
1765: Walter Long/Standfast Smith
1766: Benjamin Colborne/O Harman
1767: George Grist

1768: Robert Cottle
1769: Samuel Rake
1770: Francis Mereweather
1771: Humphrey Tugwell
1773: William Parsons
1774: Charles Penruddock
1775: Ambrose Goddard
1776: Sir James Tylney Long Bt
1777: Thomas Kington
1778: John Pullin
1779: John Awdry
1780: J William Hicks
1781: Richard Coombes
1782: Matthew Brickdale MP
1783: Robert Coleman
1784: Henry Cruger MP

Presidents of The Wiltshire Society 1817-1954 only

1817: Sir Benjamin Hobhouse bart
1818: Paul Methuen MP (later 1st Baron Methuen)
1819: Henry Petty-Fitzmaurice, 3rd Marquess of Lansdowne
1820: TGB Estcourt MP
1821: Edward St Maur, 11th Duke of Somerset
1822: John Benett MP
1823: Sir John Dugdale Astley bart, MP
1824: Sir Francis Burdett bart, MP
1825: George Watson Taylor MP
1826: Henry George Herbert, 2nd Earl of Carnarvon
1827: John Charles Villiers, 3rd Earl of Clarendon
1828: Thomas Howard, 16th Earl of Suffolk
1829: Robert Gordon MP
1830: John Pearse MP

1831: Joseph Pitt MP
1832: Thomas Calley MP
1833: Edward St Maur, 11th Duke of Somerset
1834: Sir John Hobhouse bart MP
1835: Hon Sidney Herbert MP
1836: Joseph Neeld MP
1837: THSB Estcourt MP
1838: Walter Long MP
1839: WH Ludlow Bruges MP
1840: Henry Thomas Petty-Fitzmaurice, Earl of Shelburne (later 4th Marquess of Lansdowne)
1841: John Neeld MP
1842: GH Walker Henage
1843: Ambrose Hussey MP
1844: George Edward Eyre (High Sheriff)
1845: Edward Dennison, Bishop of Salisbury

1846: Wade Browne (High Sheriff)
1847: Serjeant Merewether
1848: Hon Frederick H Paul Methuen
1849: R Parry Nisbet (High Sheriff)
1850: Simon Watson Taylor MP
1851: Horatio Nelson, 3rd Earl Nelson
1852: Sir MH Hicks Beach
1853: Charles John Howard, 17th Earl of Suffolk
1854: George Brudenell-Bruce, Earl Bruce (later 2nd Marquess of Ailesbury)
1855: John Alexander Thynne, 4th Marquess of Bath
1856: Lord Ernest Bruce MP
1857: Walter Kerr Hamilton, Bishop of Salisbury
1858: MH Marsh MP
1859: Henry Alworth Merewether QC
1860: Lord Henry Frederick Thynne MP

1861: Thomas Baring MP
1862: Col Hervey Bathurst MP
1863: William Henry Ashe Holmes-à Court, 2nd Baron Heytesbury
1864: George Brudenell-Bruce, 2nd Marquess of Ailesbury
1865: Ambrose L Goddard MP
1866: Richard Penruddocke Long MP
1867: Lord Charles William Brudenell-Bruce MP
1868: Thomas Fraser Grove MP
1869: Sir Charles Pressly KCB
1870: Henry Petty-FitzMaurice, 5th Marquess of Lansdowne
1871: Sir Alexander Malet KCB
1872: John Hibberd Brewer
1873: James Charles Herbert Agar, 3rd Earl of Normanton
1874: Sir E Antrobus bart
1875: William Pleydell-Bouverie, Viscount Folkestone (later 5th Earl of Radnor)
1876: Alfred Seymour
1877: GB Sotheron Estcourt MP
1878: Hon Sidney Herbert MP (later 14th Earl of Pembroke)
1879: Henry Charles Howard, 18th Earl of Suffolk & 11th Earl of Berkshire
1880: Ernest Augustus Charles Brudenell-Bruce, 3rd Marquis of Ailesbury
1881: Prince Leopold, Duke of Albany
1882: George Herbert, 13th Earl of Pembroke
1883: Walter Hume Long MP (later 1st Viscount Long of Wraxall)
1884: Vere Benett Stanford
1885: RN Fowler MP
1886: Col Hon Paul Sanford Methuen CB, CMG
1887: Frederick Henry Paul Methuen, 2nd Baron Methuen
1888: CNP Phipps esq (High Sheriff)

1889: Lord Edmond Fitzmaurice
1890: John Alexander Thynne, 4th Marquess of Bath
1891: Sir John Dickson-Poynder bart
1892: Walter Hume Long MP (later 1st Viscount Long of Wraxall)
1893: Sir Algernon W Neeld
1894: Jacob Pleydell-Bouverie, Viscount Folkestone MP (later 6th Earl of Radnor)
1895: Henry Charles Petty-Fitzmaurice, 5th Marquess of Lansdowne KG
1896-7: Thomas Henry Thynne, 5th Marquess of Bath
1898: John M Fuller esq, MP
1899: Algernon St Maur, 15th Duke of Somerset
1900-1: Sidney Herbert, 14th Earl of Pembroke
1902: Hon Percy Scawen Wyndham
1903: Hugh Morrison esq
1904: Lt-Col Sir Audley D Neeld bart
1905: WF Lawrence esq, MP
1906: FP Goddard esq
1907: Col Sir Edmund Antrobus bart
1908: Edward Murray Colston esq (later 2nd Baron Roundway)
1909-10: Sir Edward Tennant bart, MP (later 1st Baron Glenconner)
1911: Col Thomas Charles Pleydell Calley
1912: Sir Eyre Coote
1913: Henry Petty-Fitzmaurice MP, Earl of Kerry
1914-20: Reginald Herbert, 15th Earl of Pembroke
1921: Jacob Pleydell-Bouverie, 6th Earl of Radnor
1922: W Heward Bell esq, JP
1923: The Bishop of Salisbury St Clair Donaldson
1924: Thomas Henry Thynne, 5th

Marquess of Bath
1925: Major Gerard J Buxton (High Sheriff)
1926: Brig-Gen Edward Hamilton Seymour, 16th Duke of Somerset
1927: Edward Murray Colston, 2nd Baron Roundway
1928: Major Eric Long MP
1929: Col RW Awdry
1930: Lt-Col WC Heward Bell
1931: Lord Weymouth (Henry Frederick Thynne, later 6th Marquess of Bath)
1932: George Brudenell-Bruce, 6th Marquess of Ailesbury
1933: Herbert Leaf esq (former Mayor of Marlborough)
1934: Brigadier-General E Harding-Newman (High Sheriff)
1935: Brig-Gen E Harding-Newman
1936: Capt HP Holt
1937: Capt HP Holt
1938: G Kidston
1939: JG Morrison
1940: Lt-Col FGG Bailey
1941: Lt-Col FGG Bailey
1942: No President nominated
1943: Rt Hon Sir Eric Phipps
1944: Lt-Col William Llewellen Palmer
1945: Commander Brudnell Hunt-Grubbe
1946: Commander Brudnell Hunt-Grubbe
1947: Egbert Barnes Esq
1948: WH Yeatman-Biggs Esq
1949: WH Yeatman-Biggs Esq
1950: Lt-Col William Llewellen Palmer
1951: RE Money-Kyrle Esq
1952: Brig-Gen FE Fowle
1953: Sir Noel Arkell
1954: Major CE Awdry

Bristol churches where services were held for The Wiltshire Feast (Wiltshire Society #2)

1726: St Stephen (still exists as an active C of E church, and has a Ramsay MacDonald connection)

1728: All Saints (closed Anglican church, which stands adjacent to The Tolzey)

1729: All Saints

1731: St Peter (still stands as a ruined memorial as bombed during the Second World War)

1732: Christ Church (located on the corner of Broad Street and Wine Street, still open for worship)

1739: St Thomas (St Thomas the Martyr – the nave was rebuilt in 1791-93, although the tower is 14th century, redundant C of E church)

1741: Christ Church

1742: St Thomas

1745: Christ Church

1746: St Nicholas (destroyed in the Bristol Blitz, but rebuilt 1974/75)

1747: St Mary Redcliffe (still open)

1749: St James (St James Priory – still open, but now a Catholic place of worship)

1750: Temple Church (largely destroyed in the Bristol Blitz, but the shell remains)

1751: St Peter

1752: St Nicholas

1753: St Peter

1754: St James

1755: St Philip (St Philip & St Jacob – still active as an Anglican place of worship)

1756: St Peter

1757: St James

1758: St Mary Le Port Church (destroyed during the Bristol Blitz, although the ruins remain)

1759: St Peter

1761: All Saints

1763: Abbey Church, Bath/St James

1764: St Michael (damaged during the Bristol Blitz and currently used as a creative space)

1765: St James

1766: Abbey Church, Bath/St James

1767: Christ Church

1768: St James

1769: St James

1770: St James

1771: St Nicholas

1773: St Augustine (likely to be the Church of St Augustine the Less, which was demolished in 1962)

1774: St Augustine

1775: St Augustine

1776: St Augustine

1777: St Mary Le Port Church

1778: St Thomas

1779: St Augustine

1780: St Augustine

1782: St Nicholas

1783: St James

Selected Bibliography

Andrews, Mark/Kelly, Andy/Stillman, Tim: *Arsenal – Champions of the South* (Legends Publishing, 2018)

Clark, Peter: *British Clubs & Societies 1580-1800: The Origins of an Associational World* (Oxford: Oxford University Press, 2001, Copyright Oxford Publishing Ltd. Reproduced with permission of the Licensor through PLSclear)

Firth, Peter E: *The Men Who Made Kingston* (Peter E Firth, 1995)

Goldney, Frederick Hastings, *A History of Freemasonry in Wiltshire* (London: Virtue & Co., 1880)

Halliwell, James Orchard: *A Dictionary of Archaic and Provincial Words* (Charleston: Nabu Press, 2011)

Henley, HR: *The Apprentice Registers of the Wiltshire Society 1817-1922* (Devizes: Wiltshire Record Society, 1997)

Key, Newton E: *The Political Culture and Political Rhetoric of County Feasts and Feast Sermons 1654-1714* (Cambridge: Cambridge University Press, 2014)

Lane's Masonic Records 1717-1894 (via dhi.ac.uk)

Matheson, Rosa: *Doing Time Inside* (The History Press, 2011)

Smith, William, *A Pocket Companion for Free-Masons* (London: E Rider, 1735)

Sutton, Mark: *Tell Them of Us* (Melvyn Mckeown, 2006)

Swindon Advertiser/Swindon Evening Advertiser/Evening Advertiser/North Wilts Herald (Swindon: multiple issues, 1886-1954)

Wiltshire Times (Trowbridge: multiple issues)

Simpson, George: *Wiltshire Notes and Queries: An Illustrated Quarterly Antiquarian & Genealogical Magazine* Vol. II 1896-1898 (Devizes: 1911)

Extracts from: *The Tatler* (1934, 1935, 1936 & 1950) and *The Bystander* (1936), reproduced by kind permission of Mary Evans Picture Library Ltd/Illustrated London News Group. Licensed from Mary Evans Picture Library Ltd.

Portrait photograph of Sir Richard Burbidge courtesy of Harrods Company Archive. Copyright Harrods Ltd.

pglwilts.org.uk
radnorstreetcemetery.blog (Frances Bevan)
royal-arsenal-history.com
www.ancestry.co.uk
www.arthurlloyd.co.uk
www.britishnewspaperarchive.co.uk
www.chitternenowandthen.uk
www.dover-kent.com
www.farmersboys.com
www.findagrave.com
www.iwm.org.uk
www.lso.co.uk
www.pubology.co.uk
www.swindonadvertiser.co.uk

Find out more

The authors have deposited a file containing transcriptions of the annual dinners with Swindon Libraries/Local Studies and the Wiltshire & Swindon History Centre (Chippenham).

Do you have any additional information?

The authors would like to receive additional information on *The Moonies in London/The Association of Wiltshiremen in London*, including documents or the whereabouts of any artefacts relating to their story. Please email Noel Ponting at shresearch2@gmail.com

Milton Keynes UK
Ingram Content Group UK Ltd.
UKHW050805070624
443665UK00004B/114